TEN GREAT ECONOMISTS
From Marx to Keynes

TEN GREAT ECONOMISTS
From Marx to Keynes

JOSEPH A. SCHUMPETER

NEW YORK
Oxford University Press
1951

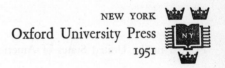

CONTENTS

FOREWORD

THESE essays were written over the course of the forty years between 1910 and 1950, the three earliest (Walras, Böhm-Bawerk, Menger) in German, the others in English. With the exception of the essay on Marx, they were written for various economic journals either on the occasion of the death of an economist or to celebrate some anniversary, such as the fiftieth anniversary of Marshall's *Principles,* or the hundredth anniversary of Pareto's birth. Because they were written rather hurriedly for special occasions, Schumpeter thought them hardly worthy of publication in book form. But there were many demands for them—since the journals in which they originally appeared were difficult to obtain—and some months before his death in January 1950, he finally consented to their publication by the Oxford University Press.

The ten main essays are those Schumpeter himself selected with a single exception—the one on Karl Marx. He had planned to include 'The Communist Manifesto in Sociology and Economics,' written for the *Journal of Political Economy* (June 1949) to commemorate somewhat belatedly the hundredth anniversary of the publication of the *Communist Manifesto.* For this has been substituted Part 1 ('The Marxian Doctrine') of *Capitalism, Socialism and Democracy* because it was a more comprehensive treatment of Marx as a prophet, sociologist, economist, and teacher. I am very much indebted to Mr. Cass Canfield and to Harper & Brothers for their generous permission to include this essay in *Ten Great Economists.* I take this opportunity to thank the editors and publishers of the *Quarterly Journal of Economics,* the *American Economic Review,* the *Economic Journal,* and *Econometrica* for consenting to the inclusion of the articles which originally appeared in those journals: the old *Zeitschrift für Volkswirtschaft* no longer exists.

The three short essays in the Appendix on Knapp, Wieser, and Bortkiewicz were included at the suggestion of Professor Gottfried Haberler, who felt that they should be republished and that they belong in a volume with the other biographical essays. These were all written for the *Economic Journal,* which Schumpeter served as Austrian correspondent from 1920 to 1926 and as German correspondent from 1927 to 1932, when he left the University of Bonn to come to Harvard.

There was a close tie between the author and the subjects of these biographical essays. He not only admired their work but also, with a single exception, knew them [1] all personally and for some of them felt a warm personal friendship. Again the exception is Karl Marx, who died in 1883, the year in which both Schumpeter and Keynes, the youngest of the ten, were born. With Marx he had one thing in common—a kind of vision of the economic process. In his own *Theory of Economic Development,* Schumpeter attempts to present 'a purely economic theory of economic change which does not merely rely on external factors propelling the economic system from one equilibrium to another.' In the Preface to the Japanese edition of that work, he says: 'It was not clear to me at the outset what to the reader will perhaps be obvious at once, namely, that this idea and this aim [Schumpeter's own] are exactly the same as the idea and the aim which underlie the economic teaching of Karl Marx. In fact, what distinguishes him from the economists

---

[1] This applies to the men covered in the ten main essays. Of the three economists in the appendix, he knew Wieser very well, and he probably met both Knapp and Bortkiewicz.

of his own time and those who preceded him, was precisely a vision of economic evolution as a distinct process generated by the economic system itself. In every other respect he only used and adapted the concepts and propositions of Ricardian economics, but the concept of economic evolution, which he put into an unessential Hegelian setting, is quite his own. It is probably due to this fact that one generation of economists after another turns back to him again, although they may find plenty to criticize in him.' Again, in the manuscript of the *History of Economic Analysis* we find: 'In his general schema of thought, development was not what it was with all the other economists of that period, an appendix to economic statics, but the central theme. And he concentrated his analytic powers on the task of showing how the economic process, changing itself by virtue of its own inherent logic, is incessantly changing the social framework—the whole of society in fact.' The vision they had in common, but it led to very different results: it led Marx to condemn capitalism and Schumpeter to be its ardent exponent.

For Schumpeter the progress of economics as a science depended on vision and technique. As he admired Marx for his vision of the economic process, he admired Walras, whom he met only once, for his pure theory. In the *History of Economic Analysis* he says of the latter: '. . . economics is a big omnibus which contains many passengers of incommensurable interests and abilities. However, *so far as pure theory is concerned,* Walras is in my opinion the greatest of all economists. His system of economic equilibrium, uniting as it does the quality of "revolutionary" creativeness with the quality of classic synthesis, is the only work by an economist that will stand comparison with the achievements of theoretical physics.'

Marx and Walras were poles apart: the one attempted a logical explanation of economic change; the other gave us a 'theoretical apparatus which for the first time in the history of our science effectively embraced the pure logic of the interdependence between economic quantities.'

It was characteristic of Schumpeter [2] that he admired, and found useful, history and pure theory, econometrics and great compilations of factual material, sociology and statistics; and this breadth of interest is reflected in these biographical essays.

He knew Menger, Böhm-Bawerk, and Wieser during his student days in Vienna. Menger, who with his two disciples, Böhm-Bawerk and Wieser, may be regarded as the co-founders of the Austrian or Viennese School of economics, had already retired from active teaching; and Schumpeter met him only once or twice. But the author of these essays was an active participant in the seminars of Wieser and Böhm-Bawerk (1904-6); later he carried on a famous controversy on the rate of interest with Böhm-Bawerk (*Zeitschrift für Volkswirtschaft,* 1913); he was one of three speakers at the celebration of Wieser's seventieth birthday in 1921.

Although he had high regard for the work of the Austrian School in which he was trained, he was even more interested in another school that developed a marginal utility theory of value— the School of Lausanne, which grew out of the work of Walras. In a sense the real founder of this school was Pareto, the brilliant pupil of Walras, who succeeded the latter in the chair of Political Economy at Lausanne. Until recently their work was too 'mathematical' and too 'theoretical' for English and American economists, who also found it difficult (and perhaps a waste of time) to read economists in other languages. The Lausanne School did, however, acquire at an early date two first-rate American followers in Irving Fisher and H. L. Moore. Three of the ten essays in this book are devoted to Walras, Pareto, and Fisher. In the essay on Pareto (note 10) J.A.S. describes a meeting where they conversed about economists and Pareto bestowed high praise on Irving Fisher: 'It was a revelation to me to hear him [Pareto] bestow high praise on [Fisher's] *Capital and Income.*'

[2] Haberler said of him in the *Quarterly Journal of Economics* (August 1950) that he had his superiors in special fields. 'But as a master of all branches of economics and as a universal scholar, Schumpeter held a unique position among contemporary economists.'

After receiving his degree at Vienna in 1906, Schumpeter went to England for a few months. There he paid his respects to some of the English economists and met Marshall for the first time in 1907. This meeting is described briefly in a note in the review of Keynes's *Essays in Biography* which J.A.S. wrote for the *Economic Journal,* December 1933. Commenting on Keynes's essay on Marshall, he wrote: 'It is as I saw him [Marshall] when I looked at him across his breakfast table in 1907 to tell him: "Professor, after our conversation (about my scientific plans) I feel exactly as I would if I were an indiscreet lover bent on an adventurous marriage and you a benevolent old uncle trying to persuade me to desist." He answered: "And this is as it should be. For if there is anything to it, the uncle will preach in vain." ' Schumpeter's own essay in this volume indicates how much he thought of the work of Marshall; after its publication in the *American Economic Review,* he received a note from Mary Marshall (Cambridge [England], July 19, 1941) which said: *'The American Economic Review* has just come and I have been reading your semi-centennial appraisal of Marshall's *Principles* with great interest. I have always known how much you appreciated his work and I am so glad that you have taken this opportunity of expressing this appreciation so warmly and well. Its last paragraph especially delights me. I also join in your admiration for Mr. Keynes's "Memorial of Alfred Marshall." '

The American economists (Taussig, Fisher, Mitchell) discussed in these essays were probably met for the first time when Schumpeter came to the United States in the academic year 1913-14 to act as Austrian Exchange Professor at Columbia University. Before this he knew their work and had corresponded at least with Taussig. There is a letter to him from the latter written from Cambridge, Mass. (November 27, 1912), in which Taussig compliments the young economist on his English and goes on to discuss a theoretical problem raised by Schumpeter. 'I have no quarrel with your reasoning; but my own disposition is to approach these subjects from a more realistic point of view.' Taussig presents some drawings of supply schedules and then goes on: 'The application of the same reasoning to labor as has been applied to capital and land, and the development of a "rent" theory of labor, have been much in my mind; and I have sketched the outline of a considerable article dealing with this topic. You know, of course, the manner in which reasoning of this sort has been attempted by my friend, J. B. Clark, and more recently and more carefully by Irving Fisher. The last word on this topic has not been said. I am not so immodest as to think that I shall myself be able to say that last word, but I hope to make some contribution to the subject.' The friendship thus inaugurated continued until Taussig's death in 1940. In fact, during his first years at Harvard (1932-7), Schumpeter lived with Taussig at 2 Scott Street.

Similarly there was both admiration and affection for Irving Fisher and Wesley Mitchell. With Fisher he was associated in the founding of the Econometric Society. There was much jovial badinage when Schumpeter visited Fisher's somewhat austere establishment in New Haven (where tobacco, alcohol, coffee, and, I believe, meat were eschewed), and coffee was brewed especially for the 'depraved' visitor. The conversation at such a week end in New Haven has been described in an article in the *Revue d'économie politique* (1950, No. 3) by Professor G. H. Bousquet, of the University of Algiers. The obituary of Wesley Mitchell in this volume was finished just a week or two before Schumpeter's own death. Both Mitchell and Schumpeter worked on business cycles and both believed that the successful study of this phenomenon of capitalist development required the most extensive factual research. Schumpeter collected his own data laboriously and almost without research assistance, because that was the way he worked, but he had the greatest admiration for a man who could organize the National Bureau and use its resources intelligently and effectively.

Keynes he did not meet until 1927, although Keynes had long been one of the editors of the *Economic Journal* and Schumpeter had been its Austrian correspondent since 1920. For some reason, not easy to explain, the relation between these two was not a close one personally or professionally.

The translation of the three essays on Walras, Menger, and Böhm-Bawerk presented certain difficulties. As Paul Sweezy has pointed out in his introduction to *Imperialism and Social Classes* and as Haberler had pointed out earlier in his essay in the *Quarterly Journal of Economics,* Schumpeter's German style is extremely difficult to translate. Haberler said: 'His somewhat involved literary style which can be perhaps best described as "baroque" gives adequate expression to the complex structure of his mind. It is characterized by long sentences, numerous qualifying phrases, qualifications of qualifications, casuistic distinctions of meanings. These qualities of his style are especially pronounced, as one would expect, in his German writings, because the German language offers more freedom for complicated constructions.' Schumpeter was aware of this fact, especially with reference to the essay on Böhm-Bawerk. He believed that the essay on Böhm-Bawerk was much too long and that it would have to be cut and rewritten for English-speaking readers. He was quite emphatic that it would be 'impossible' otherwise.

The essay on Böhm-Bawerk has been cut to about half its original length. The work of cutting was done by Haberler and by the translator, Professor Herbert Zassenhaus, a former student of the author. I wish here to express my gratitude to Professor Haberler and to the three translators (Wolfgang Stolper, Hans W. Singer, and Herbert Zassenhaus) for their generous interest and assistance —also to Paul Sweezy, who read over all the translations with me and helped me to smooth the English and clarify the meaning in many instances. In some cases, I had to take liberties with certain passages in the translations where a literal translation was involved or obscure. This was especially true in the essay on Böhm-Bawerk. Any shortcomings in the translations, therefore, are due to me and are my responsibility alone.

The remaining essays, which were all written in English, are printed here as they were originally published. They have not been altered or revised in any way except for corrections of minor misprints and small changes to insure uniformity in such technical details as capitalization, punctuation, and footnote arrangement.

Elizabeth Boody Schumpeter

Taconic, Connecticut
February 2, 1951

TEN GREAT ECONOMISTS
From Marx to Keynes

KARL MARX
1818-1883

THE MARXIAN DOCTRINE*

Most of the creations of the intellect or fancy pass away for good after a time that varies between an after-dinner hour and a generation. Some, however, do not. They suffer eclipses but they come back again, and they come back not as unrecognizable elements of a cultural inheritance, but in their individual garb and with their personal scars which people may see and touch. These we may well call the great ones—it is no disadvantage of this definition that it links greatness to vitality. Taken in this sense, this is undoubtedly the word to apply to the message of Marx. But there is an additional advantage to defining greatness by revivals: it thereby becomes independent of our love or hate. We need not believe that a great achievement must necessarily be a source of light or faultless in either fundamental design or details. On the contrary, we may believe it to be a power of darkness; we may think it funda-

* From *Capitalism, Socialism and Democracy*, copyright 1942 by Joseph A. Schumpeter. Reprinted by permission of Harper & Bros.

mentally wrong or disagree with it on any number of particular points. In the case of the Marxian system, such adverse judgment or even exact disproof, by its very failure to injure fatally, only serves to bring out the power of the structure.

The last twenty years have witnessed a most interesting Marxian revival. That the great teacher of the socialist creed should have come into his own in Soviet Russia is not surprising. And it is only characteristic of such processes of canonization that there is, between the true meaning of Marx's message and bolshevist practice and ideology, at least as great a gulf as there was between the religion of humble Galileans and the practice and ideology of the princes of the church or the warlords of the Middle Ages.

But another revival is less easy to explain—the Marxian revival in the United States. This phenomenon is so interesting because until the 'twenties there was no Marxian strain of importance in either the American labor movement or in the thought of the American intellectual. What Marxism there was always had been superficial, insignificant, and without standing. Moreover, the bolshevist type of revival produced no similar spurt in those countries which had previously been most steeped in Marxology. In Germany notably, which of all countries had the strongest Marxian tradition, a small orthodox sect indeed kept alive during the postwar socialist boom as it had during the previous depression. But the leaders of socialist thought (not only those allied to the Social Democratic party but also those who went much beyond its cautious conservatism in practical questions) betrayed little taste for reverting to the old tenets and, while worshiping the deity, took good care to keep it at a distance and to reason in economic matters exactly like other economists. Outside of Russia, therefore, the American phenomenon stands alone. We are not concerned with its causes. But it is worth while to survey the contours and the meaning of the message so many Americans have made their own.[1]

[1] References to Marx's writings will be confined to a minimum, and no data about his life will be given. This seems unnecessary because any reader who wishes for a list of the former and a general outline of the latter

I. MARX THE PROPHET

It was not by a slip that an analogy from the world of religion was permitted to intrude into the title of this chapter. There is more than analogy. In one important sense, Marxism *is* a religion. To the believer it presents, first, a systèm of ultimate ends that embody the meaning of life and are absolute standards by which to judge events and actions; and, secondly, a guide to those ends which implies a plan of salvation and the indication of the evil from which mankind, or a chosen section of mankind, is to be saved. We may specify still further: Marxist socialism also belongs to that subgroup which promises paradise on this side of the grave. I believe that a formulation of these characteristics by an hierologist would give opportunities for classification and comment which might possibly lead much deeper into the sociological essence of Marxism than anything a mere economist can say.

The least important point about this is that it explains the success of Marxism.[1] Purely scientific achievement, had it even been much more perfect than it was in the case of Marx, would never have won the immortality in the historical sense which is his. Nor would his arsenal of party slogans have done it. Part of his success, although a very minor part, is indeed attributable to the barrelful of white-hot phrases, of impassioned accusations and wrathful gesticulations, ready for use on any platform, that he put at the disposal of his flock. All that needs to be said about this aspect of the matter is that this ammunition has served and is serving its purpose very well, but

finds all he needs for our purposes in any dictionary, but especially in the *Encyclopaedia Britannica* or the *Encyclopaedia of the Social Sciences*. A study of Marx begins most conveniently with the first volume of *Das Kapital* (first English translation by S. Moore and E. Aveling, edited by F. Engels, 1886). In spite of a huge amount of more recent work, I still think that F. Mehring's biography is the best, at least from the standpoint of the general reader.

[1] The religious quality of Marxism also explains a characteristic attitude of the orthodox Marxist toward opponents. To him, as to any believer in a Faith, the opponent is not merely in error but in sin. Dissent is disapproved of not only intellectually but also morally. There cannot be any excuse for it once the Message has been revealed.

that the production of it carried a disadvantage: in order to forge such weapons for the arena of social strife Marx had occasionally to bend, or to deviate from, the opinions that would logically follow from his system. However, if Marx had not been more than a purveyor of phraseology, he would be dead by now. Mankind is not grateful for that sort of service and forgets quickly the names of the people who write the librettos for its political operas.

But he was a prophet, and in order to understand the nature of this achievement we must visualize it in the setting of his own time. It was the zenith of bourgeois realization and the nadir of bourgeois civilization, the time of mechanistic materialism, of a cultural milieu which had as yet betrayed no sign that a new art and a new mode of life were in its womb, and which rioted in most repulsive banality. Faith in any real sense was rapidly falling away from all classes of society, and with it the only ray of light (apart from what may have been derived from Rochdale attitudes and savings banks) died from the workman's world, while intellectuals professed themselves highly satisfied with Mill's *Logic* and the Poor Law.

Now, to millions of human hearts the Marxian message of the terrestrial paradise of socialism meant a new ray of light and a new meaning of life. Call Marxist religion a counterfeit if you like, or a caricature of faith—there is plenty to be said for this view—but do not overlook or fail to admire the greatness of the achievement. Never mind that nearly all of those millions were unable to understand and appreciate the message in its true significance. That is the fate of all messages. The important thing is that the message was framed and conveyed in such a way as to be acceptable to the positivistic mind of its time—which was essentially bourgeois no doubt, but there is no paradox in saying that Marxism is essentially a product of the bourgeois mind. This was done, on the one hand, by formulating with unsurpassed force that feeling of being thwarted and ill treated which is the auto-therapeutic attitude of the unsuccessful many, and, on the other hand, by proclaiming that socialistic deliverance from those ills was a certainty amenable to rational proof.

Observe how supreme art here succeeds in weaving together those extra-rational cravings which receding religion had left running about like masterless dogs, and the rationalistic and materialistic tendencies of the time, ineluctable for the moment, which would not tolerate any creed that had no scientific or pseudo-scientific connotation. Preaching the goal would have been ineffectual; analyzing a social process would have interested only a few hundred specialists. But preaching in the garb of analysis and analyzing with a view to heartfelt needs, this is what conquered passionate allegiance and gave to the Marxist that supreme boon which consists in the conviction that what one is and stands for can never be defeated but must conquer victoriously in the end. This, of course, does not exhaust the achievement. Personal force and the flash of prophecy work independently of the contents of the creed. No new life and no new meaning of life can be effectively revealed without. But this does not concern us here.

Something will have to be said about the cogency and correctness of Marx's attempt to prove the inevitability of the socialist goal. One remark, however, suffices as to what has been called above his formulation of the feelings of the unsuccessful many. It was, of course, not a true formulation of actual feelings, conscious or subconscious. Rather we could call it an attempt at replacing actual feelings by a true or false revelation of the logic of social evolution. By doing this and by attributing—quite unrealistically—to the masses his own shibboleth of 'class consciousness,' he undoubtedly falsified the true psychology of the workman (which centers in the wish to become a small bourgeois and to be helped to that status by political force), but in so far as his teaching took effect he also expanded and ennobled it. He did not weep any sentimental tears about the beauty of the socialist idea. This is one of his claims to superiority over what he called the Utopian Socialists. Nor did he glorify the workmen into heroes of daily toil as bourgeois love to do when trembling for their dividends. He was perfectly free from any tendency, so conspicuous in some of his weaker followers, toward licking the workman's boots. He had probably a clear perception of what the masses are and he looked far above their heads toward social goals altogether beyond what they thought or wanted. Also, he never taught any ideals as set by himself. Such vanity was quite foreign to him. As every true prophet styles himself the humble mouthpiece of his deity, so Marx pretended no more than to speak the logic of the dialectic process of history. There is dignity in all this which compensates for many pettinesses and vulgarities with which, in his work and in his life, this dignity formed so strange an alliance.

Another point, finally, should not go unmentioned. Marx was personally much too civilized to fall in with those vulgar professors of socialism who do not recognize a temple when they see it. He was perfectly able to understand a civilization and the 'relatively absolute' value of its values, however far removed from it he may have felt himself to be. In this respect no better testimony to his broad-mindedness can be offered than the *Communist Manifesto,* which is an account nothing short of glowing² of the achievements of capitalism; and even in pronouncing *pro futuro* death sentence on it, he never failed to recognize its historical necessity. This attitude, of course, implies quite a lot of things Marx himself would have been unwilling to accept. But he was undoubtedly strength-

²This may seem to be an exaggeration. But let us quote from the authorized English translation: 'The bourgeoisie . . . has been the first to show what man's activity can bring about. It has accomplished wonders far surpassing Egyptian pyramids, Roman aqueducts and Gothic cathedrals. . . The bourgeoisie . . . draws all nations . . . into civilization. . . It has created enormous cities . . . and thus rescued a considerable part of the population from the idiocy [sic!] of rural life. . . The bourgeoisie, during its rule of scarce one hundred years, has created more massive and more colossal productive forces than have all preceding generations together.' Observe that all the achievements referred to are attributed *to the bourgeoisie alone,* which is more than many thoroughly bourgeois economists would claim. This is all I meant by the passage above—and strikingly different from the views of the vulgarized Marxism of today or from the Veblenite stuff of the modern non-Marxist radical.

ened in it, and it was made more easy for him to take, because of that perception of the organic logic of things to which his theory of history gives one particular expression. Things social fell into order for him, and however much of a coffeehouse conspirator he may have been at some junctures of his life, his true self despised that sort of thing. Socialism for him was no obsession which blots out all other colors of life and creates an unhealthy and stupid hatred or contempt for other civilizations. And there is, in more senses than one, justification for the title claimed for his type of socialist thought and of socialist volition which are welded together by virtue of his fundamental position: Scientific Socialism.

II. MARX THE SOCIOLOGIST

We have now to do a thing which is very objectionable to the faithful. They naturally resent any application of cold analysis to what for them is the very fountain of truth. But one of the things they resent most is cutting Marx's work into pieces and discussing them one by one. They would say that the very act displays the incapacity of the bourgeois to grasp the resplendent whole, all parts of which complement and explain one another, so that the true meaning is missed as soon as any one part or aspect is considered by itself. We have no choice, however. By committing the offense and next taking up Marx the sociologist after Marx the prophet, I do not mean to deny either the presence of a unity of social vision which succeeds in giving some measure of analytic unity, and still more a semblance of unity, to the Marxian work, or the fact that every part of it, however independent intrinsically, has been correlated by the author with every other. Enough independence remains nevertheless in every province of the vast realm to make it possible for the student to accept the fruits of his labors in one of them while rejecting those in another. Much of the glamour of the faith is lost in the process but something is gained by salvaging important and stimulating truth which is much more valuable by itself than it would be if tied to hopeless wreckage.

This applies first of all to Marx's philosophy, which we may as well get out of our way once and for all. German-trained and speculative-minded as he was, he had a thorough grounding and a passionate interest in philosophy. Pure philosophy of the German kind was his starting point and the love of his youth. For a time he thought of it as his true vocation. He was a Neo-Hegelian, which roughly means that while accepting the master's fundamental attitudes and methods he and his group eliminated, and replaced by pretty much their opposites, the conservative interpretations put upon Hegel's philosophy by many of its other adherents. This background shows in all his writings wherever the opportunity offers itself. It is no wonder that his German and Russian readers, by bent of mind and training similarly disposed, should seize primarily upon this element and make it the master key to the system.

I believe this to be a mistake and an injustice to Marx's scientific powers. He retained his early love during the whole of his lifetime. He enjoyed certain formal analogies which may be found between his and Hegel's argument. He liked to testify to his Hegelianism and to use Hegelian phraseology. But this is all. Nowhere did he betray positive science to metaphysics. He himself says as much in the preface to the second edition of the first volume of *Das Kapital,* and that what he says there is true and no self-delusion can be proved by analyzing his argument, which everywhere rests upon social fact, and the true sources of his propositions none of which lies in the domain of philosophy. Of course, those commentators or critics who themselves started from the philosophic side were unable to do this because they did not know enough about the social sciences involved. The propensity of the philosophic system-builder, moreover, made them averse to any other interpretation but the one which proceeds from some philosophic principle. So they saw philosophy in the most matter-of-fact statements about economic experience, thereby shunting discussion on to the wrong track, misleading friends and foes alike.

Marx the sociologist brought to bear on his task an equipment which consisted primarily of an extensive command over historical and contemporaneous fact. His knowledge of the latter was always somewhat antiquated, for he was the most bookish of men and therefore fundamental materials, as distinguished from the material of the newspapers, always reached him with a lag. But hardly any historical work of his time that was of any general importance or scope escaped him, although much of the monographic literature did. While we cannot extol the completeness of his information in this field as much as we shall his erudition in the field of economic theory, he was yet able to illustrate his social visions not only by large historical frescoes but also by many details most of which were as regards reliability rather above than below the standards of other sociologists of his time. These facts he embraced with a glance that pierced through the random irregularities of the surface down to the grandiose logic of things historical. In this there was not merely passion. There was not merely analytic impulse. There were both. And the outcome of his attempt to formulate that logic, the so-called Economic Interpretation of History,[1] is doubtless one of the greatest individual achievements of sociology to this day. Before it, the question sinks into insignificance whether or not this achievement was entirely original and how far credit has in part to be given to predecessors, German and French.

The economic interpretation of history does *not* mean that men are, consciously or unconsciously, wholly or primarily, actuated by economic motives. On the contrary, the explanation of the role and mechanism of non-economic motives and the analysis of the way in which social reality mirrors itself in the individual psyches is an essential element of the theory and one of its most significant contributions. Marx did not hold that religions, metaphysics, schools of art, ethical ideas, and political volitions were either reducible to economic *motives* or of no importance. He only tried to unveil the economic *conditions* which shape them and which account for their

---

[1] First published in that scathing attack on Proudhon's *Philosophie de la Misère,* entitled *Das Elend der Philosophie,* 1847. Another version was included in the *Communist Manifesto,* 1848.

rise and fall. The whole of Max Weber's [2] facts and arguments fits
perfectly into Marx's system. Social groups and classes and the ways
in which these groups or classes explain to themselves their own
existence, location, and behavior were of course what interested him
most. He poured the vials of his most bilious wrath on the historians
who took those attitudes and their verbalizations (the ideologies or,
as Pareto would have said, *derivations*) at their face value and who
tried to interpret social reality by means of them. But if ideas or
values were not for him the prime movers of the social process,
neither were they mere smoke. If I may use the analogy, they had
in the social engine the role of transmission belts. We cannot touch
upon that most interesting post-war development of these principles
which would afford the best instance by which to explain this, the
Sociology of Knowledge.[3] But it was necessary to say this much
because Marx has been persistently misunderstood in this respect.
Even his friend Engels, at the open grave of Marx, defined the
theory in question as meaning precisely that individuals and groups
are swayed primarily by economic motives, which in some important respects is wrong and for the rest piteously trivial.

While we are about it, we may as well defend Marx against
another misunderstanding: the *economic* interpretation of history
has often been called the *materialistic* interpretation. It has been
called so by Marx himself. This phrase greatly increased its popular-
ity with some, and its unpopularity with other people. But it is entirely meaningless. Marx's philosophy is no more materialistic than is
Hegel's, and his theory of history is not more materialistic than is
any other attempt to account for the historic process by the means
at the command of empirical science. It should be clear that this is
logically compatible with any metaphysical or religious belief—ex-

[2] This refers to Weber's investigations into the sociology of religions
and particularly to his famous study, *Die protestantische Ethik und der Geist
des Kapitalismus,* republished in his collected works.

[3] The German word is *Wissenssoziologie,* and the best names to mention are those of Max Scheler and Karl Mannheim. The latter's article on the
subject in the German Dictionary of Sociology (*Handwörterbuch der So-
ziologie*) can serve as an introduction.

actly as any physical picture of the world is. Medieval theology itself supplies methods by which it is possible to establish this compatibility.[4]

What the theory really says may be put into two propositions: (1) The forms or conditions of production are the fundamental determinant of social structures which in turn breed attitudes, actions, and civilizations. Marx illustrates his meaning by the famous statement that the 'hand-mill' creates feudal, and the 'steam-mill,' capitalist societies. This stresses the technological element to a dangerous extent, but may be accepted on the understanding that mere technology is not all of it. Popularizing a little and recognizing that by doing so we lose much of the meaning, we may say that it is our daily work which forms our minds, and that it is our location within the productive process which determines our outlook on things—or the sides of things we see—and the social elbowroom at the command of each of us. (2) The forms of production themselves have a logic of their own; that is to say, they change according to necessities inherent in them so as to produce their successors merely by their own working. To illustrate by the same Marxian example: the system characterized by the 'hand-mill' creates an economic and social situation in which the adoption of the mechanical method of milling becomes a practical necessity that individuals or groups are powerless to alter. The rise and working of the 'steam-mill' in turn creates new social functions and locations, new groups and views, which develop and interact in such a way as to outgrow their own frame. Here, then, we have the propeller which is responsible first of all for economic and, in consequence of this, for any other social change, a propeller the action of which does not itself require any impetus external to it.

Both propositions undoubtedly contain a large amount of truth and are, as we shall find at several turns of our way, invaluable working hypotheses. Most of the current objections completely

[4] I have met several Catholic radicals, a priest among them, all devout Catholics, who took this view and in fact declared themselves Marxists in everything except in matters relating to their faith.

fail, all those for instance which in refutation point to the influence of ethical or religious factors, or the one already raised by Eduard Bernstein, which with delightful simplicity asserts that 'men have heads' and can hence act as they choose. After what has been said above, it is hardly necessary to dwell on the weakness of such arguments: of course men 'choose' their course of action which is not directly enforced by the objective data of the environment; but they choose from standpoints, views, and propensities that do not form another set of independent data but are themselves molded by the objective set.

Nevertheless, the question arises whether the economic interpretation of history is more than a convenient approximation which must be expected to work less satisfactorily in some cases than it does in others. An obvious qualification occurs at the outset. Social structures, types, and attitudes are coins that do not readily melt. Once they are formed they persist, possibly for centuries, and since different structures and types display different degrees of this ability to survive, we almost always find that actual group and national behavior more or less departs from what we should expect it to be if we tried to infer it from the dominant forms of the productive process. Though this applies quite generally, it is most clearly seen when a highly durable structure transfers itself bodily from one country to another. The social situation created in Sicily by the Norman conquest will illustrate my meaning. Such facts Marx did not overlook but he hardly realized all their implications.

A related case is of more ominous significance. Consider the emergence of the feudal type of landlordism in the kingdom of the Franks during the sixth and seventh centuries. This was certainly a most important event that shaped the structure of society for many ages and *also influenced conditions of production, wants and technology included*. But its simplest explanation is to be found in the function of military leadership previously filled by the families and individuals who (retaining that function, however) became feudal landlords after the definitive conquest of the new territory. This does not fit the Marxian schema at all well and could easily be so construed as to point in a different direction. Facts of this nature can no doubt also be brought into the fold by means of auxiliary hypotheses, but the necessity of inserting such hypotheses is usually the beginning of the end of a theory.

Many other difficulties that arise in the course of attempts at historical interpretation by means of the Marxian schema could be met by admitting some measure of interaction between the sphere of production and other spheres of social life.[5] But the glamour of fundamental truth that surrounds it depends precisely on the strictness and simplicity of the one-way relation which it asserts. If this be called in question, the economic interpretation of history will have to take its place among other propositions of a similar kind— as one of many partial truths—or else to give way to another that does tell more fundamental truth. However, neither its rank as an achievement nor its handiness as a working hypothesis is impaired thereby.

To the faithful, of course, it is simply the master key to all the secrets of human history. And if we sometimes feel inclined to smile at rather naïve applications of it, we should remember what sort of arguments it replaced. Even the crippled sister of the economic interpretation of history, the Marxian Theory of Social Classes, moves into a more favorable light as soon as we bear this in mind.

Again, it is in the first place an important contribution that we have to record. Economists have been strangely slow in recognizing the phenomenon of social classes. Of course they always classified the agents whose interplay produced the processes they dealt with. But these classes were simply sets of individuals that displayed some common character: thus, some people were classed as landlords or workmen because they owned land or sold the services of their labor. Social classes, however, are not the creatures of the classifying observer but live entities that exist as such. And their existence entails consequences that are entirely missed by a schema which looks upon society as if it were an amorphous assemblage of individuals

[5] In his later life, Engels admitted that freely. Plekhanov went still further in this direction.

or families. It is fairly open to question precisely how important the phenomenon of social classes is for research in the field of purely economic theory. That it is very important for many practical applications and for all the broader aspects of the social process in general is beyond doubt.

Roughly speaking, we may say that the social classes made their entrance in the famous statement contained in the *Communist Manifesto* that the history of society is the history of class struggles. Of course, this is to put the claim at its highest. But even if we tone it down to the proposition that historical events may often be interpreted in terms of class interests and class attitudes and that existing class structures are always an important factor in historical interpretation, enough remains to entitle us to speak of a conception nearly as valuable as was the economic interpretation of history itself.

Clearly, success on the line of advance opened up by the principle of class struggle depends upon the validity of the particular theory of classes we make our own. Our picture of history and all our interpretations of cultural patterns and the mechanism of social change will differ according to whether we choose, for instance, the racial theory of classes and like Gobineau reduce human history to the history of the struggle of races or, say, the division of labor theory of classes in the fashion of Schmoller or of Durkheim and resolve class antagonisms into antagonisms between the interests of vocational groups. Nor is the range of possible differences in analysis confined to the problem of the nature of classes. Whatever view we may hold about it, different interpretations will result from different definitions of class interest [6] and from different opinions about how class action manifests itself. The subject is a hotbed of prejudice to this day, and as yet hardly in its scientific stage.

[6] The reader will perceive that one's views about what classes are and about what calls them into existence do not uniquely determine what the *interests* of those classes are and how each class will act on what 'it'—its leaders, for instance, or the rank and file—considers or feels, in the long run or in the short, erroneously or correctly, to be its interest or interests. The problem of group interest is full of thorns and pitfalls of its own, quite irrespective of the nature of the groups under study.

Curiously enough, Marx has never, as far as we know, worked out systematically what it is plain was one of the pivots of his thought. It is possible that he deferred the task until it was too late, precisely because his thinking ran so much in terms of class concepts that he did not feel it necessary to bother about definitive statement at all. It is equally possible that some points about it remained unsettled in his own mind, and that his way toward a full-fledged theory of classes was barred by certain difficulties he had created for himself by insisting on a purely economic and over-simplified conception of the phenomenon. He himself and his disciples both offered applications of this under-developed theory to particular patterns of which his own *History of the Class Struggles in France* is the outstanding example.[7] Beyond that no real progress has been achieved. The theory of his chief associate, Engels, was of the division of labor type and essentially un-Marxian in its implications. Barring this we have only the sidelights and *aperçus*—some of them of striking force and brilliance—that are strewn all over the writings of the master, particularly in *Das Kapital* and the *Communist Manifesto*.

The task of piecing together such fragments is delicate and cannot be attempted here. The basic idea is clear enough, however. The stratifying principle consists in the ownership, or the exclusion from ownership, of means of production such as factory buildings, machinery, raw materials and the consumers' goods that enter into the workman's budget. We have thus, fundamentally, two and only two classes, those owners, the capitalists, and those have-nots who are compelled to sell their labor, the laboring class or proletariat. The existence of intermediate groups, such as are formed by farmers or artisans who employ labor but also do manual work, by clerks, and by the professions is of course not denied; but they are treated

[7] Another example is the socialist theory of imperialism which will be noticed later on. O. Bauer's interesting attempt to interpret the antagonisms between the various races that inhabited the Austro-Hungarian Empire in terms of the class struggle between capitalists and workers (*Die Nationalitätenfrage*, 1905) also deserves to be mentioned, although the skill of the analyst only serves to show up the inadequacy of the tool.

as anomalies which tend to disappear in the course of the capitalist process. The two fundamental classes are, by virtue of the logic of their position and quite independently of any individual volition, essentially antagonistic to each other. Rifts within each class and collisions between subgroups occur and may even have historically decisive importance. But in the last analysis, such rifts or collisions are incidental. The one antagonism that is not incidental but inherent in the basic design of capitalist society is founded upon the private control over the means to produce: the very nature of the relation between the capitalist class and the proletariat is strife—class war.

As we shall see presently, Marx tries to show how in that class war capitalists destroy each other and eventually will destroy the capitalist system too. He also tries to show how the ownership of capital leads to further accumulation. But this way of arguing as well as the very definition that makes the ownership of something the constituent characteristic of a social class only serves to increase the importance of the question of 'primitive accumulation,' that is to say, of the question how capitalists came to be capitalists in the first instance or how they acquired that stock of goods which according to the Marxian doctrine was necessary in order to enable them to start exploiting. On this question Marx is much less explicit.[8] He contemptuously rejects the bourgeois nursery tale (*Kinderfibel*) that some people rather than others became, and are still becoming every day, capitalists by superior intelligence and energy in working and saving. Now he was well advised to sneer at that story about the good boys. For to call for a guffaw is no doubt an excellent method of disposing of an uncomfortable truth, as every politician knows to his profit. Nobody who looks at historical and contemporaneous fact with anything like an unbiased mind can fail to observe that this children's tale, while far from telling the whole truth, yet tells a good deal of it. Supernormal intelligence and energy account for industrial success and in particular for the *found-*

---

[8] See *Das Kapital*, vol. i, ch. xxvi: 'The Secret of Primitive Accumulation.'

ing of industrial positions in nine cases out of ten. And precisely in the initial stages of capitalism and of every individual industrial career, saving was and is an important element in the process though not quite as explained in classic economics. It is true that one does not ordinarily attain the status of capitalist (industrial employer) by saving from a wage or salary in order to equip one's factory by means of the fund thus assembled. The bulk of accumulation comes from profits and hence presupposes profits—this is in fact the *sound* reason for distinguishing saving from accumulating. The means required in order to start enterprise are typically provided by borrowing other people's savings, the presence of which in many small puddles is easy to explain, or the deposits which banks create for the use of the would-be entrepreneur. Nevertheless, the latter does save as a rule; the function of his saving is to raise him above the necessity of submitting to daily drudgery for the sake of his daily bread and to give him breathing space in order to look around, to develop his plans, and to secure co-operation. As a matter of economic theory, therefore, Marx had a real case—though he overstated it—when he denied to saving the role that the classical authors attributed to it. Only his inference does not follow. And the guffaw is hardly more justified than it would be if the classical theory were correct.[9]

The guffaw did its work, however, and helped to clear the road for Marx's alternative theory of primitive accumulation. But this alternative theory is not as definite as we might wish. Force—robbery—subjugation of the masses facilitating their spoliation and the results of the pillage in turn facilitating subjugation—this was

---

[9] I will not stay to stress, though I must mention, that even the classical theory is not as wrong as Marx pretended it was. 'Saving up' in the most literal sense has been, especially in earlier stages of capitalism, a not unimportant method of 'original accumulation.' Moreover, there was another method that was akin to it though not identical with it. Many a factory in the seventeenth and eighteenth centuries was just a shed that a man was able to put up by the work of his hands, and required only the simplest equipment to work it. In such cases the manual work of the prospective capitalist plus a quite small fund of savings was all that was needed—and brains, of course.

all right, of course, and admirably tallied with ideas common among intellectuals of all types, in our day still more than in the day of Marx. But evidently it does not solve the problem, which is to explain how some people acquired the power to subjugate and to rob. Popular literature does not worry about it. I should not think of addressing the question to the writings of John Reed. But we are dealing with Marx.

Now at least the semblance of a solution is afforded by the historical quality of all the major theories of Marx. For him, it is essential for the *logic* of capitalism, and not only a matter of *fact,* that it grew out of a feudal state of society. Of course the same question about the causes and the mechanism of social stratification arises also in this case, but Marx substantially accepted the bourgeois view that feudalism was a reign of force [10] in which subjugation and exploitation of the masses were already accomplished facts. The class theory devised primarily for the conditions of capitalist society was extended to its feudal predecessor—as was much of the conceptual apparatus of the economic theory of capitalism [11]—and some of the most thorny problems were stowed away in the feudal compound to reappear in a settled state, in the form of data, in the analysis of the capitalist pattern. The feudal exploiter was simply replaced by the capitalist exploiter. In those cases in which feudal lords actually turned into industrialists, this alone would solve what is thus left of the problem. Historical evidence lends a certain amount of support to this view: many feudal lords, particularly in Germany, in fact did erect and run factories, often providing the

[10] Many socialist writers besides Marx have displayed that uncritical confidence in the explanatory value of the element of force and of the control over the physical means with which to exert force. Ferdinand Lassalle, for instance, has little beyond cannons and bayonets to offer by way of explanation of governmental authority. It is a source of wonder to me that so many people should be blind to the weakness of such a sociology and to the fact that it would obviously be much truer to say that power leads to control over cannons (and men willing to use them) than that control over cannons generates power.

[11] This constitutes one of the affinities of the teaching of Marx to that of K. Rodbertus.

financial means from their feudal rents and the labor from the agricultural population (not necessarily but sometimes their serfs).[12]
In all other cases the material available to stop the gap is distinctly
inferior. The only frank way of expressing the situation is that from
a Marxian standpoint there is no satisfactory explanation, that is to
say, no explanation without resorting to non-Marxian elements suggestive of non-Marxian conclusions.[13]

   This, however, vitiates the theory at both its historical and its
logical source. Since most of the methods of primitive accumulation
also account for later accumulation—primitive accumulation, as it
were, continues throughout the capitalist era—it is not possible to say
that Marx's theory of social classes is all right *except* for the difficulties about processes in a distant past. But it is perhaps superfluous
to insist on the shortcomings of a theory which not even in the most
favorable instances goes anywhere near the heart of the phenomenon
it undertakes to explain, and which never should have been taken
seriously. These instances are to be found mainly in that epoch of
capitalist evolution which derived its character from the prevalence
of the medium-sized owner-managed firm. Beyond the range of
that type, class positions, though in most cases reflected in more or
less corresponding economic positions, are more often the cause than
the consequence of the latter: business achievement is obviously not
everywhere the only avenue to social eminence and only where it is
can ownership of means of production causally determine a group's
position in the social structure. Even then, however, it is as reason-

---

[12] W. Sombart, in the first edition of his *Theorie des modernen Kapitalismus,* tried to make the most of those cases. But the attempt to base primitive accumulation entirely on the accumulation of ground rent showed its
hopelessness, as Sombart himself eventually recognized.

[13] This holds true even if we admit robbery to the utmost extent to
which it is possible to do so without trespassing upon the sphere of the intellectual's folklore. Robbery actually entered into the building up of commercial
capital at many times and places. Phoenician as well as English wealth offers
familiar examples. But even then the Marxian explanation is inadequate because in the last resort successful robbery must rest on the personal superiority of the robbers. And as soon as this is admitted, a very different theory
of social stratification suggests itself.

able to make that ownership the defining element as it would be to define a soldier as a man who happens to have a gun. The watertight division between people who (together with their descendants) are supposed to be capitalists once for all and others who (together with their descendants) are supposed to be proletarians once for all is not only, as has often been pointed out, utterly unrealistic but it misses the salient point about social classes—the incessant rise and fall of individual families into and out of the upper strata. The facts I am alluding to are all obvious and indisputable. If they do not show on the Marxian canvas, the reason can only be in their un-Marxian implications.

It is not superfluous, however, to consider the role which that theory plays within Marx's structure and to ask ourselves what analytic intention—as distinguished from its use as a piece of equipment for the agitator—he meant it to serve.

On the one hand, we must bear in mind that for Marx the theory of Social Classes and the Economic Interpretation of History were not what they are for us, viz., two independent doctrines. With Marx, the former implements the latter in a particular way and thus restricts—makes more definite—the *modus operandi* of the conditions or forms of production. These determine the social structure and, through the social structure, all manifestations of civilization and the whole march of cultural and political history. But the social structure is, for all non-socialist epochs, defined in terms of classes—those two classes—which are the true dramatis personae and at the same time the only *immediate* creatures of the logic of the capitalist system of production which affects everything else through them. This explains why Marx was forced to make his classes purely economic phenomena, and even phenomena that were economic in a very narrow sense: he thereby cut himself off from a deeper view of them, but in the precise spot of his analytic schema in which he placed them he had no choice but to do so.

On the other hand, Marx wished to define capitalism by the same trait that also defines his class division. A little reflection will convince the reader that this is not a necessary or natural thing to

do. In fact it was a bold stroke of analytic strategy which linked
the fate of the class phenomenon with the fate of capitalism in such
a way that socialism, which in reality has nothing to do with the
presence or absence of social classes, became, by definition, the only
possible kind of classless society, excepting primitive groups. This
ingenious tautology could not equally well have been secured by any
definitions of classes *and* of capitalism other than those chosen by
Marx—the definition by private ownership of means of production.
Hence there had to be just two classes, owners and non-owners,
and hence all other principles of division, much more plausible ones
among them, had to be severely neglected or discounted or else reduced to that one.

   The exaggeration of the definiteness and importance of the
dividing line between the capitalist class in that sense and the proletariat was surpassed only by the exaggeration of the antagonism
between them. To any mind not warped by the habit of fingering
the Marxian rosary it should be obvious that their relation is, in normal times, primarily one of co-operation and that any theory to the
contrary must draw largely on pathological cases for verification.
In social life, antagonism and synagogism are of course both ubiqui-
tous and in fact inseparable except in the rarest of cases. But I am
almost tempted to say that there was, if anything, less of absolute
nonsense in the old harmonistic view—full of nonsense though that
was too—than in the Marxian construction of the impassable gulf
between tool owners and tool users. Again, however, he had no
choice, not because he wanted to arrive at revolutionary results—
these he could have derived just as well from dozens of other possible schemata—but because of the requirements of his own analysis.
If class struggle was the subject matter of history and also the means
of bringing about the socialist dawn, and *if* there had to be just
those two classes, then their relation had to be antagonistic on principle or else the force in his system of social dynamics would have
been lost.

   Now, though Marx *defines* capitalism sociologically, i.e. by
the institution of private control over means of production, the

mechanics of capitalist society are provided by his economic theory. This economic theory is to show how the sociological data embodied in such conceptions as class, class interest, class behavior, exchange between classes, work out through the medium of economic values, profits, wages, investment, et cetera, and how they generate precisely the economic process that will eventually break its own institutional framework and at the same time create the conditions for the emergence of another social world. This particular theory of social classes is the analytic tool which, by linking the economic interpretation of history with the concepts of the profit economy, marshals all social facts, makes all phenomena confocal. It is therefore not simply a theory of an individual phenomenon which is to explain that phenomenon and nothing else. It has an organic function which is really much more important to the Marxian system than the measure of success with which it solves its immediate problem. This function must be seen if we are to understand how an analyst of the power of Marx could ever have borne with its shortcomings.

There are, and always have been, some enthusiasts who admired the Marxian theory of social classes as such. But far more understandable are the feelings of all those who admire the force and grandeur of that synthesis as a whole to the point of being ready to condone almost any number of shortcomings in the component parts. We shall try to appraise it for ourselves (Chapter IV). But first we must see how Marx's economic mechanics acquits itself of the task that his general plan imposes upon it.

III. MARX THE ECONOMIST

As an economic theorist Marx was first of all a very learned man. It may seem strange that I should think it necessary to give such prominence to this element in the case of an author whom I have called a genius and a prophet. Yet it is important to appreciate it. Geniuses and prophets do not usually excel in professional learning, and their originality, if any, is often due precisely to the fact that they do not. But nothing in Marx's economics can be accounted for by any want of scholarship or training in the technique of theoretical analysis. He was a voracious reader and an indefatigable worker. He missed very few contributions of significance. And whatever he read he digested, wrestling with every fact or argument with a passion for detail most unusual in one whose glance habitually encompassed entire civilizations and secular developments. Criticizing and rejecting or accepting and co-ordinating, he always went to the bottom of every matter. The outstanding proof of this is in his work, *Theories of Surplus Value,* which is a monument of theoretical ardor. This incessant endeavor to school himself and to master whatever there was to master went some way toward freeing him from prejudices and extra-scientific aims, though he certainly worked in order to verify a definite vision. To his powerful intellect, the interest in the problem as a problem was paramount in spite of himself; and however much he may have bent the import of his final *results,* while at work he was primarily concerned with sharpening the tools of analysis proffered by the science of his day, with straightening out logical difficulties, and with building on the foundation thus acquired a theory that in nature and intent was truly scientific whatever its shortcomings may have been.

It is easy to see why both friends and foes should have misunderstood the nature of his performance in the purely economic field. For the friends, he was so much more than a mere professional theorist that it would have seemed almost blasphemy to them to give too much prominence to this aspect of his work. The foes, who resented his attitudes and the setting of his theoretic argument, found it almost impossible to admit that in some parts of his work he did precisely the kind of thing which they valued so highly when presented by other hands. Moreover, the cold metal of economic theory is in Marx's pages immersed in such a wealth of steaming phrases as to acquire a temperature not naturally its own. Whoever shrugs his shoulders at Marx's claim to be considered an analyst in the scientific sense thinks of course of those phrases and not of the thought, of the impassioned language and of the glowing indictment of 'exploitation' and 'immiserization' (this is probably the best way to render the word *Verelendung,* which is no more good German than that English monster is good English. It is *immiserimento* in Italian). To be sure, all these things and many others, such as his spiteful innuendoes or his vulgar comment on Lady Orkney,[1] are important parts of the show, were important to Marx himself, and are so both for the faithful and for the unbelievers. They explain in part why many people insist on seeing in Marx's theorems something more than, and even something fundamentally different from, the analogous propositions of his master. But they do not affect the nature of his analysis.

Marx had a master then? Yes. Real understanding of his economics begins with recognizing that, as a theorist, he was a pupil of Ricardo. He was his pupil not only in the sense that his own argument evidently starts from Ricardo's propositions but also in the much more significant sense that he had learned the art of theorizing from Ricardo. He always used Ricardo's tools, and every theoretical problem presented itself to him in the form of difficulties which occurred to him in his profound study of Ricardo and of suggestions for further work which he gleaned from it. Marx himself admitted much of this, although of course he would not have admitted that his attitude toward Ricardo was typically that of a pupil who goes to the professor, hears him speak several times in almost successive sentences of redundancy of population and of population that is redundant and again of machinery making population redundant, and then goes home and tries to work the thing out. That both parties to the Marxian controversy should have been averse to admitting this is perhaps understandable.

Ricardo's is not the only influence which acted on Marx's economics, but no other than that of Quesnay, from whom Marx derived his fundamental conception of the economic process as a whole, need be mentioned in a sketch like this. The group of English writers who between 1800 and 1840 tried to develop the labor theory of value may have furnished many suggestions and details, but this is covered for our purpose by the reference to the Ricardian

[1] The friend of William III—the king who, so unpopular in his own day, had by that time become an idol of the English bourgeoisie.

current of thought. Several authors, to some of whom Marx was un-kind in inverse proportion to their distance from him and whose work ran in many points parallel to his (Sismondi, Rodbertus, John Stuart Mill), must be left out of account, as must everything not directly pertaining to the main argument—so, for instance, Marx's distinctly weak performance in the field of money, in which he did not succeed in coming up to the Ricardian standard.

Now for a desperately abbreviated outline of the Marxian argument, unavoidably unjust on many counts to the structure of *Das Kapital* which, partly unfinished, partly battered by successful attack, still stretches its mighty skyline before us!

1. Marx fell in with the ordinary run of the theorists of his own and also of a later epoch by making a theory of value the corner stone of his theoretical structure. His theory of value is the Ricardian one. I believe that such an outstanding authority as Professor Taussig disagreed with this and always stressed the differences. There is plenty of difference in wording, method of deduction, and sociological implication, but there is none in the bare theorem, which alone matters to the theorist of today.[2] Both Ricardo and Marx say that the value of every commodity is (in perfect equilibrium and perfect competition) proportional to the quantity of labor contained

---

[2] It may, however, be open to question whether this is all that mattered to Marx himself. He was under the same delusion as Aristotle, viz. that value, though a factor in the determination of relative prices, is yet something that is different from, and exists independently of, relative prices or exchange relations. The proposition that the value of a commodity *is* the amount of labor embodied in it can hardly mean anything else. If so, then there *is* a difference between Ricardo and Marx, since Ricardo's values are simply ex-change values or relative prices. It is worth while to mention this because, if we could accept this view of value, much of his theory that seems to us un-tenable or even meaningless would cease to be so. Of course we cannot. Nor would the situation be improved if, following some Marxologists, we took the view that whether a distinct 'substance' or not, Marx's labor-quantity values are merely intended to serve as tools by which to display the division of total social income into labor income and capital income (the theory of individual relative prices being then a secondary matter). For, as we shall see presently, Marx's theory of value also fails at this task (granted that we can divorce that task from the problem of individual prices).

in the commodity, provided this labor is in accordance with the existing standard of efficiency of production (the 'socially necessary quantity of labor'). Both measure this quantity in hours of work and use the same method in order to reduce different qualities of work to a single standard. Both encounter the threshold difficulties incident to this approach similarly (that is to say, Marx encounters them as he had learned to do from Ricardo). Neither has anything useful to say about monopoly or what we now call imperfect competition. Both answer critics by the same arguments. Marx's arguments are merely less polite, more prolix, and more 'philosophical' in the worst sense of this word.

Everybody knows that this theory of value is unsatisfactory. In the voluminous discussion that has been carried on about it, the right is not indeed all on one side and many faulty arguments have been used by its opponents. The essential point is not whether labor is the true 'source' or 'cause' of economic value. This question may be of primary interest to social philosophers who want to deduce from it ethical claims to the product, and Marx himself was of course not indifferent to this aspect of the problem. For economics as a positive science, however, which has to describe or explain actual processes, it is much more important to ask how the labor theory of value works as a tool of analysis, and the real trouble with it is that it does so very badly.

To begin with, it does not work at all outside of the case of perfect competition. Second, even with perfect competition it never works *smoothly* except if labor is the only factor of production and, moreover, if labor is all of one kind.[3] If either of these two conditions

---

[3] The necessity for the second assumption is particularly damaging. The labor theory of value may be able to deal with differences in quality of labor that are due to training (acquired skill): appropriate quota of the work that goes into the process of training would then have to be added to every hour of skilled work so that we might, without leaving the range of the principle, put the hour of work done by a skilled workman equal to a determined multiple of an hour of unskilled work. But this method fails in the case of 'natural' differences in quality of work due to differences in intelligence, will power, physical strength, or agility. Then recourse must be had to the difference in value of the hours respectively worked by the naturally inferior

is not fulfilled, additional assumptions must be introduced and analytical difficulties increase to an extent that soon becomes unmanageable. Reasoning on the lines of the labor theory of value is hence reasoning on a very special case without practical importance, though something might be said for it if it be interpreted in the sense of a rough approximation to the historical tendencies of relative values. The theory which replaced it—in its earliest and now outmoded form, known as the theory of marginal utility—may claim superiority on many counts but the real argument for it is that it is much more general and applies equally well, on the one hand, to the cases of monopoly and imperfect competition and, on the other hand, to the presence of other factors and of labor of many different kinds and qualities. Moreover, if we introduce into this theory the restrictive assumptions mentioned, proportionality between value and quantity of labor applied follows from it.[4] It should be clear, therefore, not only that it was perfectly absurd for Marxists to question, as at first they tried to do, the validity of the marginal utility theory of value (which was what confronted them), but also that it is incorrect to call the labor theory of value 'wrong.' In any case it is dead and buried.

and the naturally superior workmen—a value that is not itself explainable on the labor-quantity principle. In fact, Ricardo does precisely this: he simply says that those different qualities will somehow be put into their right relation by the play of the market mechanism so that we may after all speak of an hour's work done by workman A being equivalent to a definite multiple of the work done by workman B. But he completely overlooks that in arguing in this way he appeals to another principle of valuation and really surrenders the labor-quantity principle which thus fails from the start, within its own precincts, and before it has the chance to fail because of the presence of factors other than labor. |

[4] In fact, it follows from the marginal utility theory of value that for equilibrium to exist each factor must be so distributed over the productive uses open to it that the last unit allocated to any use produces the same value as the last unit allocated to each of the other uses. If there be no other factors except labor of one kind and quality, this obviously means that the relative values or prices of all commodities must be proportional to the numbers of man-hours contained in them, provided there is perfect competition and mobility.

2. Though neither Ricardo nor Marx seems to have been fully aware of all the weaknesses of the position in which they had placed themselves by adopting this starting point, they perceived some of them quite clearly. In particular, they both grappled with the problem of eliminating the element of Services of Natural Agents, which of course are deprived of their proper place in the process of production and distribution by a theory of value that rests upon quantity of labor alone. The familiar Ricardian theory of the rent of land is essentially an attempt to accomplish that elimination and the Marxian theory is another. As soon as we are in possession of an analytical apparatus which takes care of rent as naturally as it does of wages, the whole difficulty vanishes. Hence nothing more need be said about the intrinsic merits or demerits of Marx's doctrine of absolute as distinguished from differential rent, or about its relation to that of Rodbertus.

But even if we let that pass we are still left with the difficulty arising out of the presence of capital in the sense of a stock of means of production that are themselves produced. To Ricardo it presented itself very simply: in the famous Section iv of the first chapter of his *Principles* he introduces and accepts as a fact, without attempting to question it, that, where capital goods such as plant, machinery, and raw materials are used in the production of a commodity, this commodity will sell at a price which will yield a net return to the owner of those capital goods. He realized that this fact has something to do with the period of time that elapses between the investment and the emergence of salable products and that it will enforce deviations of the actual values of these from proportionality to the man-hours 'contained' in them—including the man-hours that went into the production of the capital goods themselves—whenever these periods are not the same in all industries. To this he points as coolly as if it followed from, instead of contradicting, his fundamental theorem about value, and beyond this he does not really go, confining himself to some secondary problems that arise in this connection and obviously believing that his theory still describes the basic determinant of value.

Marx also introduced, accepted, and discussed that same fact and never questioned it as a fact. He also realized that it seems to give the lie to the labor theory of value. But he recognized the inadequacy of Ricardo's treatment of the problem and, while accepting the problem itself in the shape in which Ricardo presented it, set about to attack it in earnest, devoting to it about as many hundreds of pages as Ricardo devoted sentences.

3. In doing so he not only displayed much keener perception of the nature of the problem involved, but he also improved the conceptual apparatus he received. For instance, he replaced to good purpose Ricardo's distinction between fixed and circulating capital by the distinction between constant and variable (wage) capital, and Ricardo's rudimentary notions about duration of the processes of production by the much more rigorous concept of 'organic structure of capital,' which turns on the relation between constant and variable capital. He also made many other contributions to the theory of capital. We will, however, confine ourselves now to his explanation of the net return to capital, his Theory of Exploitation.

The masses have not always felt themselves to be frustrated and exploited. But the intellectuals that formulated their views for them have always told them that they were, without necessarily meaning by it anything precise. Marx could not have done without the phrase even if he had wanted to. His merit and achievement were that he perceived the weakness of the various arguments by which the tutors of the mass mind before him had tried to show how exploitation came about and which even today supply the stock in trade of the ordinary radical. None of the usual slogans about bargaining power and cheating satisfied him. What he wanted to prove was that exploitation did not arise from individual situations occasionally and accidentally; but that it resulted from the very logic of the capitalist system, unavoidably and quite independently of any individual intention.

This is how he did it. The brain, muscles, and nerves of a laborer constitute, as it were, a fund or stock of potential labor (*Arbeitskraft,* usually translated not very satisfactorily by labor power).

This fund or stock Marx looks upon as a sort of substance that exists in a definite quantity and in capitalist society is a commodity like any other. We may clarify the thought for ourselves by thinking of the case of slavery: Marx's idea is that there is no essential difference, though there are many secondary ones, between the wage contract and the purchase of a slave—what the employer of 'free' labor buys is not indeed, as in the case of slavery, the laborers themselves but a definite quota of the sum total of their potential labor.

Now since labor in that sense (not the labor *service* or the actual man-hour) is a commodity, the law of value must apply to it. That is to say, it must in equilibrium and perfect competition fetch a wage proportional to the number of labor *hours* that entered into its 'production.' But what number of labor *hours* enters into the 'production' of the stock of potential labor that is stored up within a workman's skin? Well, the number of labor *hours* it took and takes to rear, feed, clothe, and house the laborer.[5] This constitutes the value of that stock, and if he sells parts of it—expressed in days or weeks or years—he will receive wages that correspond to the labor value of these parts, just as a slave trader selling a slave would in equilibrium receive a price proportional to the total number of those labor *hours*. It should be observed once more that Marx thus keeps carefully clear of all those popular slogans which in one form or another hold that in the capitalist labor market the workman is robbed or cheated or that, in his lamentable weakness, he is simply compelled to accept any terms imposed. The thing is not as simple as this: he gets the full value of his labor potential.

But once the 'capitalists' have acquired that stock of potential services they are in a position to make the laborer work more hours —render more actual services—than it takes to produce that stock or potential stock. They can exact, in this sense, more actual hours of labor than they have paid for. Since the resulting products also

[5] That is, barring the distinction between 'labor power' and labor, the solution which S. Bailey (*A Critical Discourse on the Nature, Measure and Causes of Value*, 1825) by anticipation voted absurd, as Marx himself did not fail to notice (*Das Kapital*, vol. i, ch. xix).

sell at a price proportional to the man-hours that enter into their production, there is a difference between the two values—arising from nothing but the *modus operandi* of the Marxian law of values —which necessarily and by virtue of the mechanism of capitalist markets goes to the capitalist. This is the Surplus Value (*Mehrwert*).[6] By appropriating it the capitalist 'exploits' labor, though he pays to the laborers not less than the full value of their labor potential and receives from consumers not more than the full value of the products he sells. Again it should be observed that there is no appeal to such things as unfair pricing, restriction of production, or cheating in the markets for the products. Marx did of course not mean to deny the existence of such practices. But he saw them in their true perspective and hence never based any fundamental conclusions upon them.

Let us admire, in passing, the pedagogics of it: however special and removed from its ordinary sense the meaning might be which the word Exploitation now acquires, however doubtful the support which it derives from the Natural Law and the philosophies of the schoolmen and the writers of the Enlightenment, it is received into the pale of scientific argument after all and thus serves the purpose of comforting the disciple marching on to fight his battles.

As regards the merits of this scientific argument we must carefully distinguish two aspects of it, one of which has been persistently neglected by critics. At the ordinary level of the theory of a stationary economic process it is easy to show that under Marx's own assumptions the doctrine of surplus value is untenable. The labor theory of value, even if we could grant it to be valid for every other commodity, can never be applied to the commodity labor, for this would imply that workmen, like machines, are being produced according to rational cost calculations. Since they are not, there is no warrant for assuming that the value of labor power will be proportional to the man-hours that enter into its 'production.' Logically Marx would have improved his position had he accepted Lassalle's

[6] The rate of surplus value (degree of exploitation) is defined as the ratio between surplus value and the variable (wage) capital.

Iron Law of Wages or simply argued on Malthusian lines as Ricardo did. But since he very wisely refused to do that, his theory of exploitation loses one of its essential props from the start.[7]

Moreover, it can be shown that perfectly competitive equilibrium cannot exist in a situation in which all capitalist-employers make exploitation gains. For in this case they would individually try to expand production, and the mass effect of this would unavoidably tend to increase wage rates and to reduce gains of that kind to zero. It would no doubt be possible to mend the case somewhat by appealing to the theory of imperfect competition, by introducing friction and institutional inhibitions of the working of competition, by stressing all the possibilities of hitches in the sphere of money and credit and so on. Only a moderate case could be made out in this manner, however, one that Marx would have heartily despised.

But there is another aspect of the matter. We need only look at Marx's analytic aim in order to realize that he need not have accepted battle on the ground on which it is so easy to beat him. This is so easy only as long as we see in the theory of surplus value nothing but a proposition about stationary economic processes in perfect equilibrium. Since what he aimed at analyzing was not a state of equilibrium which according to him capitalist society can never attain, but on the contrary a process of incessant change in the economic structure, criticism along the lines above is not completely decisive. Surplus values may be impossible in perfect equilibrium but can be ever present because that equilibrium is never allowed to establish itself. They may always *tend* to vanish and yet be always there because they are constantly re-created. This defense will not rescue the labor theory of value, particularly as applied to the commodity labor itself, or the argument about exploitation as it stands. But it will enable us to put a more favorable interpretation on the result, although a satisfactory theory of those surpluses will strip them of the specifically Marxian connotation. This aspect proves to be of considerable importance. It throws a new light also on other

[7] We shall see later how Marx tried to replace that prop.

parts of Marx's apparatus of economic analysis and goes far toward explaining why that apparatus was not more fatally damaged by the successful criticisms directed against its very fundaments.

4. If, however, we go on at the level on which discussion of Marxian doctrines ordinarily moves, we get deeper and deeper into difficulties or rather we perceive that the faithful do when they try to follow the master on his way. To begin with, the doctrine of surplus value does not make it any easier to solve the problems, alluded to above, which are created by the discrepancy between the labor theory of value and the plain facts of economic reality. On the contrary it accentuates them because, according to it, constant capital—that is, non-wage capital—does not transmit to the product any more value than it loses in its production; only wage capital does that and the profits earned should in consequence vary, as between firms, according to the organic composition of their capitals. Marx relies on the competition between capitalists for bringing about a redistribution of the total 'mass' of surplus value such that each firm should earn profits proportional to its total capital, or that individual rates of profits should be equalized. We readily see that the difficulty belongs to the class of spurious problems that always result from attempts to work an unsound theory,[8] and the solution to the class of counsels of despair. Marx, however, believed not only that the latter availed to establish the emergence of uniform rates of profits and to explain how, because of it, relative prices of commodities will deviate from their values in terms of labor,[9] but also that

[8] There is, however, one element in it which is not unsound and the perception of which, however dim, should be recorded to Marx's credit. It is not, as almost all economists believe even today, an unquestionable fact that produced means of production would yield a net return in a perfectly stationary economy. If they in practice normally do seem to yield net returns, that may well be due to the fact that the economy never is stationary. Marx's argument about the net return to capital might be interpreted as a devious way of recognizing this.

[9] His solution of that problem he embodied in manuscripts from which his friend Engels compiled the posthumous third volume of *Das Kapital*. Therefore we have not before us what Marx himself might ultimately have wished to say. As it was, most critics felt no hesitation in convicting him of

his theory offered an explanation of another 'law' that held a great
place in classical doctrine, namely, the statement that the rate of
profit has an inherent tendency to fall. This follows in fact fairly
plausibly from the increase in relative importance of the constant
part of the total capital in the wage-good industries: if the relative
importance of plant and equipment increases in those industries,
as it does in the course of capitalist evolution, and if the rate of
surplus value or the degree of exploitation remains the same, then
the rate of return to total capital will in general decrease. This argument has elicited much admiration, and was presumably looked
upon by Marx himself with all the satisfaction we are in the habit
of feeling if a theory of ours explains an observation that did not
enter into its construction. It would be interesting to discuss it on its
own merits and independently of the mistakes Marx committed in
deriving it. We need not stay to do so, for it is sufficiently condemned by its premises. But a cognate though not identical proposition provides both one of the most important 'forces' of Marxian
dynamics and the link between the theory of exploitation and the
next story of Marx's analytic structure, usually referred to as the
Theory of Accumulation.

The main part of the loot wrung from exploited labor (according to some of the disciples, practically all of it) capitalists turn

having by the third volume flatly contradicted the doctrine of the first. On
the face of it that verdict is not justified. If we place ourselves on Marx's
standpoint, as it is our duty in a question of this kind, it is not absurd to look
upon surplus value as a 'mass' produced by the social process of production
considered as a unit and to make the rest a matter of the distribution of that
mass. And if that is not absurd, it is still possible to hold that the relative
prices of commodities, as deduced in the third volume, follow from the labor-
quantity theory in the first volume. Hence it is not correct to assert, as some
writers from Lexis to Cole have done, that Marx's theory of value is completely divorced from, and contributes nothing to, his theory of prices. But
Marx stands to gain little by being cleared of contradiction. The remaining
indictment is quite strong enough. The best contribution to the whole question of how values and prices are related to each other in the Marxian system,
that also refers to some of the better performances in a controversy that was
not exactly fascinating, is L. von Bortkiewicz, 'Wertrechnung und Preis-
rechnung im Marxschen System,' *Archiv für Sozialwissenschaft und Sozialpolitik,* 1907.

into capital—means of production. In itself and barring the connotations called up by Marx's phraseology, this is of course no more than a statement of a very familiar fact ordinarily described in terms of saving and investment. For Marx however this mere fact was not enough: if the capitalist process was to unfold in inexorable logic, that fact had to be part of this logic which means, practically, that it had to be necessary. Nor would it have been satisfactory to allow this necessity to grow out of the social psychology of the capitalist class, for instance in a way similar to Max Weber's who made Puritan attitudes—and abstaining from hedonist enjoyment of one's profits obviously fits well into their pattern—a causal determinant of capitalist behavior. Marx did not despise any support he felt able to derive from this method.[10] But there had to be something more substantial than this for a system designed as his was, something which compels capitalists to accumulate irrespective of what they feel about it, and which is powerful enough to account for that psychological pattern itself. And fortunately there is.

In setting forth the nature of that compulsion to save, I shall for the sake of convenience accept Marx's teaching on one point: that is to say, I shall assume as he does that saving by the capitalist class *ipso facto* implies a corresponding increase in real capital.[11] This movement will in the first instance always occur in the variable part of total capital, the wage capital, even if the intention is to increase the constant part and in particular that part which Ricardo called fixed capital—mainly machinery.

[10] For instance, in one place (*Das Kapital,* vol. i, p. 654, of the Everyman edition) he surpasses himself in picturesque rhetoric on the subject— going, I think, further than is proper for the author of the economic interpretation of history. Accumulating may or may not be 'Moses and all the prophets'(!) for the capitalist class and such flights may or may not strike us as ridiculous—with Marx, arguments of that type and in that style are always suggestive of some weakness that must be screened.

[11] For Marx, saving or accumulating is identical with conversion of 'surplus value into capital.' With that I do not propose to take issue, though individual attempts at saving do not necessarily and automatically increase real capital. Marx's view seems to me to be so much nearer the truth than the opposite view sponsored by many of my contemporaries that I do not think it worth while to challenge it here.

When discussing Marx's theory of exploitation, I have pointed out that in a perfectly competitive economy exploitation gains would induce capitalists to expand production, or to attempt to expand it, because from the standpoint of every one of them that would mean more profit. In order to do so they would have to accumulate. Moreover the mass effect of this would tend to reduce surplus values through the ensuing rise in wage rates, if not also through an ensuing fall in the prices of products—a very nice instance of the contradictions inherent in capitalism that were so dear to Marx's heart. And that tendency itself would, also for the individual capitalist, constitute another reason why he should feel compelled to accumulate,[12] though again that would in the end make matters worse for the capitalist class as a whole. There would hence be a sort of compulsion to accumulate even in an otherwise stationary process which, as I mentioned before, could not reach stable equilibrium until accumulation had reduced surplus value to zero and thus destroyed capitalism itself.[13]

Much more important and much more drastically compelling is something else, however. As a matter of fact, capitalist economy is not and cannot be stationary. Nor is it merely expanding in a steady manner. It is incessantly being revolutionized *from within*

[12] Less would of course in general be saved out of a smaller than out of a bigger income. But more will be saved out of any given income if it is not expected to last or if it is expected to decrease than would be saved out of the same income if it were known to be at least stable at its current figure.

[13] To some extent Marx recognizes this. But he thinks that if wages rise and thereby interfere with accumulation, the rate of the latter will decrease 'because the stimulus of gain is blunted' so that 'the mechanism of the process of capitalist production removes the very obstacles it temporarily creates.' (*Das Kapital,* vol. i, ch. xxv, section i.) Now *this* tendency of the capitalist mechanism to equilibrate itself is surely not above question and any assertion of it would require, to say the least, careful qualification. But the interesting point is that we should call that statement most un-Marxian if we happened to come across it in the work of another economist and that, as far as it is tenable, it greatly weakens the main drift of Marx's argument. In this point as in many others, Marx displays to an astonishing degree the shackles of the bourgeois economics of his time which he believed himself to have broken.

by new enterprise, i.e. by the intrusion of new commodities or new methods of production or new commercial opportunities into the industrial structure as it exists at any moment. Any existing structures and all the conditions of doing business are always in a process of change. Every situation is being upset before it has had time to work itself out. Economic progress, in capitalist society, means turmoil. And, as we shall see in the next part, in this turmoil competition works in a manner completely different from the way it would work in a stationary process, however perfectly competitive. Possibilities of gains to be reaped by producing new things or by producing old things more cheaply are constantly materializing and calling for new investments. These new products and new methods compete with the old products and old methods not on equal terms but at a decisive advantage that may mean death to the latter. This is how 'progress' comes about in capitalist society. In order to escape being undersold, *every* firm is in the end compelled to follow suit, to invest in its turn and, in order to be able to do so, to plow back part of its profits, i.e. to accumulate.[14] Thus, everyone else accumulates.

Now Marx saw this process of industrial change more clearly and he realized its pivotal importance more fully than any other economist of his time. This does not mean that he correctly understood its nature or correctly analyzed its mechanism. With him, that mechanism resolves itself into mere mechanics of masses of capital. He had no adequate theory of enterprise and his failure to distinguish the entrepreneur from the capitalist, together with a faulty theoretical technique, accounts for many cases of *non sequitur* and for many mistakes. But the mere vision of the process was in itself sufficient for many of the purposes that Marx had in mind. The *non sequitur* ceases to be a fatal objection if what does not follow

[14] That is of course not the only method of financing technological improvement. But it is practically the only method that Marx considered. Since it actually is a very important one, we may here follow him in this, though other methods, particularly that of borrowing from banks, i.e. of creating deposits, produce consequences of their own, insertion of which would really be necessary in order to draw a correct picture of the capitalist process.

from Marx's argument can be made to follow from another one; and even downright mistakes and misinterpretations are often redeemed by the substantial correctness of the general drift of the argument in the course of which they occur—in particular they may be rendered innocuous for the further steps of the analysis which, to the critic who fails to appreciate this paradoxical situation, seem condemned beyond appeal.

We had an example of this before. Taken as it stands, Marx's theory of surplus value is untenable. But since the capitalist process does produce recurrent waves of temporary surplus gains over cost which, though in a very un-Marxian way, other theories can account for all right, Marx's next step, inscribed to accumulation, is not completely vitiated by his previous slips. Similarly, Marx himself did not satisfactorily establish that compulsion to accumulate, which is so essential to his argument. But no great harm results from the shortcomings of his explanation because, in the way alluded to, we can readily supply a more satisfactory one ourselves, in which among other things the fall of profits drops into the right place by itself. The aggregate rate of profit on total industrial capital need not fall in the long run, either for the Marxian reason that the constant capital increases relatively to the variable capital [15] or for any other. It is sufficient that, as we have seen, the profit of every individual plant is incessantly being threatened by actual or potential competition

[15] According to Marx, profits can of course also fall for another reason, i.e. because of a fall in the rate of surplus value. That may be due either to increases in wage rates or to reductions, by legislation for instance, of the daily hours of work. It is possible to argue, even from the standpoint of Marxian theory, that this will induce 'capitalists' to substitute labor-saving capital goods for labor, and hence also increase investment temporarily irrespective of the impact of new commodities and of technological progress. Into these questions we cannot enter however. But we may note a curious incident. In 1837, Nassau W. Senior published a pamphlet entitled *Letters on the Factory Act,* in which he tried to show that the proposed reduction of the duration of the working day would result in the annihilation of profits in the cotton industry. In *Das Kapital,* vol. i, ch. vii, section 3 Marx surpasses himself in fierce indictments against that performance. Senior's argument is in fact little short of foolish. But Marx should have been the last person to say so for it is quite in keeping with his own theory of exploitation.

from new commodities or methods of production which sooner or later will turn it into a loss. So we get the driving force required and even an analogon to Marx's proposition that constant capital does not produce surplus value—for no individual assemblage of capital goods remains a source of surplus gains forever—without having to rely on those parts of his argument which are of doubtful validity.

Another example is afforded by the next link in Marx's chain, his Theory of Concentration, that is, his treatment of the tendency of the capitalist process to increase the size both of industrial plants and of units of control. All he has to offer in explanation,[16] when stripped of his imagery, boils down to the unexciting statements that 'the battle of competition is fought by cheapening commodities' which 'depends, *caeteris paribus,* on the productiveness of labor'; that this again depends on the scale of production; and that 'the larger capitals beat the smaller.'[17] This is much like what the current textbook says on the matter, and not very deep or admirable in itself. In particular it is inadequate because of the exclusive emphasis placed on the size of the individual 'capitals' while in his description of effects Marx is much hampered by his technique which is unable to deal effectively with either monopoly or oligopoly.

Yet the admiration so many economists outside the fold profess to feel for this theory is not unjustified. For one thing, to predict the advent of big business was, considering the conditions of Marx's day, an achievement in itself. But he did more than that. He neatly hitched concentration to the process of accumulation or rather he visualized the former as part of the latter, and not only as part of its factual pattern but also of its logic. He perceived some of the consequences correctly—for instance that 'the increasing bulk of individual masses of capital becomes the material basis of an

[16] See *Das Kapital,* vol. i, ch. xxv, section 2.
[17] This conclusion, often referred to as the theory of expropriation, is with Marx the only purely economic basis of that struggle by which capitalists destroy one another.

uninterrupted revolution in the mode of production itself'—and others at least in a one-sided or distorted manner. He electrified the atmosphere surrounding the phenomenon by all the dynamos of class war and politics—that alone would have been enough to raise his exposition of it high above the dry economic theorems involved, particularly for people without any imagination of their own. And, most important of all, he was able to go on, almost entirely unhampered by the inadequate motivation of individual traits of his picture and by what to the professional appears to be lack of stringency in his argument, for after all the industrial giants actually were in the offing and so was the social situation which they were bound to create.

5. Two more items will complete this sketch: Marx's theory of *Verelendung* or, to use the English equivalent I have ventured to adopt, of immiserization, and his (and Engels') theory of the trade cycle. In the former, both analysis and vision fail beyond remedy; both show up to advantage in the latter.

Marx undoubtedly held that in the course of capitalist evolution real wage rates and the standard of life of the masses would fall in the better-paid, and fail to improve in the worst-paid, strata and that this would come about not through any accidental or environmental circumstances but by virtue of the very logic of the capitalist process.[18] As a prediction, this was of course singularly infelicitous and Marxists of all types have been hard put to it to make the best of the clearly adverse evidence that confronted them. At first, and in some isolated instances even to our day, they displayed a remarkable tenacity in trying to save that 'law' as a statement of an actual

---

[18] There is a first-line defense which Marxists, like most apologists, are wont to set against the critical intention lurking behind any such clear-cut statement. It is that Marx did not entirely fail to see the other side of the medal and that he very often 'recognized' cases of rising wages and so on—as indeed nobody could possibly fail to do—the implication being that he fully anticipated whatever a critic might have to say. So prolix a writer who interlards his argument with such rich layers of historical analysis naturally gives more scope for such defense than any of the fathers of the church did. But what is the good of 'recognizing' recalcitrant fact if it is not allowed to influence conclusions?

tendency borne out by wage statistics. Then attempts were made to read into it a different meaning, that is to say, to make it refer not to rates of real wages or to the absolute share that goes to the working class but to the relative share of labor incomes in total national income. Though some passages in Marx will in fact bear interpretation in this sense, this clearly violates the meaning of most. Moreover, little would be gained by accepting this interpretation, because Marx's main conclusions presuppose that the *absolute* per capita share of labor should fall or, at the very least, not increase: if he really had been thinking of the relative share that would only add to Marxian troubles. Finally the proposition itself would still be wrong. For the relative share of wages and salaries in total income varies but little from year to year and is remarkably constant over time—it certainly does not reveal any tendency to fall.

There seems, however, to be another way out of the difficulty. A tendency may fail to show in our statistical time series—which may even show the opposite one as they do in this case—and yet it might be inherent in the system under investigation, for it might be suppressed by exceptional conditions. This is in fact the line that most modern Marxists take. The exceptional conditions are found in colonial expansion or, more generally, in the opening up of new countries during the nineteenth century, which is held to have brought about a 'closed season' for the victims of exploitation.[19] In the next part we shall have occasion to touch upon this matter. Meanwhile, let us note that facts lend some *prima facie* support to this argument which is also unexceptionable in logic and therefore might resolve the difficulty if that tendency were otherwise well established.

But the real trouble is that Marx's theoretical structure is anything but trustworthy in that sector: along with the vision, the analytic groundwork is there at fault. The basis of the theory of immiserization is the theory of the 'industrial reserve army,' i.e. of the

[19] This idea was suggested by Marx himself, though it has been developed by the Neo-Marxists.

unemployment created by the mechanization of the process of production.[20] And the theory of the reserve army is in turn based upon
the doctrine expounded in Ricardo's chapter on machinery. Nowhere else—excepting of course the theory of value—does Marx's
argument so completely depend on that of Ricardo without adding
anything essential.[21] I am speaking of course of the pure theory of
the phenomenon only. Marx did add, as always, many minor touches
such as the felicitous generalization by which the replacement of
skilled by unskilled workers is made to enter into the concept of
unemployment; also he added an infinite wealth of illustration and
phraseology; and, most important of all, he added the impressive
setting, the wide backgrounds of his social process.

Ricardo had at first been inclined to share the view, very common at all times, that the introduction of machines into the productive process could hardly fail to benefit the masses. When he came
to doubt that opinion or, at all events, its general validity, he with
characteristic frankness revised his position. No less characteristically, he leaned backwards in doing so and, using his customary
method of 'imagining strong cases,' produced a numerical example,
well known to all economists, to show that things could also turn
out the other way. He did not mean to deny, on the one hand, that
he was proving no more than a possibility—a not unlikely one
though—or, on the other hand, that in the end net benefit to labor
would result from mechanization through its ulterior effects on
total output, prices and so on.

[20] This kind of unemployment must of course be distinguished from
others. In particular, Marx notices the kind which owes its existence to the
cyclical variations in business activity. Since the two are not independent and
since in his argument he often relies on the latter type rather than on the
former, difficulties of interpretation arise of which not all critics seem to be
fully aware.

[21] To any theorist this must be obvious, from a study not only of the
sedes materiae, Das Kapital, vol. i, ch. xv, sections 3, 4, 5, and especially 6
(where Marx deals with the theory of compensation, to be noted above), but
also of chs. xxiv and xxv where, in a partially different garb, the same things
are repeated and elaborated.

The example is correct as far as it goes.[22] The somewhat more refined methods of today support its result to the extent that they admit the possibility it aimed at establishing as well as the opposite one; they go beyond it by stating the formal conditions which determine whether the one or the other consequence will ensue. That is of course all that pure theory can do. Further data are necessary in order to predict the actual effect. But for our purpose, Ricardo's example presents another interesting feature. He considers a firm owning a given amount of capital and employing a given number of workmen that decides to take a step in mechanization. Accordingly, it assigns a group of those workmen to the task of constructing a machine which when installed will enable the firm to dispense with part of that group. Profits may eventually remain the same (after the competitive adjustments which will do away with any temporary gain) but gross revenue will be destroyed to the exact amount of the wages previously paid to the workmen that have now been 'set free.' Marx's idea of the replacement of variable (wage) capital by constant capital is almost the exact replica of this way of putting it. Ricardo's emphasis upon the ensuing *redundancy* of population is likewise exactly paralleled by Marx's emphasis upon *surplus* population which term he uses as an alternative to the term 'industrial reserve army.' Ricardo's teaching is indeed being swallowed hook, line and sinker.

But what may pass muster as long as we move within the restricted purpose Ricardo had in view becomes utterly inadequate—in fact the source of another *non sequitur,* not redeemed this time by a correct vision of ultimate results—as soon as we consider the superstructure Marx erected on that slender foundation. Some such feeling he seems to have had himself. For with an energy that has something desperate about it he clutched the conditionally pessimistic result of his teacher as if the latter's strong case were the only possible one, and with energy even more desperate he fought those

[22] Or it can be made correct without losing its significance. There are a few doubtful points about the argument that are probably due to its lamentable technique—which so many economists would love to perpetuate.

authors who had developed the implications of Ricardo's hint at compensations that the machine age might hold out to labor even where the immediate effect of the introduction of machinery spelled injury (theory of compensation, the pet aversion of all Marxists).

He had every reason for taking this course. For he badly needed a firm foundation for his theory of the reserve army which was to serve two fundamentally important purposes, besides some minor ones. First, we have seen that he deprived his doctrine of exploitation of what I have called an essential prop by his aversion, quite understandable in itself, to making use of the Malthusian theory of population. That prop was replaced by the ever-present, because ever-recreated [23] reserve army. Second, the particularly narrow view of the process of mechanization he adopted was essential in order to motivate the resounding phrases in Chapter xxxii of the first volume of *Das Kapital* which in a sense are the crowning finale not only of that volume but of Marx's whole work. I will quote them in full—more fully than the point under discussion requires—in order to give my readers a glimpse of Marx in the attitude which accounts equally well for the enthusiasm of some and for the contempt of others. Whether a compound of things that are not so or the very heart of prophetic truth, here they are:

'Hand in hand with this centralization, or this expropriation of many capitalists by few, develops . . . the entanglement of all nations in the net of the world market, and with this, the international character of the capitalist régime. Along with the constantly diminishing number of the magnates of capital, who usurp and monopolize all advantages of this process of transformation, grows the mass of misery, oppression, slavery, degradation, exploitation; but with this too grows the revolt of the working class, a class always increasing in numbers, and disciplined, united, organized by

[23] It is of course necessary to stress the incessant creation. It would be quite unfair to Marx's words as well as meaning to imagine, as some critics have done, that he assumed that the introduction of machinery threw people out of work who then would remain individually unemployed ever after. He did not deny absorption, and criticism that is based on the proof that any unemployment created will each time be absorbed entirely misses the target.

the very mechanism of the process of capitalist production itself. The monopoly of capital becomes a fetter upon the mode of production, which has sprung up and flourished along with it, and under it. Centralization of the means of production and socialization of labor at last reach a point where they become incompatible with their capitalist integument. This integument bursts. The knell of capitalist private property sounds. The expropriators are expropriated.'

6. Marx's performance in the field of business cycles is exceedingly difficult to appraise. The really valuable part of it consists of dozens of observations and comments, most of them of a casual nature, which are scattered over almost all his writings, many of his letters included. Attempts at reconstruction from such *membra disjecta* of a body that nowhere appears in the flesh and perhaps did not even exist in Marx's own mind except in an embryonic form, may easily yield different results in different hands and be vitiated, by the understandable tendency of the admirer to credit Marx, by means of suitable interpretation, with practically all those results of later research of which the admirer himself approves.

The common run of friends and foes never realized and does not realize now the kind of task which confronts the commentator because of the nature of Marx's kaleidoscopic contribution to that subject. Seeing that Marx so frequently pronounced upon it and that it was obviously very relevant to his fundamental theme, they took it for granted that there must be some simple and clear-cut Marxian cycle theory which it should be possible to make grow out of the rest of his logic of the capitalist process much as, for instance, the theory of exploitation grows out of the labor theory. Accordingly they set about finding such a theory, and it is easy to guess what it was that occurred to them.

On the one hand, Marx no doubt extols—though he does not quite adequately motivate—the tremendous power of capitalism to develop society's capacity to produce. On the other hand, he incessantly places emphasis on the growing misery of the masses. Is it not the most natural thing in the world to conclude that crises or depressions are due to the fact that the exploited masses cannot buy what that ever-expanding apparatus of production turns out or stands ready to turn out, and that for this and also other reasons which we need not repeat the rate of profits drops to bankruptcy level? Thus we seem indeed to land, according to which element we want to stress, at the shores of either an under-consumption or an over-production theory of the most contemptible type.

The Marxian explanation has in fact been classed with the under-consumption theories of crises.[24] There are two circumstances that may be invoked in support. First, in the theory of surplus value and also in other matters, the affinity of Marx's teachings with that of Sismondi and Rodbertus is obvious. And these men did espouse the under-consumption view. It was not unnatural to infer that Marx might have done the same. Second, some passages in Marx's works particularly the brief statement about crises contained in the *Communist Manifesto* undoubtedly lend themselves to this interpretation, though Engels' utterances do so much more.[25] But this is of

[24] Though this interpretation has become a fashion, I will mention two authors only, one of whom is responsible for a modified version of it, while the other may testify to its persistence: Tugan-Baranowsky, *Theoretische Grundlagen des Marxismus,* 1905, who condemned Marx's theory of crises on that ground; and M. Dobb, *Political Economy and Capitalism,* 1937, who is more sympathetic toward it.

[25] Engels' somewhat commonplace view of the matter is best expressed in his polemical book entitled *Herrn Eugen Dührings Umwälzung der Wissenschaft,* 1878, in what has become one of the most frequently quoted passages in socialist literature. He presents there a very graphic account of the morphology of crises that is good enough no doubt for the purposes of popular lectures, but also the opinion, standing in the place in which one would look for an explanation, that 'the expansion of the market cannot keep pace with the expansion of production.' Also he approvingly refers to Fourier's opinion, conveyed by the self-explanatory phrase, *crises pléthoriques.* It cannot be denied however that Marx wrote part of ch. x and shares responsibility for the whole book.

I observe that the few comments on Engels that are contained in this sketch are of a derogatory nature. This is unfortunate and not due to any intention to belittle the merits of that eminent man. I do think however that it should be frankly admitted that intellectually and especially as a theorist he stood far below Marx. We cannot even be sure that he always got the latter's meaning. His interpretations must therefore be used with care.

no account since Marx, showing excellent sense, expressly repudiated it.[26]

The fact is that he had no simple theory of business cycles.
And none can be made to follow logically from his 'laws' of the
capitalist process. Even if we accept his explanation of the emergence of surplus value and agree to allow that accumulation, mechanization (relative increase of constant capital) and surplus population, the latter inexorably deepening mass misery, do link up into
a logical chain that ends in the catastrophe of the capitalist system—
even then we are left without a factor that would necessarily impart
cyclical fluctuation to the process and account for an *immanent*
alternation of prosperities and depressions.[27] No doubt plenty of
accidents and incidents are always at hand for us to draw upon in
order to make up for the missing fundamental explanation. There
are miscalculations, mistaken expectations and other errors, waves
of optimism and pessimism, speculative excesses and reactions to
speculative excesses, and there is the inexhaustible source of 'external factors.' All the same, Marx's mechanical process of accumulation going on at an even rate—and there is nothing to show
why, on principle, it should not—the process he describes *might*
also go on at even rates; as far as its logic is concerned, it is essentially prosperityless and depressionless.

Of course this is not necessarily a misfortune. Many other
theorists have held and do hold simply that crises happen whenever
something of sufficient importance goes wrong. Nor was it altogether a handicap because it released Marx, for once, from the
thralldom of his system and set him free to look at facts without

[26] *Das Kapital,* vol. ii, p. 476, of the English translation of 1907. See,
however, also *Theorien über den Mehrwert,* vol. ii, ch. iii.

[27] To the layman, the opposite seems so obvious that it would not be
easy to establish this statement, even if we had all the space in the world.
The best way for the reader to convince himself of its truth is to study
Ricardo's argument on machinery. The process there described might cause
any amount of unemployment and yet go on indefinitely without causing a
breakdown other than the final one of the system itself. Marx would have
agreed with this.

having to do violence to them. Accordingly, he considers a wide variety of more or less relevant elements. For instance, he uses somewhat superficially the intervention of money in commodity transactions—and nothing else—in order to invalidate Say's proposition about the impossibility of a general glut; or easy money markets in order to explain disproportionate developments in the lines characterized by heavy investment in durable capital goods; or special stimuli such as the opening of markets or the emergence of new social wants in order to motivate sudden spurts in 'accumulation.' He tries, not very successfully, to turn the growth of population into a factor making for fluctuations.[28] He observes, though he does not really explain, that the scale of production expands 'by fits and starts' that are 'the preliminary to its equally sudden contraction.' He aptly says that 'the superficiality of Political Economy shows itself in the fact that it looks upon expansion and contraction of credit, which is a mere symptom of the periodic changes of the industrial cycle, as their cause.' [29] And the chapter of incidents and accidents he of course lays under heavy contribution.

All that is common sense and substantially sound. We find practically all the elements that ever entered into any serious analysis of business cycles, and on the whole very little error. Moreover, it must not be forgotten that the mere perception of the existence of cyclical movements was a great achievement at the time. Many economists who went before him had an inkling of it. In the main, however, they focused their attention on the spectacular breakdowns that came to be referred to as 'crises.' And those crises they failed to see in their true light, that is to say, in the light of the cyclical

[28] In this also he does not stand alone. However it is but fair to him to expect that he would eventually have seen the weaknesses of this approach, and it is relevant to note that his remarks on the subject occur in the third volume and cannot be trusted to render what might have been his final view.

[29] *Das Kapital,* vol. i, ch. xxv, section 3. Immediately after this passage he takes a step in a direction that is also very familiar to the student of modern business cycle theories: 'Effects, in their turn become causes, and the varying accidents of the whole process, *which always reproduces its own conditions* [my italics], take on the form of periodicity.'

process of which they are mere incidents. They considered them, without looking beyond or below, as isolated misfortunes that will happen in consequence of errors, excesses, misconduct, or of the faulty working of the credit mechanism. Marx was, I believe, the first economist to rise above that tradition and to anticipate—barring the statistical complement—the work of Clément Juglar. Though, as we have seen, he did not offer an adequate explanation of the business cycle, the phenomenon stood clearly before his eyes and he understood much of its mechanism. Also like Juglar, he unhesitatingly spoke of a decennial cycle 'interrupted by minor fluctuations.' [30] He was intrigued by the question of what the cause of that period might be and considered the idea that it might have something to do with the life of machinery in the cotton industry. And there are many other signs of preoccupation with the problem of business cycles as distinguished from that of crises. This is enough to assure him high rank among the fathers of modern cycle research.

Another aspect must be mentioned. In most cases Marx used the term crisis in its ordinary sense, speaking of the crisis of 1825 or that of 1847 as other people do. But he also used it in a different sense. Believing that capitalist evolution would some day disrupt the institutional framework of capitalist society, he thought that before the actual breakdown occurred, capitalism would begin to work with increasing friction and display the symptoms of fatal illness. To this stage, to be visualized of course as a more or less prolonged historical period, he applied the same term. And he displays a tendency to link those recurrent crises with this unique crisis of the capitalist order. He even suggests that the former may in a sense be looked upon as previews of the ultimate breakdown. Since to many readers this

[30] Engels went further than this. Some of his notes to Marx's third volume reveal that he suspected also the existence of a longer swing. Though he was inclined to interpret the comparative weakness of prosperities and the comparative intensity of depressions in the seventies and eighties as a structural change rather than as the effect of the depression phase of a wave of longer span (exactly as many modern economists do with respect to the postwar developments and especially to those of the last decade) some anticipation of Kondratieff's work on Long Cycles might be seen in this.

might look like a clue to Marx's theory of crises in the ordinary sense, it is necessary to point out that the factors which according to Marx will be responsible for the ultimate breakdown cannot, without a good dose of additional hypotheses, be made responsible for the recurrent depressions,[31] and that the clue does not get us beyond the trivial proposition that the 'expropriation of the expropriators' may be an easier matter in a depression than it would be in a boom.

7. Finally, the idea that capitalist evolution will burst—or outgrow—the institutions of capitalist society (*Zusammenbruchstheorie*, the theory of the inevitable catastrophe) affords a last example of the combination of a *non sequitur* with profound vision which helps to rescue the result.

Based as Marx's 'dialectic deduction' is on the growth of misery and oppression that will goad the masses into revolt, it is invalidated by the *non sequitur* that vitiates the argument which was to establish that inevitable growth of misery. Moreover, otherwise orthodox Marxists have long ago begun to doubt the validity of the proposition that concentration of industrial control is necessarily incompatible with the 'capitalist integument.' The first of them to voice this doubt by means of a well-organized argument was Rudolf Hilferding,[32] one of the leaders of the important group of Neo-Marxists, who actually inclined toward the opposite inference, viz. that through concentration capitalism might gain in stability.[33] De-

[31] In order to convince himself of this, the reader need only glance again at the quotation on pp. 46-47. In fact, though Marx so often plays with the idea, he avoids committing himself to it, which is significant because it was not his way to miss the opportunity for a generalization.

[32] *Das Finanzkapital*, 1910. Doubts based on a number of secondary circumstances that were held to show that Marx made too much of the tendencies he thought he had established and that social evolution was a much more complex and a much less consistent process than he made out, had of course often arisen before. It is sufficient to mention E. Bernstein; see ch. xxvi. But Hilferding's analysis does not plead extenuating circumstances, but fights that conclusion on principle and on Marx's own ground.

[33] This proposition has often (even by its author) been confused with the proposition that business fluctuations tend to become milder as time goes on. That may or may not be so (1929-32 would not disprove it) but greater stability of the capitalist *system*, i.e. a somewhat less temperamental behavior

ferring to the next part what I have to say upon the matter, I will state that Hilferding seems to me to go too far although there is, as we shall see, no foundation for the belief, at present current in this country, that big business 'becomes a fetter upon the mode of production,' and although Marx's conclusion does in fact not follow from his premises.

However, even though Marx's facts and reasoning were still more at fault than they are, his result might nevertheless be true so far as it simply avers that capitalist evolution will destroy the foundations of capitalist society. I believe it is. And I do not think I am exaggerating if I call profound a vision in which that truth stood revealed beyond doubt in 1847. It is a commonplace now. The first to make it that was Gustav Schmoller. His Excellency, Professor von Schmoller, Prussian Privy Councillor and Member of the Prussian House of Lords, was not much of a revolutionary or much given to agitatorial gesticulations. But he quietly stated the same truth. The Why and How of it he likewise left unsaid.

It is hardly necessary to sum up elaborately. However imperfect, our sketch should suffice to establish: first, that nobody who cares at all for purely economic analysis can speak of unqualified success; second, that nobody who cares at all for bold construction can speak of unqualified failure.

In the court that sits on theoretical technique, the verdict must be adverse. Adherence to an analytic apparatus that always had been inadequate and was in Marx's own day rapidly becoming obsolete; a long list of conclusions that do not follow or are downright wrong; mistakes which if corrected change essential inferences, sometimes into their opposites—all this can be rightfully charged against Marx, the theoretical technician.

Even in that court, however, qualification of the verdict will be necessary on two grounds.

of our time series of prices and quantities, does not necessarily imply, nor is it necessarily implied by, greater stability, i.e. a greater ability of the capitalist *order* to withstand attack. Both things are related, of course, but they are not the same.

First, though Marx was often—sometimes hopelessly—wrong, his critics were far from being always right. Since there were excellent economists among them, the fact should be recorded to his credit, particularly because most of them he was not able to meet himself.

Second, so should Marx's contributions, both critical and positive, to a great many individual problems. In a sketch like this, it is not possible to enumerate them, let alone to do them justice. But we have had a view of some of them in our discussion of his treatment of the business cycle. I have also mentioned some that improved our theory of the structure of physical capital. The schemata which he devised in that field, though not irreproachable, have again proved serviceable in recent work that looks quite Marxian in places.

But a court of appeal—even though still confined to theoretical matters—might feel inclined to reverse this verdict altogether. For there is one truly great achievement to be set against Marx's theoretical misdemeanors. Through all that is faulty or even unscientific in his analysis runs a fundamental idea that is neither—the idea of a theory, not merely of an indefinite number of disjointed individual patterns or of the logic of economic quantities in general, but of the actual sequence of those patterns or of the economic process as it goes on, under its own steam, in historic time, producing at every instant that state which will of itself determine the next one. Thus, the author of so many misconceptions was also the first to visualize what even at the present time is still the economic theory of the future for which we are slowly and laboriously accumulating stone and mortar, statistical facts and functional equations.

And he not only conceived that idea, but he tried to carry it out. All the shortcomings that disfigure his work must, because of the great purpose his argument attempted to serve, be judged differently even where they are not, as they are in some cases, fully redeemed thereby. There is however one thing of fundamental importance for the methodology of economics which he actually achieved. Economists always have either themselves done work in economic history or else used the historical work of others. But the facts of economic history were assigned to a separate compartment. They entered theory, if at all, merely in the role of illustrations, or possibly of verifications of results. They mixed with it only mechanically. Now Marx's mixture is a chemical one; that is to say, he introduced them into the very argument that produces the results. He was the first economist of top rank to see and to teach systematically how economic theory may be turned into historical analysis and how the historic narrative may be turned into *historic raisonnée.*[34] The analogous problem with respect to statistics he did not attempt to solve. But in a sense it is implied in the other. This also answers the question how far, in the way explained at the end of the preceding chapter, Marx's economic theory succeeds in implementing his sociological setup. It does not succeed; but in failing, it establishes both a goal and a method.

IV. MARX THE TEACHER

The main components of the Marxian structure are now before us. What about the imposing synthesis as a whole? The question is not otiose. If ever it is true, it is in this case that the whole is more than the sum of the parts. Moreover, the synthesis may have so spoiled the wheat or so utilized the chaff, both of which are present in almost every spot, that the whole might be more true or more false than any part of it is, taken by itself. Finally, there is the Message that proceeds only from the whole. Of the latter however no more will be said. Each of us must settle for himself what it means to him.

Our time revolts against the inexorable necessity of specialization and therefore cries out for synthesis, nowhere so loudly as in

[34] If devoted disciples should therefore claim that he set the goal for the historical school of economics, that claim could not be lightly dismissed, though the work of the Schmoller school was certainly quite independent of Marx's suggestion. But if they went on to claim that Marx, and Marx only, knew how to rationalize history, whereas the men of the historical school only knew how to describe facts without getting at their meaning, they would be spoiling their case. For those men as a matter of fact knew how to analyze. If their generalizations were less sweeping and their narratives less selective, that is all to their credit.

the social sciences in which the non-professional element counts for so much.[1] But Marx's system illustrates well that, though synthesis may mean new light, it also means new fetters.

We have seen how in the Marxian argument sociology and economics pervade each other. In intent, and to some degree also in actual practice, they are one. All the major concepts and propositions are hence both economic and sociological and carry the same meaning on both planes—if, from our standpoint, we may still speak of two planes of argument. Thus, the economic *category* 'labor' and the social *class* 'proletariat' are, on principle at least, made congruent, in fact identical. Or the economists' functional distribution—that is to say, the explanation of the way in which incomes emerge as returns to productive services irrespective of what social class any recipient of such a return may belong to—enters the Marxian system only in the form of distribution between social classes and thus acquires a different connotation. Or capital in the Marxian system is capital only if in the hands of a distinct capitalist class. The same things, if in the hands of the workmen, are not capital.

There cannot be any doubt about the access of vitality which comes to analysis thereby. The ghostly concepts of economic theory begin to breathe. The bloodless theorem descends into *agmen, pulverem et clamorem;* without losing its logical quality, it is no longer a mere proposition about the logical properties of a system of abstractions; it is the stroke of a brush that is painting the wild jumble of social life. Such analysis conveys not only richer meaning of what all economic analysis describes but it embraces a much broader field —it draws every kind of class action into its picture, whether or not this class action conforms to the ordinary rules of business procedure. Wars, revolutions, legislation of all types, changes in the structure

---

[1] The non-professional element is particularly strongly represented among those admirers of Marx who, going beyond the attitude of the typical Marxian *economist,* still take at face value everything he wrote. This is very significant. In every national group of Marxists there are at least three laymen to every trained economist and even this economist is as a rule a Marxist only in that qualified sense defined in the introduction to this part: he worships at the shrine, but he turns his back upon it when he does his research.

of governments, in short all the things that non-Marxian economics treats simply as external disturbances do find their places side by side with, say, investment in machinery or bargains with labor— everything is covered by a single explanatory schema.

At the same time, such procedure has its shortcomings. Conceptual arrangements that are subject to a yoke of this kind may easily lose in efficiency as much as they gain in vividness. The pair, worker-proletarian, may serve as a telling if somewhat trite example. In non-Marxian economics all returns to services of persons partake of the nature of wages, whether those persons are tophole lawyers, movie stars, company executives or street sweepers. Since all these returns have, from the standpoint of the economic phenomenon involved, much in common, this generalization is not futile or sterile. On the contrary, it may be enlightening, even for the sociological aspect of things. But by equating labor and proletariat we obscure it; in fact, we entirely banish it from our picture. Similarly, a valuable economic theorem may by its sociological metamorphosis pick up error instead of richer meaning and vice versa. Thus, synthesis in general and synthesis on Marxian lines in particular might easily issue in both worse economics and worse sociology.

Synthesis in general, i.e. co-ordination of the methods and results of different lines of advance, is a difficult thing which few are competent to tackle. In consequence it is ordinarily not tackled at all and from the students who are taught to see only individual trees we hear discontented clamor for the forest. They fail to realize however that the trouble is in part an *embarras de richesse* and that the synthetic forest may look uncommonly like an intellectual concentration camp.

Synthesis on Marxian lines, i.e. co-ordination of economic and sociological analysis with a view to bending everything to a single purpose, is of course particularly apt to look like that. The purpose— that *histoire raisonnée* of capitalist society—is wide enough but the analytic setup is not. There is indeed a grand wedding of political facts and of economic theorems; but they are wedded by force and neither of them can breathe. Marxists claim that their system solves

all the great problems that baffle non-Marxian economics; so it does
but only by emasculating them. This point calls for some elaboration.

I said a moment ago that Marx's synthesis embraces all those
historical events—such as wars, revolutions, legislative changes—
and all those social institutions—such as property, contractual relations, forms of government—that non-Marxian economists are wont
to treat as disturbing factors or as data, which means that they do
not propose to explain them but only to analyze their *modi operandi*
and consequences. Such factors or data are of course necessary in
order to delimit the object and range of any research program whatsoever. If they are not always expressly specified, that is only because everyone is expected to know what they are. The trait peculiar
to the Marxian system is that it subjects those historical events and
social institutions themselves to the explanatory process of economic
analysis or, to use the technical lingo, that it treats them not as
data but as variables.

Thus the Napoleonic Wars, the Crimean War, the American
Civil War, the World War of 1914, the French Frondes, the great
French Revolution, the revolutions of 1830 and 1848, English free
trade, the labor movement as a whole as well as any of its particular
manifestations, colonial expansion, institutional changes, the national
and party politics of every time and country—all this enters the
domain of Marxian economics which claims to find theoretical explanations in terms of class warfare, of attempts at and revolt against
exploitation, of accumulation and of qualitative change in the capital
structure, of changes in the rate of surplus value and in the rate of
profit. No longer has the economist to be content with giving technical answers to technical questions; instead, he teaches humanity
the hidden meaning of its struggles. No longer is 'politics' an independent factor that may and must be abstracted from in an investigation of fundamentals and, when it does intrude, plays according
to one's preferences either the role of a naughty boy who viciously
tampers with a machine when the engineer's back is turned, or else
the role of a *deus ex machina* by virtue of the mysterious wisdom
of a doubtful species of mammals deferentially referred to as 'states-

men.' No—politics itself is being determined by the structure and state of the economic process and becomes a conductor of effects as completely within the range of economic theory as any purchase or sale.

Once more, nothing is easier to understand than the fascination exerted by a synthesis which does for us just this. It is particularly understandable in the young and in those intellectual denizens of our newspaper world to whom the gods seem to have granted the gift of eternal youth. Panting with impatience to have their innings, longing to save the world from something or other, disgusted with textbooks of undescribable tedium, dissatisfied emotionally and intellectually, unable to achieve synthesis by their own effort, they find what they crave for in Marx. There it is, the key to all the most intimate secrets, the magic wand that marshals both great events and small. They are beholding an explanatory schema that at the same time is—if I may for a moment lapse into Hegelianism—most general and most concrete. They need no longer feel out of it in the great affairs of life—all at once they see through the pompous marionettes of politics and business who never know what it is all about. And who can blame them, considering available alternatives?

Yes, of course—but apart from that, what does this service of the Marxian synthesis amount to? I wonder. The humble economist who describes England's transition to free trade or the early achievements of English factory legislation is not, and never was, likely to forget to mention the structural conditions of the English economy that produced those policies. If he does not do so in a course or book on pure theory, that merely makes for neater and more efficient analysis. What the Marxist has to add is only the insistence on the principle, and a particularly narrow and warped theory by which to implement it. This theory yields results no doubt, and very simple and definite ones to boot. But we need only apply it systematically to individual cases in order to grow thoroughly weary of the unending jingle about the class war between owners and non-owners and to become aware of a painful sense of inadequacy or, worse still, of triviality—of the former, if we do not swear by the underlying schema; of the latter, if we do.

Marxists are in the habit of pointing triumphantly to the success of the Marxian diagnosis of the economic and social tendencies that are supposed to be inherent in capitalist evolution. As we have seen, there is some justification for this: more clearly than any other writer of his day Marx discerned the trend toward big business and not only that but also some of the features of the consequent situations. We have also seen that in this case vision lent its aid to analysis so as to remedy some of the shortcomings of the latter and to make the import of the synthesis truer than the contributing elements of the analysis were themselves. But this is all. And against the achievement must be set the failure of the prediction of increasing misery, the joint result of wrong vision and faulty analysis, on which a great many Marxian speculations about the future course of social events had been based. He who places his trust in the Marxian synthesis as a whole in order to understand present situations and problems is apt to be woefully wrong.[2] This seems in fact to be felt by many a Marxist just now.

In particular there is no reason for taking pride in the manner in which the Marxian synthesis accounts for the experience of the last decade. Any prolonged period of depression or of unsatisfactory recovery will verify any pessimistic forecast exactly as well as it verifies the Marxian one. In this case an impression to the contrary

---

[2] Some Marxists would reply that non-Marxian economists have simply nothing to contribute to our understanding of our time so that the disciple of Marx is nevertheless better off in that respect. Waiving the question of whether it is better to say nothing or to say something that is wrong, we should bear in mind that this not true, for both economists and sociologists of non-Marxian persuasions have as a matter of fact contributed substantially though mostly on individual questions. Least of all can this Marxist claim be based on a comparison of Marx's teachings with that of the Austrians or of the Walras or Marshall schools. The members of these groups were in most cases wholly, in all cases mainly, interested in economic theory. This performance is hence incommensurable with Marx's synthesis. It could only be compared with Marx's theoretical apparatus and in that field comparison is all to their advantage.

is created by the talk of disheartened bourgeois and elated intellectuals which naturally acquired a Marxian hue from their fears and hopes. But no actual fact warrants any specifically Marxian diagnosis, still less an inference to the effect that what we have been witnessing was not simply a depression, but the symptoms of a structural change in the capitalist process such as Marx expected to occur. For, as will be noted in the next part, all the phenomena observed such as supernormal unemployment, lack of investment opportunity, shrinkage of money values, losses and so on, come within the well-known pattern of periods of predominating depression such as the seventies and eighties on which Engels commented with a restraint that should set an example to ardent followers of today.

Two outstanding examples will illustrate both the merits and the demerits of the Marxian synthesis considered as a problem-solving engine.

First we will consider the Marxist theory of Imperialism. Its roots are all to be found in Marx's chief work, but it has been developed by the Neo-Marxist school which flourished in the first two decades of this century and, without renouncing communion with the old defenders of the faith, such as Karl Kautsky, did much to overhaul the system. Vienna was its center; Otto Bauer, Rudolf Hilferding, Max Adler were its leaders. In the field of imperialism their work was continued, with but secondary shifts of emphasis, by many others, prominent among whom were Rosa Luxemburg and Fritz Sternberg. The argument runs as follows.

Since, on the one hand, capitalist society cannot exist and its economic system cannot function without profits and since, on the other hand, profits are constantly being eliminated by the very working of that system, incessant effort to keep them alive becomes the central aim of the capitalist class. Accumulation accompanied by qualitative change in the composition of capital is, as we have seen, a remedy which though alleviating for the moment the situation of the individual capitalist makes matters worse in the end. So capital, yielding to the pressure of a falling rate of profits—it falls, we recall, both because constant capital increases relative to variable capital and because, if wages tend to rise and hours are being shortened, the rate of surplus value falls—seeks for outlets in countries in which there is still labor that can be exploited at will and in which the process of mechanization has not as yet gone far. Thus we get an export of capital into undeveloped countries which is essentially an export of capital equipment or of consumers' goods to be used in order to buy labor or to acquire things with which to buy labor.[3] But it is also export of capital in the ordinary sense of the term because the exported commodities will not be paid for—at least not immediately—by goods, services or money from the importing country. And it turns into colonization if, in order to safeguard the investment both against hostile reaction of the native environment— or if you please, against its resistance to exploitation—and against competition from other capitalist countries, the undeveloped country is brought into political subjection. This is in general accomplished by military force supplied either by the colonizing capitalists themselves or by their home government which thus lives up to the definition given in the *Communist Manifesto:* 'the executive of the modern State [is] . . . a committee for managing the common affairs of the whole bourgeoisie.' Of course, that force will not be used for defensive purposes only. There will be conquest, friction between the capitalist countries and internecine war between rival bourgeoisies.

Another element completes this theory of imperialism as it is now usually presented. So far as colonial expansion is prompted by a falling rate of profit in the capitalist countries, it should occur in

[3] Think of luxuries to be traded to chieftains against slaves or to be traded against wage goods with which to hire native labor. For the sake of brevity, I do not take account of the fact that capital export in the sense envisaged will in general arise as a part of the total trade of the two countries which also includes commodity transactions unconnected with the particular process we have in mind. These transactions of course greatly facilitate that capital export, but do not affect its principle. I shall also neglect other types of capital exports. The theory under discussion is not, and is not intended to be, a general theory of international trade and finance.

the later stages of capitalist evolution—Marxists in fact speak of imperialism as a stage, preferably the last stage, of capitalism. Hence it would coincide with a high degree of concentration of capitalist control over industry and with a decline of the type of competition that characterized the times of the small or medium-sized firm. Marx himself did not lay much stress on the resulting tendency toward monopolistic restriction of output and on the consequent tendency toward protecting the domestic game preserve against the intrusion of poachers from other capitalist countries. Perhaps he was too competent an economist to trust this line of argument too far. But the Neo-Marxists were glad to avail themselves of it. Thus we get not only another stimulus for imperialist policy and another source of imperialist imbroglios but also, as a by-product, a theory of a phenomenon that is not necessarily imperialist in itself, modern protectionism.

Note one more hitch in that process that will stand the Marxist in good stead in the task of explaining further difficulties. When the undeveloped countries have been developed, capital export of the kind we have been considering will decline. There may then be a period during which the mother country and the colony will exchange, say, manufactured products for raw materials. But in the end the exports of manufacturers will also have to decline while colonial competition will assert itself in the mother country. Attempts to retard the advent of that state of things will provide further sources of friction, this time between each old capitalist country and its colonies, of wars of independence and so on. But in any case colonial doors will eventually be closed to domestic capital which will no longer be able to flee from vanishing profits at home into richer pastures abroad. Lack of outlets, excess capacity, complete deadlock, in the end regular recurrence of national bankruptcies and other disasters—perhaps world wars from sheer capitalist despair— may confidently be anticipated. History is as simple as that.

This theory is a fair—perhaps it is the best—example of the way in which the Marxian synthesis attempts to solve problems and acquires authority by doing so. The whole thing seems to follow beautifully from two fundamental premises that are both firmly embedded in the groundwork of the system: the theory of classes and the theory of accumulation. A series of vital facts of our time seems to be perfectly accounted for. The whole maze of international politics seems to be cleared up by a single powerful stroke of analysis. And we see in the process why and how class action, always remaining intrinsically the same, assumes the form of political or of business action according to circumstances that determine nothing but tactical methods and phraseology. If, the means and opportunities at the command of a group of capitalists being what they are, it is more profitable to negotiate a loan, a loan will be negotiated. If, the means and opportunities being what they are, it is more profitable to make war, war will be made. The latter alternative is no less entitled to enter economic theory than the former. Even mere protectionism now grows nicely out of the very logic of capitalist evolution.

Moreover, this theory displays to full advantage a virtue that it has in common with most of the Marxian concepts in the field of what is usually referred to as applied economics. This is its close alliance with historical and contemporaneous fact. Probably not one reader has perused my résumé without being struck by the ease with which supporting historical instances crowded in upon him at every single step of the argument. Has he not heard of the oppression by Europeans of native labor in many parts of the world, of what South and Central American Indians suffered at the hands of the Spaniards for instance, or of slave-hunting and slave-trading and coolieism? Is capital export not actually ever-present in capitalist countries? Has it not almost invariably been accompanied by military conquest that served to subdue the natives and to fight other European powers? Has not colonization always had a rather conspicuous military side, even when managed entirely by business corporations such as the East India Company or the British South Africa Company? What better illustration could Marx himself have desired than Cecil Rhodes and the Boer War? Is it not pretty obvious that colonial ambitions were, to say the least, an important factor in European troubles, at all events since about 1700? As for the present time, who has not heard, on the one hand, about the 'strategy of raw materials' and, on the other hand, of the repercussions on Europe of the growth of native capitalism in the tropics? And so on. As to protectionism—well, that is as plain as anything can be.

But we had better be careful. An apparent verification by prima facie favorable cases which are not analyzed in detail may be very deceptive. Moreover, as every lawyer and every politician knows, energetic appeal to familiar facts will go a long way toward inducing a jury or a parliament to accept also the construction he desires to put upon them. Marxists have exploited this technique to the full. In this instance it is particularly successful, because the facts in question combine the virtues of being superficially known to everyone and of being thoroughly understood by very few. In fact, though we cannot enter into detailed discussion here, even hasty reflection suffices to suggest a suspicion that 'it is not so.'

A few remarks will be made in the next part on the relation in which the bourgeoisie stands to imperialism. We shall now consider the question whether, if the Marxian interpretation of capital export, colonization, and protectionism were correct, it would also be adequate as a theory of all the phenomena we think of when using that loose and misused term. Of course we can always define imperialism in such a way as to mean just what the Marxian interpretation implies; and we can always profess ourselves convinced that all those phenomena *must* be explainable in the Marxian manner. But then the problem of imperialism—always granting that the theory is in itself correct—would be 'solved' only tautologically.[4]

---

[4] The danger of empty tautologies being put over on us is best illustrated by individual cases. Thus, France conquered Algeria, Tunisia, and Morocco, and Italy conquered Abyssinia, by military force without there being any significant capitalist interests to press for it. As a matter of fact, presence of such interests was a pretense that was very difficult to establish, and the subsequent development of such interests was a slow process that went on, unsatisfactorily enough, under government pressure. If that should not look very Marxist, it will be replied that action was taken under pressure of potential or anticipated capitalist interests or that in the last analysis some capitalist interest or objective necessity 'must' have been at the bottom of it. And

Whether the Marxian approach or, for that matter, any purely economic approach yields a solution that is not tautological would still have to be considered. This, however, need not concern us here, because the ground gives way before we get that far.

At first sight, the theory seems to fit some cases tolerably well. The most important instances are afforded by the English and Dutch conquests in the tropics. But other cases, such as the colonization of New England, it does not fit at all. And even the former type of case is not satisfactorily described by the Marxian theory of imperialism. It would obviously not suffice to recognize that the lure of gain played a role in motivating colonial expansion.[5] The Neo-Marxists did not mean to aver such a horrible platitude. If these cases are to count for them, it is also necessary that colonial expansion came about, in the way indicated, under pressure of accumulation on the rate of profit, hence as a feature of decaying, or at all events of fully matured, capitalism. But the heroic time of colonial adventure was precisely the time of early and immature capitalism when accumulation was in its beginnings and any such pressure—also, in particular, any barrier to exploitation of domestic labor—was conspicuous by its absence. The element of monopoly was not absent. On the contrary it was far more evident than it is today. But that only adds to the absurdity of the construction which makes both monopoly and conquest specific properties of latter-day capitalism.

we can then hunt for corroboratory evidence that will never be entirely lacking, since capitalist interests, like any others, will in fact be affected by, and take advantage of, any situation whatsoever, and since the particular conditions of the capitalist organism will always present some features which may without absurdity be linked up with those policies of national expansion. Evidently it is preconceived conviction and nothing else that keeps us going in a task as desperate as this; without such a conviction it would never occur to us to embark upon it. And we really need not take the trouble; we might just as well say that 'it must be so' and leave it at that. This is what I meant by tautological explanation.

[5] Nor is it sufficient to stress the fact that each country actually did 'exploit' its colonies. For that was exploitation of a country as a whole by a country as a whole (of all classes by all classes) and has nothing to do with the specifically Marxian kind of exploitation.

Moreover, the other leg of the theory, class struggle, is in no better condition. One must wear blinkers to concentrate on that aspect of colonial expansion which hardly ever played more than a secondary role, and to construe in terms of class struggle a phenomenon which affords some of the most striking instances of class cooperation. It was as much a movement toward higher wages as it was a movement toward higher profits, and in the long run it certainly benefited (in part because of the exploitation of *native* labor) the proletariat more than it benefited the capitalist interest. But I do not wish to stress its *effects*. The essential point is that its *causation* has not much to do with class warfare, and not more to do with class structure than is implied in the leadership of groups and individuals that belonged to, or by colonial enterprise rose into, the capitalist class. If however we shake off the blinkers and cease to look upon colonization or imperialism as a mere incident in class warfare, little remains that is specifically Marxist about the matter. What Adam Smith has to say on it does just as well—better in fact.

The by-product, the Neo-Marxian theory of modern protectionism, still remains. Classical literature is full of invectives against the 'sinister interests'—at that time mainly, but never wholly, the agrarian interests—which in clamoring for protection committed the unforgivable crime against public welfare. Thus the classics had a causal theory of protection all right—not only a theory of its effects —and if now we add the protectionist interests of modern big business we have gone as far as it is reasonable to go. Modern economists with Marxist sympathies really should know better than to say that even now their bourgeois colleagues do not see the relation between the trend toward protectionism and the trend toward big units of control, though these colleagues may not always think it necessary to stress so obvious a fact. Not that the classics and their successors to this day were right about protection: their interpretation of it was, and is, as one-sided as was the Marxian one, besides being often wrong in the appraisal of consequences and of the interests involved. But for at least fifty years they have known about the monopoly component in protectionism all that Marxists ever knew, which was not difficult considering the commonplace character of the discovery.

And they were superior to the Marxist theory in one very important respect. Whatever the value of their economics—perhaps it was not great—they mostly [6] stuck to it. In this instance, that was an advantage. The proposition that many protective duties owe their existence to the pressure of large concerns that desire to use them for the purpose of keeping their prices at home above what they otherwise would be, possibly in order to be able to sell more cheaply abroad, is a platitude but correct, although no tariff was ever wholly or even mainly due to this particular cause. It is the Marxian synthesis that makes it inadequate or wrong. If our ambition is simply to understand all the causes and implications of modern protectionism, political, social and economic, then it is inadequate. For instance, the consistent support given by the American people to protectionist policy, whenever they had the opportunity to speak their minds, is accounted for not by any love for or domination by big business, but by a fervent wish to build and keep a world of their own and to be rid of all the vicissitudes of the rest of the world. Synthesis that overlooks such elements of the case is not an asset but a liability. But if our ambition is to reduce all the causes and implications of modern protectionism, whatever they may be, to the monopolistic element in modern industry as the sole *causa causans* and if we formulate that proposition accordingly, then it becomes wrong. Big business has been able to take advantage of the popular sentiment and it has fostered it; but it is absurd to say that it has created it. Synthesis that yields—we ought rather to say, postulates— such a result is inferior to no synthesis at all.

Matters become infinitely worse if, flying in the face of fact plus common sense, we exalt that theory of capital export and

[6] They did not always confine themselves to their economics. When they did not, results were anything but encouraging. Thus, James Mill's purely economic writings, while not particularly valuable, cannot be simply dismissed as hopelessly substandard. The real nonsense—and platitudinous nonsense at that—is in his articles on government and cognate subjects.

colonization into the fundamental explanation of international politics which thereupon resolves into a struggle, on the one hand, of monopolistic capitalist groups with each other and, on the other hand, of each of them with their own proletariat. This sort of thing may make useful party literature but otherwise it merely shows that nursery tales are no monopoly of bourgeois economics. As a matter of fact, very little influence on foreign policy has been exerted by big business—or by the *haute finance* from the Fuggers to the Morgans —and in most of the cases in which large-scale industry as such, or banking interests as such, have been able to assert themselves, their naïve dilettantism has resulted in discomfiture. The attitudes of capitalist groups toward the policy of their nations are predominantly adaptive rather than causative, today more than ever. Also, they hinge to an astonishing degree on short-run considerations equally remote from any deeply laid plans and from any definite 'objective' class interests. At this point Marxism degenerates into the formulation of popular superstitions.[7]

There are other instances of a similar state of things in all parts of the Marxian structure. To mention one, the definition of the nature of governments that was quoted from the *Communist Manifesto* a little while ago has certainly an element of truth in it. And in many cases that truth will account for governmental attitudes toward the more obvious manifestations of class antagonisms. But so far as true, the theory embodied in that definition is trivial. All that is worth while troubling about is the Why and How of that

---

[7] This superstition is exactly on a par with another that is harbored by many worthy and simple-minded people who explain modern history to themselves on the hypothesis that there is somewhere a committee of supremely wise and malevolent Jews who behind the scenes control international or perhaps all politics. Marxists are not victims of this particular superstition but theirs is on no higher plane. It is amusing to record that, when faced with either doctrine, I have always experienced great difficulty in replying in anything like a fashion satisfactory to myself. This was not only due to the circumstance that it is always difficult to establish denial of factual assertions. The main difficulty came from the fact that people, lacking any first-hand knowledge of international affairs and their personnel, also lack any organ for the perception of absurdity.

vast majority of cases in which the theory either fails to conform to fact or, even if conforming, fails to describe correctly the actual behavior of those 'committees for managing the common affairs of the bourgeoisie.' Again, in practically all cases the theory can be made tautologically true. For there is no policy short of exterminating the bourgeoisie that could not be held to serve some economic or extra-economic, short-run or long-run, bourgeois interest, at least in the sense that it wards off still worse things. This, however, does not make that theory any more valuable. But let us turn to our second example of the problem-solving power of the Marxian synthesis.

The badge of Scientific Socialism which according to Marx is to distinguish it from Utopian Socialism consists in the proof that socialism is inevitable irrespective of human volition or of desirability. As has been stated before, all this means is that by virtue of its very logic capitalist evolution tends to destroy the capitalist and to produce the socialist order of things. How far has Marx succeeded in establishing the existence of these tendencies?

As regards the tendency toward self-destruction, the question has already been answered. The doctrine that the capitalist economy will inevitably break down for purely economic reasons has not been established by Marx, as Hilferding's objections would suffice to show. On the one hand, some of his propositions about future facts that are essential to the orthodox argument, especially the one about the inevitable increase of misery and oppression, are untenable; on the other hand, the breakdown of the capitalist order would not necessarily follow from these propositions, even if they were all true. But other factors in the situation that the capitalist process tends to develop were correctly seen by Marx, as was, so I hope to show, the ultimate outcome itself. Concerning the latter, it may be necessary to replace the Marxian nexus by another, and the term 'breakdown' may then turn out to be a misnomer, particularly if it be understood in the sense of a breakdown caused by the failure of the capitalist engine of production; but this does not affect the essence of the doctrine, however much it may affect its formulation and some of its implications.

As regards the tendency toward socialism, we must first realize that this is a distinct problem. The capitalist or any other order of things may evidently break down—or economic and social evolution may outgrow it—and yet the socialist phoenix may fail to rise from the ashes. There may be chaos and, unless we define as socialism any non-chaotic alternative to capitalism, there are other possibilities. The particular type of social organization that the average orthodox Marxist—before the advent of bolshevism at any rate—seemed to anticipate is certainly only one of many possible cases.

Marx himself, while very wisely refraining from describing socialist society in detail, emphasized conditions of its emergence: on the one hand, the presence of giant units of industrial control—which, of course, would greatly facilitate socialization—and, on the other hand, the presence of an oppressed, enslaved, exploited, but also very numerous, *disciplined,* united, and organized proletariat. This suggests much about the final battle that is to be the acute stage of the secular warfare between the two classes which will then be arrayed against other other for the last time. It also suggests something about what is to follow; it suggests the idea that the proletariat as such will 'take over' and, through its dictatorship, put a stop to the 'exploitation of man by man' and bring about classless society. If our purpose were to prove that Marxism is a member of the family of chiliastic creeds this would indeed be quite enough. Since we are concerned not with that aspect but with a scientific forecast, it clearly is not. Schmoller was on much safer ground. For though he also refused to commit himself to details, he obviously visualized the process as one of progressive bureaucratization, nationalization, and so on, ending in state socialism which, whether we like it or not, at least makes definite sense. Thus Marx fails to turn the socialist possibility into a certainty even if we grant him the breakdown theory in its entirety; if we do not, then failure follows *a fortiori.*

In no case, however—whether we accept Marx's reasoning or any other—will the socialist order be realized automatically; even if

capitalist evolution provided all conditions for it in the most Marxian manner conceivable, distinct action would still be necessary to
bring it about. This of course is in accordance with Marx's teaching. His revolution is but the particular garb in which his imagination liked to clothe that action. The emphasis on violence is perhaps understandable in one who in his formative years had experienced all the excitement of 1848 and who was, though quite able to
despise revolutionary ideology, yet never able to shake off its
trammels. Moreover, the greater part of his audience would hardly
have been willing to listen to a message that lacked the hallowed
clarion call. Finally, though he saw the possibility of peaceful transition, at least for England, he may not have seen its likelihood. In his
day it was not so easy to see, and his pet idea of the two classes in
battle array made it still more difficult to see it. His friend Engels
actually went to the trouble of studying tactics. But though the revolution can be relegated to the compound of non-essentials, the necessity for distinct action still remains.

This should also solve the problem that has divided the disciples: revolution or evolution? If I have caught Marx's meaning,
the answer is not hard to give. Evolution was for him the parent of
socialism. He was much too strongly imbued with a sense of the inherent logic of things social to believe that revolution can replace
any part of the work of evolution. The revolution comes in nevertheless. But it only comes in order to write the conclusion under a
complete set of premises. The Marxian revolution therefore differs
entirely, in nature and in function, from the revolutions both of the
bourgeois radical and of the socialist conspirator. It is essentially
revolution in the fullness of time. It is true that disciples who dislike this conclusion, and especially its application to the Russian
case,[8] can point to many passages in the sacred books that seem to
contradict it. But in those passages Marx himself contradicts his

[8] Karl Kautsky, in his preface to *Theorien über den Mehrwert,* even
claimed the revolution of 1905 for Marxian socialism, although it is patent
that the Marxian phraseology of a few intellectuals was all that was socialist
about it.

deepest and most mature thought which speaks out unmistakably from the analytic structure of *Das Kapital* and—as any thought must that is inspired by a sense of the inherent logic of things— carries, beneath the fantastic glitter of dubious gems, a distinctly conservative implication. And, after all, why not? No serious argument ever supports any 'ism' unconditionally.[9] To say that Marx, stripped of phrases, admits of interpretation in a conservative sense is only saying that he can be taken seriously.

[9] This argument could be carried much further. In particular, there is nothing specifically socialist in the labor theory of value; this of course everyone would admit who is familiar with the historical development of that doctrine. But the same is true (excepting of course the phrase) of the theory of exploitation. We need only recognize that existence of the surpluses so dubbed by Marx is—or at least was—a necessary condition for the emergence of all that we comprise in the term civilization (which in fact it would be difficult to deny), and there we are. In order to be a socialist, it is of course not necessary to be a Marxist; but neither is it sufficient to be a Marxist in order to be a socialist. Socialist or revolutionary conclusions can be impressed on any scientific theory; no scientific theory necessarily implies them. And none will keep us in what Bernard Shaw somewhere describes as sociological rage, unless its author goes out of his way in order to work us up.

MARIE ESPRIT LEON WALRAS*
1834-1910

T HE simple greatness which lies in unconditional surrender to one task is what strikes us when we look back today on this scholarly life. Its inherent logic, inevitability, and power impress us as a natural event. Exclusive meditation on the problems of pure economics formed its content. Nothing else. Nothing disturbs the unity of the whole picture. No other element is of importance in it; it alone affects us. Slowly but steadily, as if by its weight, the achievement of this life's work impresses itself upon us.

The external events of this life are quickly told. I take from Walras' autobiography [1] the material for the modest frame surrounding the picture which has such historic scientific significance. Walras was born on December 16, 1834, in Evreux, Departement d'Eure. The course of his studies shows the thinker's unfitness for

* This article appeared originally under the title 'Marie Ésprit Léon Walras' in *Zeitschrift für Volkswirtschaft, Sozialpolitik und Verwaltung*, vol. xix (1910), pp. 397-402. It was translated from the German by Dr. Wolfgang F. Stolper, who studied under Professor Schumpeter both at Bonn and at Harvard, and is now Associate Professor of Economics at the University of Michigan.

[1] *Giornale degli Economisti*, December 1908.

74

practical matters: failures such as we should expect of one who prepared for the École Polytechnique by studying Descartes and Newton; lack of enthusiasm for outworn paths such as every searching mind experiences. There was an unsatisfying attempt to study at the École des Mines. He then tried journalism, worked for various enterprises, all with characteristic lack of success. For us, however, it is important that already in his first publication in 1859—an attempt to refute the basic ideas of Proudhon—he was convinced that economic theory could be treated mathematically. From that moment on he knew what he wanted, from that moment on his whole strength was dedicated to *one* end. Here—in the method and not in any specific problems—is the origin of his work. He felt impelled in this direction, though he did not immediately know how far he would be able to go. Then, too, the necessary setting and leisure were lacking—in his autobiography he describes with caustic bitterness the atmosphere in the scientific circles of France; and in general he did not succeed in taking root.

At this juncture chance rendered great service to science. In 1860 Walras had participated in a 'Tax Congress' in Lausanne—the discussions of which became the inspiration of his second great publication—and the connections he made there led ten years later to his appointment to the newly founded chair of economics. This meant much for science as well as for Walras. And everyone who esteems Walras' work highly will be moved deeply by that part in his *Autobiography* in which he describes, not without solemnity, how he went to the *prefecture* to obtain the permission (necessary because of the threat of mobilization) to leave the country, and how he then traveled to Lausanne 'on December 7, 1870, from Caen, via Angers, Poitiers, Moulins, and Lyon.' Once arrived he went to work, and he continued to work until his life's task had been done and his strength had failed.

In 1892 he retired from his chair, but maintained his connection with the University as *Honorarprofessor*. He continued to work in his small apartment in a house near Clarens. There he died on January 4, 1910.

I have to report on only one other external matter: the shadow which the indifference to his written work threw on the last thirty years of his life. It is an old story. The fate of truth as well as that of beauty is a sad one on this earth. And when moreover the novelty consists essentially in the manner of looking at things and not in discoveries and inventions which appeal to the interest and understanding of wide circles, when finally the 'vision' is as far removed from the current interests of the profession as was the case with Walras, it is readily understood that external success could come neither easily nor quickly. If all this is taken into account, we need not be dissatisfied with what was actually achieved; perhaps we shall be astonished at *so much* success rather than at *so little*. Walras founded a school, and, mainly through Marshall, his influence extended beyond it. It has become long since manifest who was being judged when the Académie des Sciences Morales et Politiques rejected his work. And without fanfare, the deep and wide effects of this work continue to grow. Though for a long time Walras did not have any defenders, he lived to see the time when he could take pleasure in the knowledge that his ideas needed no defense and that they had moved beyond the realm of scientific fashion. But this was not how he thought, and he never overcame the memory of struggles and failure. His autobiography ends with bitter words and he seems to have been given to bitter thoughts— thus an element of the tragic hovers over this life outwardly so quiet.

The celebration of his jubilee in the spring of 1909 affected him like a ray of sunshine after a rainy day. Sympathies and feelings of admiration of which he had been unaware found there an expression. He received more recognition than he ever dared to hope. It was the great moment of his life.

The theory of economic equilibrium is Walras' claim to immortality, that great theory whose crystal-clear train of thought has illuminated the structure of purely economic relationships with the light of *one* fundamental principle. The monument with which the University of Lausanne has honored him rightly has no other inscription than: *équilibre économique*. To be sure, his fundamental idea led him to many results of practical importance. No one has more convincingly advocated the nationalization of land, and few contributions in the field of monetary policy compare with his. But all this is nothing beside the knowledge he has provided for us. All three volumes in which he synthesized the writings of a lifetime [2] belong to the richest books of our science, but *aere perennius* is the train of thought contained in Sections II-VI of the first volume.

Walras started from Cournot. He soon discovered, so he tells us, that Cournot's demand curve, which represents the amounts demanded as a function of price, is strictly applicable only to the exchange of two goods, but that it offers only an approximation for the exchange of more than two goods. He at first limited himself to the former case and in an exact manner derived the supply curve of the one good from the demand curve of the other: then he derived the equilibrium prices for the two goods from the point of intersection of the two curves. From these curves, which refer to the total amounts of the goods on the market under investigation, he derived the individual demand and utility curves for the amounts of every individual economic unit and thus arrived at the foundation stone of his structure, the marginal utility concept. In this stage the theory was published in 1873, and it was further developed in subsequent years. The agreement of his results with those of Menger and Jevons is as striking as the differences in their starting points and methods. It is an achievement of fundamental importance which is contained in these simple theorems.

Further problems follow from this first one in an unbroken chain of reasoning. First the problem of the exchange of more than two goods, which presents more difficulties to a scientific formulation than the layman may think. Next Walras arrived at the problem of production by juxtaposing to the market for a given amount of consumer's goods, which he had thus far considered in isolation, an analogously constructed market for the factors of production.

---

[2] *Éléments d'économie politique pure*, 4th edition, 1900 (1st edition, 1874); *Études d'économie sociale*, 1896; *Études d'économie politique appliquée*, 1898.

These were connected in *one* way through the *entrepreneur faisant ni bénéfice ni perte,* in *another* way by the fact that total receipts from all sales of means of production must, under pure competition and in equilibrium, equal total receipts from the sales of all consumer's goods. When account is taken, on the one hand, of the condition that utility must be maximized for every person engaged in exchange, and on the other hand, of the so-called coefficients of production which are variable in definite ways, the theory of the interactions of 'cost' and 'utility,' and with it the fundamental principle of the whole course of the economic process, results in a solution of brilliant simplicity.

Walras introduces the problem of capitalization by assuming that some sellers of productive services *save* and invest these savings in 'new capital goods' which because of this demand come on the market in definite quantities. The price of these 'new capital goods' is formed on the basis of their services. This price furnishes in turn the basis for the capital values of the 'old production goods,' which solves the problem of capitalization or of the derivation of the capital values of all goods. This view has its faults. But we notice them only because we compare it today with the achievement of Böhm-Bawerk. If it sinned in some respects, as did many other earlier interest theories, it yet differs favorably from them in many others. Walras' theory of interest may perhaps best be compared with Ricardo's, but they are to each other as edifice to foundation.

Of all the parts of his system, his theory of money has undergone most changes in the course of time until it is rated as one of the most mature fruits in this field. A good part of Walras' work between 1876 and 1899 was devoted to the theory of money. While in the first edition of the *Éléments* he still started with the 'necessary circulation' (*circulation à deservir*), he later built his monetary theory on the individual need for means of payments (*encaisse désirée*). The difference is essential. It is impossible to speak of the economy's need for a medium of exchange as such in the same sense in which one speaks of a man's need for bread. Such an individual desire for means of payments is however perfectly analogous to the demand for bread; it is something which may be subsumed under the law of diminishing marginal utility. This principle is then brilliantly utilized, and a beautiful theory of the formation of the price of money develops from the 'equations of circulation.' Since, however, I cannot here go into details, it may suffice to say that in particular Walras' treatment of the problem of bimetallism is nothing short of classic and will be definitive for a long time to come.

The whole of pure economics rests with Walras on the two conditions that every economic unit wants to maximize utility and that demand for every good equals supply. All his theorems follow from these two assumptions. Edgeworth, Barone, and others may have supplemented his work; Pareto and others may have gone beyond it in individual points: the significance of his work is not thereby touched. Whoever knows the origin and the workings of the exact natural sciences knows also that their great achievements are, in method and essence, of the same kind as Walras'. To find exact forms for the phenomena whose interdependence is given us by experience, to reduce these forms to, and derive them from, each other: this is what the physicists do, and this is what Walras did. And Walras did it in a new field which could not draw on centuries of preparatory work. He did it immediately with very favorable results. He did it in spite of outer and inner difficulties. He did it without help and without collaborators, until he himself had created them—without any encouragement other than that which he found within himself. He did it though he knew, though he *must* have known, that he could expect success or recognition in his own generation neither among economists nor among mathematicians. He walked a solitary path without the moral support to which the practical man as well as the scientist is usually accustomed. Thus his portrait shows all the characteristics which distinguish the truly creative mind from those that are created. So much for the *man*. The *work* will find its recognition—sooner or later.

CARL MENGER *
1840-1921

I T IS an acid test of the power of an argument whether it can be looked upon as decisive in its own right, or whether it stands in need of a long string of supporting subsidiary arguments. Similarly, it is an acid test of the significance of a man's lifework whether one can discern in it a single achievement which by itself signifies greatness, or whether it can be portrayed only as a mosaic into which many small pieces have been assembled. Menger was one of those thinkers who can claim a single decisive achievement that made scientific history. His name will be forever linked with a new explanatory principle which has revolutionized the whole field of economic theory. Whatever significant or lovable traits one may ascribe to his character, whatever additional scientific achievements one may adduce, whatever one may say about his devoted teaching and outstanding scholarship—all that is pushed into the background behind the lofty height on which this figure stands. Menger's biog-

* This article appeared originally under the title 'Carl Menger' in the *Zeitschrift für Volkswirtschaft und Sozialpolitik,* New Series, vol. 1 (1921), pp. 197-206. It was translated by Dr. Hans W. Singer, a former student of Professor Schumpeter at the University of Bonn, now Acting Chief, Economic Development Section, United Nations.

rapher, of course, will put all this material together into a composite picture of a strong and attractive personality. But this picture derives its significance from his one great achievement, and there is no need for those details to lend fame to Menger's name.

Menger has left us after twenty years of the strictest retirement, during which he explored and enjoyed at leisure the fields of his interests. Thus, we have gained sufficient distance to enable us to discuss his life's work as part of the history of our science. And it is indeed imposing. The background from which Menger's scientific personality emerged can be briefly sketched. Out of practical doubts, out of the needs of practical policy, a small fund of knowledge on economic matters had developed since the sixteenth century; questions of monetary and commercial policy had since that time—that is to say, since the modern exchange economy began to transcend the bounds of village and manor—led to discussions which in a primitive fashion linked together the causes and effects of striking economic events. The slow trend in the direction of an individualized economy and free trade was accompanied by an ever swelling stream of pamphlets and books by authors who were usually more inclined to solve the actual economic problems of the day than to think about more fundamental problems. During the eighteenth century, there emerged a consolidated science which had its own schools, results, disputes, textbook summaries, and scholarly experts. This was the first epoch of our science, an epoch which we may think of as culminating in Adam Smith. There then followed a period of analysis and specialization, with the English Classics dominating the field with which we are here concerned, since it is in this field that Menger's achievement lies. Ricardo stamped his name on this epoch. In its course, a coherent system of doctrines was evolved which claimed scientific character and general validity within wide limits; pure economic theory had arrived.

It will never be quite clear why such rapid success should have been followed by such complete defeat. Several of the leading brains of the new discipline were still at work; they had not yet passed beyond the stage of dealing with fundamentals; but already we witness paralyzing stagnation inside the circle of economists and general distrust, hostility, or neglect outside it. The fault lay partly in the inherent defects of what had been achieved, the primitive nature of some of the methods used, the superficiality of some of the thinking, and the clearly visible inadequacy of some of the results. All this, however, should not have been fatal since it was capable of improvement. But nobody started this work of improvement, nobody showed interest in the internal structure of the new theoretical edifice, because—and here lies the other cause of the failure—public opinion as well as the experts turned away for a different reason: the new doctrine had been in too much of a hurry to try to solve practical questions and to enter the quarrels of political and social parties with a claim to scientific validity. Thus, the defeat of liberalism became also the defeat of the new doctrine. As a result, especially since in some countries—particularly in Germany—there was antagonism to social theory generally and a tendency to cling to the intellectual heritage of philosophical and historical tradition, little more than the economic and social policy façade of the classical theory was transmitted to the next generation, while the way into its internal structure was actually blocked. The younger people were scarcely aware how much of scientific knowledge and even more of further possibilities there was to be had. And thus it looked as if theory had been no more than an interlude in the history of ideas, an attempted foundation for the economic policies of a particular fleeting period. It was, of course, inevitable that little pools of theory should be preserved here and there among experts. In isolated cases, achievements of major significance were accomplished, but essentially the field lay untilled. The names of Thünen and Hermann in Germany do not change this verdict. The socialist theory alone built on the classical methodological foundations without petrifying.

With the autonomy of scientific greatness, the lifework of Carl Menger stands out in sharp relief against this background. Without external stimulation, and certainly without external help, he atttacked the half-ruined edifice of economic theory. What drove him on was not interest in economic policies or the history of ideas, nor a desire to add to the accumulated store of facts, but mainly the quest of the born theorist for new principles of knowledge, for new tools for marshalling the facts. And while usually the researcher scores at best a partial success, the solution of one of the many individual problems of a discipline, Menger belongs to those who have demolished the existing structure of a science and put it on entirely new foundations. The old theory was vanquished, not by the historians and sociologists who brushed it aside, not by the makers of economic and social policies who rejected its practical conclusions, but by one who recognized its inner organic deficiencies and who made it into something new by tackling it on its own ground.

It is always awkward to formulate the fundamental principle of a theory for a wider circle, for the final formulation of a fundamental principle always seems somewhat obvious. The intellectual achievement of an analyst does not consist in the content of the statement which expresses the fundamental principle, but in his knowing how to make it fertile and how to derive from it all the problems of the science concerned. If you tell someone that the fundamental principle of mechanics is expressed in the statement that a body is in equilibrium if it does not move in any direction, the layman will hardly understand the usefulness of the theorem or the intellectual achievement that went into its formulation. Thus if we say that the fundamental idea of Menger's theory is that people value goods because they need them, we must understand that this will not impress the layman—and even the majority of professional economists are laymen in theoretical matters. The critics of Menger's theory have always maintained that no one could ever have been unaware of the fact of subjective valuation, and that nothing could be more unfair than to put forward such a triviality as an objection to the Classics. But the answer is very simple: it can be demonstrated that almost every one of the classical economists tried to start with this recognition and then threw it aside because he could make no progress with it, because he believed that, in the mechanism of the capitalist economy, subjective valuation had lost its function as the engine of the vehicle. And like subjective valuation itself, so also the phenomena of demand based on it were regarded as useless in comparison to the objective facts of costs. Even today, the critics of Menger's school will declare now and then that the subjective theory of value can at best explain the prices of fixed stocks of consumption goods but nothing else.

What matters, therefore, is not the discovery that people buy, sell, or produce goods because and in so far as they value them from the point of view of satisfaction of needs, but a discovery of quite a different kind: the discovery that this simple fact and its sources in the laws of human needs are wholly sufficient to explain the basic facts about all the complex phenomena of the modern exchange economy, and that in spite of striking appearances to the contrary, human needs are the driving force of the economic mechanism beyond the Robinson Crusoe economy or the economy without exchange. The chain of thought which leads to this conclusion starts with the recognition that price formation is the specific economic characteristic of the economy—as distinct from all the other social, historical, and technical characteristics—and that all specifically economic events can be comprehended within the framework of price formation. From a purely economic standpoint, the economic system is merely a system of dependent prices; all special problems, whatever they may be called, are nothing but special cases of one and the same constantly recurring process, and all specifically economic regularities are deduced from the laws of price formation. Already in the preface of Menger's work, we find this recognition as a self-evident assumption. His essential aim is to discover the law of price formation. As soon as he succeeded in basing the solution of the pricing problem, in both its 'demand' and 'supply' aspects, on an analysis of human needs and on what Wieser has called the principle of 'marginal utility,' the whole complex mechanism of economic life suddenly appeared to be unexpectedly and transparently simple. All that remained to be done was merely elaboration and advance along the road of increasingly complicated details.

The main work, which contains the solution of this fundamental problem and clearly hints at all future developments, and
which, together with the roughly simultaneous, independent writings of Jevons and Walras, must be considered as the foundation
of modern economic theory, bears the title *Grundsätze der Volkswirtschaftslehre, Erster Allgemeiner Teil* and appeared in 1871.
Calmly, firmly, and clearly, perfectly certain of his cause, in careful
elaboration of each sentence, he presents to us the great reform of
the theory of value. Menger's admirers have often compared his
achievement with that of Copernicus; his critics have ridiculed the
comparison even more frequently. Today it has become possible to
form an opinion on this issue: Menger reformed a science in which
rigidly exact thought was much more recent and imperfect than in
the science which Copernicus placed on new foundations. To that
extent, the technical achievement of the latter was much greater
and more difficult, not to mention the fact that it lay in a field
where results cannot be tested by the layman and are shrouded in
mystery. But in essence and quality, Menger's work is in the same
category, just as an army commander who leads a small army to
success in a neglected theater of war may rank in personal achievement with Napoleon and Alexander, even though the classification
would surprise someone not familiar with the circumstances. Comparisons are generally deceptive and likely to lead to useless discussions. But since they are a means of defining a man's position for
those who are not experts in the narrowest sense, we shall risk a
comparison of Menger with other economists. If we compare him,
for example, to Adam Smith, it strikes us immediately that his
achievement is much narrower than that of the Scottish professor.
Adam Smith gave expression to the practical needs of his time, and
his name is inseparably linked to the economic policy of the epoch.
Menger's achievement is purely scientific, and as a scientific contribution, again purely analytical. His work can be compared to only
a part of Smith's. Smith was not at all original, and more particularly in basic scientific problems he was remarkably superficial.

Menger burrowed deep, and entirely by himself he discovered truths
which were quite inaccessible to Smith.

Ricardo was more his peer. Here we have two theoretical
talents, though within the realm of theory, two fundamentally different talents. Ricardo's fertility and acuteness lie in the many practical conclusions and insights which he managed to call forth from
very primitive foundations. Menger's greatness lies precisely in those
foundations, and from the standpoint of pure science it is he who
should be ranked higher. Ricardo is a prerequisite for Menger—a
prerequisite which Menger himself certainly could not have created.
But Menger is the vanquisher of the Ricardian theory.

Since Menger and his school soon came to be considered as
the only serious competitor of the Marxist theory, a comparison with
Marx may also be attempted. Here again one must completely disregard Marx the sociologist and prophet, and confine oneself to the
purely theoretical skeleton of his work. Menger competed with only
one sector of Marx's work. In this sector, however, he excels Marx
considerably, both in force of originality and in success. In the field
of pure theory, Marx is the pupil of Ricardo and even of some of
Ricardo's followers, especially of the socialist and semi-socialist value
theorists who wrote in England during the 1820's. Menger is nobody's pupil, and what he created stands. To avoid misunderstanding: no economic sociology or sociology of economic development
can be derived from Menger's work. It makes only a small contribution to the picture of economic history and the struggle of social
classes, but Menger's theory of value, price, and distribution is the
best we have up to now.

I have said that Menger was nobody's pupil. In fact, he had
only one forerunner who had already recognized his basic idea in
its full significance—namely, Gossen. Menger's success roused the
forgotten book by that solitary thinker from its slumber. Apart
from that, there are, of course, many hints of a subjective theory of
value, and even of a price theory based on it, from the scholastic
school onwards, especially by Genovesi and Isnard, and then again
by some German theorists during the first decades of the nineteenth

century. But all this amounted to little more than that matter of obvious fact which we have mentioned before. In order to see more in these hints, one must have already worked out their significance through one's own labors. On the other hand, any scientific achievement is always the blossoming of old trees. Otherwise mankind does not know what to do with it, and the blossom falls to the earth, unregarded. But in so far as there can be any originality in scientific life, or in human life generally, Menger's theory belongs entirely to him—to him and to Jevons and Walras.

This also explains the way in which his gift was received and its early fate. His gift was the fruit of his thought and struggle during the third decade of his life, that period of sacred fertility which, in the case of every thinker, creates what is subsequently worked out. Born on February 23, 1840, he was just thirty-one years old when his book appeared. Originally, it was addressed to Vienna, for by it he wanted to qualify to teach; and the magnitude of his personal achievement can be realized only if we remember in what a desert he planted his trees. For long there had been no sign of life in the field of our discipline. One must go back as far as 1848, to Sonnenfels whose book was the first official textbook, to find even a good average performance. Everything presentable was imported from Germany. The men whom Menger encountered when he started at the University had hardly any understanding of his ideas or of the whole field which he could make bear fruit. They gave him that chilly reception of which he later told us. Finally, however, he established himself, became a professor, and the course of time brought him the usual honors of the man of science; but he never forgot that first struggle. In Germany, furthermore, he remained neglected, if only because the field was dominated by social policy on the one hand, and by research into details of economic history on the other hand. Quite alone, without a platform from which his voice could have carried into the world, without any sphere of influence, and without that apparatus which traditionally is everywhere at the disposal of the holder of an eminent chair, he saw himself confronted by a complete lack of comprehension, which in turn gave rise to hostility.

Anyone who understands the inner history of scientific progress will be aware of all the tactics employed in small circles in order to gain acceptance for new ideas. Menger did not know how that is done; and even if he had known, he lacked the means of conducting his own campaigns. But his powerful strength penetrated through all the jungles and triumphed over all the hostile armies. That, in the first place, was entirely his own merit. There is within the human soul a fine and intimate connection, not always apparent and often seemingly absent, between the intellectual energy which can liberate itself from traditional views and burrow independently into the depths of things, and the faculty of founding schools—that peculiar fascination which attracts and convinces the future thinkers. In the case of Menger, the concentration of his intellectual work led directly to concentration on proclaiming his results. Although he never again expressed himself on the subject of the theory of value, yet he implanted his principles into a whole generation of students. Beyond that, he correctly perceived that in Germany it was not so much his own theory, but rather all theory, that was rejected, and he took up the battle to establish the rightful place of theoretical analysis in social matters. To this battle—all too well known as the *Methodenstreit*—we owe his work on the methodology of social sciences in which he tried, with systematic thoroughness and by formulations which have not often been bettered to the present day, to clear the field of exact research from an undergrowth of methodological confusion. This contribution, too, is of permanent value, even though subsequent advances in the theory of knowledge may have carried us beyond it in many respects. It would be unfair to his chief contribution to present this later work as equally important; yet its educational influence on his contemporaries was incalculable. It had no influence outside Germany, and there was no need for it to have had. For outside Germany, the ideas which it tried to establish had for the most part already been commonly accepted. For the development of the science in Germany it was a milestone.

Furthermore, a kind fate favored him, in the propagation of his ideas, with such good fortune as rarely falls to the lot of founders of schools: an alliance with two intellectual peers who could directly continue his work at the same level of original power, Böhm-Bawerk and Wieser. The work and efforts of these two men—which were directly linked to his own and which, despite their own calling to intellectual leadership, did not prevent them from constantly referring back to Menger—created the 'Austrian School,' which slowly conquered the scientific world of this special field for its basic ideas. Success was slow in coming. It appeared frequently in a form which is psychologically comprehensible, but all the same not very pleasant, and which we can always observe in the history of science if a group lacks what one can only call the means of scientific advertising. Thus the essential things were accepted, but this acceptance was accompanied not by grateful acknowledgment, but instead by formal rejection based on subsidiary issues. This is what happened in Italy. The leading English theorists also were not quite free from this weakness. The reception in America and also—when it finally took place—in France was much more cordial and generous, and this was particularly the case in the Scandinavian countries and in Holland. Only after this degree of success had been achieved was the new tendency accepted in Germany as an accomplished fact. So Menger finally lived to see his doctrines discussed in scientific circles wherever our discipline flourishes, and to see his basic ideas slowly and imperceptibly transcend the plane of current discussion and become part of the uncontested store of scientific knowledge. He himself was keenly aware of that, and even though —like a true scholar—he was sometimes furious about some little pinprick or other administered by a colleague, he was nevertheless conscious of having made scientific history and of the fact that his name could never vanish from the history of science.

All of us know that today no scientific achievement can be permanent in the sense that it is not subject to amendment by the progress of research. Menger's own successors, and in another direction all those researchers in our subject who follow Walras, have already made changes in the structure as he conceived it, and will doubtless continue to do so in the future. In another sense, however, his achievement had become timeless. This is so in the sense that today it is beyond question that he succeeded in taking an enormous step forward on the road of knowledge, and that his work will stand out from the mass of ephemeral publications, most of which are destined for oblivion, and will be recognizable through the generations.

If the one achievement were less great, there would be other things yet to mention: above all, his theory of money written for the *Handwörterbuch der Staatswissenschaften,* his contributions to the theory of capital and to practical currency problems. We would have to mention his work as a teacher, which is unforgettably stamped upon the memory of the older among us, far beyond the narrow circle of specialists, and also the amazing range of his interests. But all this counts for little beside his theory of value and price, which is, so to speak, the expression of his real personality.

But we mourn not only the thinker but also the lovable man. Thousands of memories which are dear to us linger in the minds of all who knew him.

ALFRED MARSHALL
1842-1924

ALFRED MARSHALL'S *PRINCIPLES*:
A SEMI-CENTENNIAL APPRAISAL [*][1]

FIFTEEN years or so ago I gave a series of lectures at the London School of Economics in which I incidentally paid my respects to the great shade of Marshall. Somebody in the audience thereupon wrote me a letter expressing a feeling, couched in the form of a question, to the effect that Marshall's message would pass away much as Mill's

[*] Reprinted from the *American Economic Review,* vol. XXXI, no. 2, June 1941. Copyright 1941 by American Economic Association.

[1] This article is a reconstruction, from notes, of a 'paper' read to the American Economic Association, at the New Orleans meeting, on 29 December 1940. Here and there, some comments have been added from an earlier and unpublished essay of mine which in turn had been revised in the light of the information contained in Mr. Keynes's 'Memoir of Marshall,' first published in the *Econ. Jour.,* and reprinted in *Memorials of Alfred Marshall* (ed. A. C. Pigou, 1925) and in J. M. Keynes, *Essays in Biography,* 1933. I hereby acknowledge my debt to that 'Memoir,' which I regard as one of the outstanding masterpieces of biographical literature. References are to the 1933 volume.

message had, or for that matter that of Adam Smith. I will put what I have to say in the form of an answer to that question.

In one sense Marshallian economics has passed away already. His vision of the economic process, his methods, his results, are no longer ours. We may love and admire that mighty structure which, battered by the impact of criticisms and of new ideas, still spreads its majestic lines in the background of our own work. We may love and admire it as we love and admire a madonna by the Perugino, recognizing that she embodies to perfection the thought and feeling of her time, yet recognizing also how far we have traveled from her.

This, of course, is no more than the inevitable result of the work done during these fifty years which would have had to be entirely barren if Marshall's *Principles* could be to us anything else than what is conveyed by that equivocal term, a 'classic.' It is the common fate of all classics in all fields. *Si licet parva componere magnis,* there is a significant analogy between the relation of modern economic theory to the theory of the *Principles* and the relation of modern physics to the physics of the nineties. It was in 1894, if my memory serves me, that H. A. Lorentz said he felt that theoretical physics had attained perfection and therefore had ceased to be very interesting. Now that feeling of certainty is gone. Gone are the beautifully simple and clear-cut contour lines. Instead, we see the disorder of a battlefield—unco-ordinated masses of fact and pieces of technique, no prospect at all of fitting this heap ever again into an architectural structure. Something very similar has happened to economics. I do not now mean to refer to the vicissitudes of the capitalist system and to the change in moral and political attitude that has occurred with respect to it. It is not Marshall's views on practical problems, social questions, and the like that are so obsolete. They may be, but whether they are or not is immaterial for the purpose of this paper. What matters is that his analytical apparatus is obsolete and that it would be so even if nothing had happened to change our political attitudes. If history had stood still and nothing except analysis had gone on, the verdict would have to be the same.

In another sense, however, Marshall's teaching can never pass away. Its influence will last for an indefinite time not only because teaching of such breadth and force merges into the inheritance of subsequent generations, but also because there is about it a peculiar quality which effectively resists decay. Reared in an atmosphere that was full of the slogans of evolutionary progress, Marshall was one of the first economists to realize that economics is an evolutionary science (although his critics not only overlooked this element of his thought but in some instances actually indicted his economics on the very ground that it neglected the evolutionary aspect), and in particular that the human nature he professed to deal with is malleable and changing, a function of changing environments. But again, this is not what matters to us just now. What does matter is that he carried his 'evolution-mindedness' into his theoretical work. There was no air of finality about it. Unlike Mill, he would never have said that some problem or other was settled for all time to come and that there was nothing about it that called for further explanation either by himself or any other writer. On the contrary, he was fully aware that he was building an essentially temporary structure. He always pointed beyond himself and toward lands into which it was not given to him to enter. New problems, ideas, and methods that are enemies to the work of other men thus came to his own work as allies. Within the vast fortified camp that he built, there was room—in fact, there was accommodation prepared in advance—for them all. Many as were and are the revolts against his rule, most of them were but local. And sometimes the insurgents discovered—or other people discovered for them—that he had anticipated their goals and that there really was no point in revolting.

II

The *Principles* were the fruits of work that extended over more than twenty years.[2] When finally they appeared in 1890, suc-

[2] During those twenty years, Marshall published several articles and, in collaboration with his wife, his (or her) *Economics of Industry,* 1879. In

cess was instantaneous and complete. This success is not difficult to explain. The book was a great performance. And this performance was presented in a most attractive garb that suited to perfection the humors of the time and the prevailing conditions in the field of economics—indeed it does as much credit to the judgment as it does to the genius of the author.

The precise nature of the performance, however, is less easy to define. Full justice cannot be rendered to it by going straight to the core of the analytic apparatus the *Principles* presents. For behind, beyond, and all around that kernel there is an economic sociology of ninetenth century English capitalism which rests on historical bases of impressive extent and solidity. Marshall was, in fact, an economic historian of the first rank, though he may not have been much of a historical technician. And his mastery of historical fact and his analytic habit of mind did not dwell in separate compartments but formed so close a union that the live fact intrudes into the theorem and the theorem into purely historical observations. This shows, of course, very much more obviously in *Industry and Trade* than it does in the *Principles,* in which, even in the historical introduction, historical fact has been so severely scaled down as to be almost lost to follower and critic alike. But it is there nevertheless and so are the results of his tireless and sympathetic observation of contemporaneous business life which he understood as few academic economists ever did. In its very nature the latter achievement implies certain limitations. The practice of the middle-sized English business firm of his time no doubt absorbed a greater share of the attention of the analyst than it should have done in an exposition making large claims to generality. But within those limits a realism was attained which greatly surpasses that of Adam Smith—the only comparable instance. This may be one of the reasons why no institutionalist opposition rose against him in England.

the same year, at the instigation of Henry Sidgwick, the two famous little monographs, *The Pure Theory of Foreign Trade* and *The Pure Theory of Domestic Values,* were privately printed and circulated both in England and abroad. Most of their contents entered into the *Principles* and into the Appendix J of *Money, Credit and Commerce.*

To be sure, such opposition did arise in this country. Nor is this difficult to understand. A simplified Marshallism, which disregarded historical backgrounds, pervaded the routine of college teaching until many of the more lively intellects got thoroughly sick of it. It is but natural that in breaking away from a traditionalized Marshall they should have thought that they were breaking away from the real Marshall, and that in trying to cut their way toward economic reality they should have overlooked the fact that there was a Marshallian signpost pointing to realization of their program.

The analytic core or kernel of the *Principles* consists of course in a theory of economic statics. Its originality does not stand out as, on the merits of the case, it should because for us it is just one member of a family which had grown up or was growing up at that time. Moreover, the other members of that family were no doubt independent of Marshall, whereas his habits of work and his methods of publication make it impossible for the historian of economic thought to be equally positive about his version. I do not wish to be misunderstood. Mr. Keynes's biography of his teacher bears witness to, and presents evidence for, Marshall's subjective originality which seems to me quite convincing.[3] Marshall himself kept dignified silence on the matter and indicated his feelings only by being scrupulously fair to the classics, in particular to Ricardo and Mill, and by taking up a position of armed neutrality against Menger, Jevons, and the greatest of all theorists, Walras. The following reconstruction cannot, however, be far from the truth.

We know from Mr. Keynes's pages that it was not primarily intellectual curiosity that brought Marshall into the economist's camp. He was driven to it from ethical speculations by a generous impulse to help in the great task of alleviating the misery and degradation he observed among the English poor. When talking about his preoccupation with the subject, he was constantly rebuffed by a friend steeped in the economist's wisdom of the time, and that was why he turned to Mill's *Principles* for enlightenment. There

[3] Keynes, op. cit. pp. 180*ff.*

are other indications from Marshall's work which suggest that he first learned his economics from that source. He also took up Ricardo in 1867. And even if we did not know, we could easily infer what would happen when a mind thoroughly trained in mathematics turns to those two authors with a will: such a mind would, first, be shocked at the haziness and carelessness that both authors, but especially Mill, displayed with respect to cogency of proofs and determinateness of results; secondly, it would at once set about eliminating restrictions and generalizing propositions. Not much more than that is really needed to transform Mill's structure into the Marshallian one.

Of course that is a very considerable performance. Many a theoretical physicist has gained immortality for less. Marshall himself acknowledges the help of Cournot and Thünen and the profound influence of both is indeed obvious. The demand and supply curves of the partial or particular equilibrium analysis are Cournot's curves (though Fleeming Jenkins should not be forgotten) and the marginal analysis, which in any case would automatically occur to the mathematical mind, is Thünen's. As regards marginal utility in particular, there was Jevons' *Brief Account of a General Mathematical Theory of Political Economy,* presented to the Cambridge meeting of the British Association in 1862, which paper contained the idea under the name of 'coefficient of utility.' The two parts of Walras' *Éléments d'économie politique pure* were published in 1874 and 1877. These contained the theoretical skeleton of the static model in question much more fully than did Marshall's *Principles.* But, given the economist's reading habits, it is not likely that at the time they were known to Marshall, and all the rest of the authors to whom technical priority belongs would have had only fragments to contribute.

This seems to account for Marshall's tendency to impute to Mill and Ricardo practically all that the reformers of economic theory had to say. Although an ardent admirer of Walras may perhaps be excused for resenting the scant notice taken of him in the *Principles,* and an ardent admirer of Marshall for lamenting the absence of more expansive generosity on his part, it follows that no serious objection can be raised to Marshall's acknowledgments to persons. But such objection is in order as regards his written and spoken comments about his great impersonal ally to which he owed so much, mathematics.

If the diagnosis above be correct, then the point is—not merely that his mathematical turn of mind was favorable to his achievement in the field of economic theory, but—that the actual use of the methods of mathematical analysis *produced* that achievement and that the transformation of the Smith-Ricardo-Mill material into a modern engine of research could hardly have been accomplished without it. It is of course possible to argue that any particular result or even the general vision of a system of interdependent economic quantities could also have been attained by methods not mathematically articulate, just as it is possible to argue that a railroad cannot take us to any place which we could not also reach by walking. But even if we choose to disregard the fact that rigorous proofs cannot be supplied except in ways which are mathematical in essence though in simple cases they need not be mathematical in form, the further fact remains that performance of the Marshallian kind *practically* presupposes a mathematical schema. And this Marshall always refused to admit. He never gave full credit to the faithful ally. He hid the tool that had done the work.

Of course there were excellent reasons for this. He did not wish to frighten the layman, he wanted—strange ambition!—to be 'read by businessmen.' He was afraid, and justly, of setting an example which might induce people with a mathematical training to think that mathematics is all an economist needs. Yet one might wish that he had extended more encouragement to those who, partly inspired by his work, were then beginning to espouse the cause of exact economics. He does not seem to have realized that the danger of 'mathematics running away with us' is not confined to the field of economics, yet has not proved to be so very terrible elsewhere. No science will ever progress if there are no runaways among its votaries. Economics cannot, alone of all the branches of human knowledge, be tied down forever to what the layman can readily understand. As a matter of fact, Marshall himself cannot be fully understood by readers who have no grasp at all of the elements of the calculus. No good purpose is served by making them think that he can. Much good could have been accomplished if Marshall had resolutely stood for the line of advance which he had done more than anyone else to open.

III

Every member of a family, however, has his distinctive characteristics, and the Marshallian individual is not fully described by indicating the family to which it belongs.

The feature that will first strike the theorist's eye is the neatness of the structure. This virtue that has so much to do with success stands out particularly well if we compare Marshall's exposition with that of Walras. There is a tiresome heaviness about the latter whereas the former flows along with easy grace. All traces of effort have disappeared from the highly polished surface. Theorems are elegantly put. Proofs are simple and concise—in the skeleton appendix at least. Marshall's mathematical training disciplined even his verbal statements. It also accounts for the charming simplicity of his diagrams.

Geometrical illustrations of economic arguments had been used before, especially by Cournot. By now, many of us have grown out of humor with them, because the use of the easy two-dimensional variety unavoidably implies oversimplification. But still they are inestimable vehicles of fundamental, if elementary, propositions. They victoriously clear up many a point. They have proved a boon in countless classrooms. And practically all the most useful ones we owe to Marshall.

Secondly, the text of the *Principles* suggests and the appendix proves that Marshall had fully grasped the idea of general equilibrium, discovering 'a whole Copernican system, by which all the elements of the economic universe are kept in their places by mutual counterpoise and interaction.'[4] But in order to display the working of that system he forged and extensively used a different model that was much easier to manage though its field of application was also much more restricted. In most cases, especially in Book v, he thought primarily of medium-sized firms operating in 'industries' whose importance is not great enough to influence appreciably the course of events in the rest of the economy, and of individual commodities absorbing but small parts of their buyers' total expenditure. This 'partial' or 'particular' analysis has its shortcomings. He did not fully state—perhaps he did not fully realize himself—how many phenomena it excludes from vision and how dangerous it may be in unwary hands: to some of his disciples Professor Pigou's all too necessary emphasis on the 'smallness' of the industries dealt with has, I dare say, come as a surprise, and others have carelessly applied the Marshallian demand-supply curves to such commodities as labor. But if we frankly recognize that this method is essentially one of approximation—and if furthermore we waive our present-day objections to the concept of an industry—then we are at liberty to enjoy the rich harvest of results which it turned out and for the sake of which Marshall, deviating from strict correctness, developed what was really much more bold and novel than his method of presentation suggests.

Third, in order to reap that harvest, he devised those handy tools everyone knows, such as substitution, the elasticity coefficient, consumers' surplus, quasi-rent, internal and external economies, the representative firm, prime and supplementary cost, the long and the short run. They are such old friends of ours and have become such familiar denizens of our arsenal of analysis that we hardly realize any more what we owe to them. Of course they, or the things they stood for, were not all completely new. But even those that were not then stepped into their proper places and became really useful for the first time. Like old friends, however, they occasionally prove treacherous. Some of them, such as the representative firm and the

[4] Cf. Keynes, op. cit. p. 223.

external economies, cover rather than mend the logical difficulties we are bound to encounter when we emerge, on the one hand, from the precincts of statics and, on the other hand, from the precincts of the individual industry. The downward sloping cost and supply curves cannot be completely salvaged by those means. And the attempt to do so for a time absorbed energies that might have been better employed in radical reconstruction.

Fourth, when we again recall the reasons which Marshall may have had for the particular equilibrium aspect and when we analyze those handy tools, we cannot fail to be struck by the realism of his theoretical thought. Particular equilibrium analysis brings out the practical problems of the individual industry and of the individual firm. It is much more, of course, but it is also a scientific basis for business economics. Some of the tools are taken directly from business practice, the prime and the supplementary costs, for instance; while others, like the quasi-rent and the internal and external economies, are excellently qualified to catch business situations and to formulate business problems. Nothing at all like that has been so much as attempted by any of Marshall's peers, whereas everything else was not only attempted but also achieved by them, and in some respects more completely than by him. Thus, a full elaboration of the theory of general equilibrium could only have duplicated the work of Walras; a mere elaboration of the concepts of the particular equilibrium method would have been trite. But the one inspired by the other and the other implemented by the one— that was the achievement that was exclusively his own.

Finally, fifth, though it was essentially a static theory that he worked out, he always looked beyond it. He inserted dynamic elements whenever he could, more often, in fact, than was compatible with the static logic he nevertheless retained. The mists that lie on certain parts of his route, particularly where it touches the phenomena that lie behind his treatment of the 'element of time,' mainly arise from this source. There is a hybrid character about some of his curves which later analysis was not slow in discovering. Yet though he did not take the fortress, he effectively led his troops up to it. Nor is this all. A still more significant point comes into view if we pass from the distinction static-dynamic to the distinction stationary-evolutionary. Marshall put up, somewhat regretfully as it seems, with the static nature of his apparatus but he disliked the stationary hypothesis to the point of overlooking its usefulness for some purposes. His thought ran in terms of evolutionary change—in terms of an organic, irreversible process. And something of the flavor of it he imparted to his theorems and concepts and still more to the factual observations with which he presented them. I do not think that the theory of evolution at the back of them was satisfactory. No schema can be that does not go beyond an automatic expansion of markets—an expansion not otherwise motivated than by increase of population and by saving—which then induces internal and external economies that in turn are to account for further expansion. But still it *was* a theory of evolution, an important development of Adam Smith's suggestions, and greatly superior to what Ricardo and Mill had to offer on the subject.

IV

However, imposing as the achievement was, it would not have met with so huge a success without the garb in which it strode forth and which appealed to the spirit of the time. Fundamentally, Marshall had built an 'engine of analysis . . . machinery of universal application in the discovery of a certain class of truths . . . not a body of concrete truth, but an engine for the discovery of concrete truth.' [5] The discovery that there is such a thing as a general method of economic analysis or, to put it differently, that as far as the logic of their procedure is concerned, economists, whether dealing with international trade or with unemployment or with profits or with money or what not, are always applying substantially the same schema that is invariant to the particular subject matter in hand—this discovery was not his. Nor was it the discovery of the

[5] Taken from Mr. Keynes's 'portmanteau quotation' in his essay, op. cit. p. 208.

group of economists of which he was so outstanding a member. In order to satisfy ourselves that this truth must have been known, at least from the Physiocrats on, to all economists that knew their business, we need only look at Ricardo's work. The first chapter, supplemented by the second, is obviously a blueprint of such an 'engine for the discovery of concrete truth,' and the rest of Ricardo's chapters is nothing but a series of experiments in the application of that blueprint. But no economist before Marshall ever grasped the meaning of this so fully, preached it so energetically, acted upon it so consistently.

Now from a man who took that view of the nature and the function of economic theory, one might have expected a treatise very different from the *Principles,* one that could never have enjoyed widespread popular favor. We have already seen some of the reasons why the *Principles* was more fortunate: Marshall's historic-philosophical culture tells on almost every page—his analytic schema is embedded in a luxuriant frame that conciliates and comforts the layman. The analytic skeleton does not grin at you. It is clothed in flesh and skin which Marshall's observation of business facts found it easy to assemble. All that meant more than homely and palatable illustration. But it also meant that this theory 'went down' with the general public as no other comparable treatise on economic theory ever did.

There was something else however. In more fortunate fields of human knowledge, the analyst is allowed to do his work without constantly thinking of and pointing out its utilitarian virtues; he may even with impunity stray from any possibility of practical application—which is one of the reasons why he progresses so well. The economist has not only to struggle with much less promising problems; he is also incessantly harassed by imperious demands for the immediately 'useful' result, for service in the troubles of the hour, for professions of sympathy with the betterment of mankind, and, unlike the physicist, he is not permitted to answer that all successful production is roundabout production and that even the utilitarian result is best attained by *not* aiming at it directly. But Marshall felt no repugnance to the credo that prompts those demands. In fact, he fully subscribed to it. *L'art pour l'art* had no place in his eminently Anglo-Saxon soul. To serve his nation and his time, and to teach what would be immediately helpful, that was what he himself wished to do more than anything else. He had no objection to commonplaces about human values and loved to preach the gospel of the Noble Life.

Moreover, his idea of the Noble Life, his views about social problems, his general outlook on the public as well as on the private sphere happened to coincide with the ideas, views, and outlook of his country and his time. More precisely, his ideals and convictions were the ideals and convictions not indeed of the average Englishman of 1890, but of the average intellectual Englishman of 1890. He accepted the institutions around him, the privately owned firm and the family home in particular, and entertained no doubt about their vitality or the vitality of the civilization that had grown up around them. He accepted the utilitarianized and detheologized Christianity that prevailed. He complacently carried the flag of justice and did not question the validity of the compromise that had been struck, by means of the White Man's Burden, between a creed of utilitarian righteousness and the inheritance of the Great Mogul. He cheerfully sympathized, from a warm heart, with the ideals of socialism and patronizingly talked down to socialists from a cool head. Thus he was in a position to give his readers exactly what they craved—a message that was both high-minded and comforting —and at the same time to answer to the call of his conscience.

We may question the propriety of *professiones fidei* in a scientific treatise—though, after all, Marshall was in the same boat with Newton in that respect.[6] I for one do. More than that, we may

---

[6] I have been struck by what seems to me a curious similarity between those two great men, and I have often wondered how much of it was due to their approximately similar environments and how much merely to chance. It is not only that academic pontificality, that assertiveness of fundamental creed, that unreasonable sensitiveness to criticism which both of them displayed. There is more. Both developed methods which they were extremely reluctant to publish as such. They liked to keep their blueprints to themselves.

fail to admire the particular message. I confess that few things are
so irritating to me as is the preaching of mid-Victorian morality,
seasoned by Benthamism, the preaching from a schema of middle-
class values that knows no glamour and no passion. But that does
not alter the fact that the vast majority af Marshall's readers felt
differently, and that they welcomed an analysis which was thoroughly imbued with what to them was the only right and decent
spirit.

V

But there is something about Marshall's work that is much
greater than anything he actually accomplished—something that
assures immortality or, let us say, vitality far beyond the lifetime
of any definite achievement. Over and above the products of his
genius which he handed to us to work with and which inevitably
wear out in our hands, there are in the *Principles* subtle suggestions
or directions for further advance, manifestations of that quality of
leadership that I have made an effort to define at the start. To list
some of the former is easy; to convey a sense of the latter, difficult.

First, it was but natural that a work of such importance
should have guided the work of the generation it taught. The economic literature of the thirty years after 1890, therefore, abounds
with developments and restatements of, and corollaries to, Marshallian propositions and pieces of technique. The works of Marshall's pupil and successor, Professor Pigou, of Robertson, Laving-
ton, Shove, and many others afford countless instances that are
familiar to all of us. Even a part of Edgeworth's contributions comes
within this category. One example may suffice for the theorems and
another for the techniques.

Marshall was the first to show that perfect competition will
not always maximize output. This, so far as I know the first breach

They worked out results and presented them in ways other than those by
which they had been discovered, and after curiously long delays. Especially
in later life, they both affected to despise precisely those things in which they
were so great.

in an ancient wall, yielded the proposition that output might be increased beyond the competitive maximum by restricting industries subject to decreasing, and expanding industries subject to increasing returns. Pigou, Kahn and others, following up the suggestion, developed what eventually became a field of considerable interest and importance.

Again, the concept of elasticity of demand may not quite merit all the praise that has been bestowed on it. Still it set a fashion of reasoning in terms of elasticities which all of us find convenient. There are nearly a dozen elasticity concepts now in use. Among them, the elasticity of substitution ranks first in importance. Though it is true that it works well only under assumptions so restrictive as to be practically inapplicable to any real pattern, it serves admirably to clear up points that have been the subject of much unnecessary controversy—the question, for instance, whether the introduction of machinery into the productive process can or cannot injure the interests of labor. Now, the concept of substitution is basic for the Marshallian structure. His emphasis on the 'principle of substitution' might almost be looked upon as the main purely theoretical difference between his schema and that of Walras. Hence the new instrument consists entirely of material that is to be found in the *Principles* and had only to be joined.

Second, though Marshall's distinction between the long run and the short does not quite satisfactorily express what Marshall presumably intended to express by it, it spelled a great advance in clear and realistic thinking and is fully entitled to the homage that was rendered to it by its ready acceptance. Marshall himself used it extensively and by so doing taught us a lesson from which our generation was and is eager to profit: by slow accretion a whole branch of economics has developed, Short Time Analysis.

Third, Marshall is still more obviously the father of another comparatively recent body of economic thought, of the theory of Imperfect Competition. This, I suppose, is true quite generally, but it is particularly obvious in the case of the English version. The ideas presented to English readers by Piero Sraffa in his famous article of

1926 are there seen to arise—this is still clearer in *Costo di Produzi-one e Quantità Prodotta*—from a struggle with the logical difficulties about Marshall's descending cost curves. Moreover, there are positive suggestions in the *Principles,* in particular the comments on special markets of individual firms. And Mr. Harrod and Mrs. Robinson simply proved themselves good Marshallians as well as economists of powerful originality by building the structure we admire.

Less incontrovertible, I admit, is the fourth claim I am going to make on Marshall's behalf. I have said that though he grasped the idea of general equilibrium he yet relegated it to the background, erecting in the foreground the handier house of partial or particular analysis. Nevertheless, especially in Book vi, he launches out into wide generalizations about the economic process as a whole. What is their nature, if they are neither particular nor general analyses? Well, I suppose we have got to recognize a third type of theory—in my own workshop it is called 'aggregative.' Of course, he did not link up his treatment of such aggregative quantities with money. His failure to do so, in spite of his many and important discoveries in monetary theory—since this is a comment on the *Principles* they cannot be mentioned here—is perhaps the only fundamental criticism that I should level against him. But really, if one starts from partial analysis and then wishes to say something about the economic process as a whole, is it not natural that, despairing of the possibilities of the unwieldy idea of general equilibrium, one should turn to aggregative theory? And would not then the theory of money automatically come in, to use Mrs. Robinson's phrase, as the theory of total output and employment?

Fifth, it has been pointed out that Marshall held a definite theory of economic evolution which, though true to his habit he did not press it upon the reader's attention, stood in the very center of his thought. I shall not be suspected of harboring much sympathy for it. But I do want to point out that, not as a philosophy but as an instrument of research, it has exerted more influence than most of us seem to be aware of. H. L. Moore's trend-values can be considered to approximate equilibrium-values only on the basis of that theory.

And W. M. Persons found in it the theoretical rationale for dealing as he did with the trends in the Harvard-barometer series. This, however, leads to the item that is the most important of all.

Sixth, then, Marshall's was one of the strongest influences in the emergence of modern econometrics. Many as are the points in which the *Principles* resemble the *Wealth of Nations,* there is one in which the former are definitely superior to the latter, if, eliminating time, we reduce both to the common denominator of subjective, time-conditioned performance. Adam Smith judiciously assembled and developed whatever he thought most worth while in the thought of his own and of the preceding epoch. But he did nothing to develop one of the most significant of the achievements within his reach, the 'Political Arithmetick' of the seventeenth century, whereas Marshall, who, proportions guarded, had really less to go upon, firmly led the way toward, and prepared the ground for, an economic science that would be not only quantitative but numerical. The importance of this cannot be overestimated. Economics will never either have or merit any prestige until it can figure out results.

How clearly Marshall realized this can be seen from his address on 'The Old Generation of Economists and the New' (1897). But we owe him much more than a program; we owe him a definite approach. All we have to do in order to satisfy ourselves of this, is to glance once more at what I have described as his 'handy tools.' They are all of them eminently operational in the statistical sense. We need but try our hand at the task of constructing, from statistical material, models of a firm, a household, a market, in order to find that in doing so we run up against difficulties with which those tools are intended to cope. They are useful irrespective of that, to be sure, but we do not appreciate them fully until we realize that, whatever else they may be, they are first of all methods of measurement—*devices to facilitate numerical measurement*—and parts of a general apparatus that aims at statistical measurement. They are perhaps not the best possible ones and they are certainly not the only possible ones. But they were the first of their kind, and econometric endeavors could hardly have started from anything else.

For instance, it is obviously no coincidence that those endeavors were, on a large scale, first directed toward the derivation of statistical demand curves: Marshall's theory of demand had provided an acceptable basis. There would have been little point in imposing all those restrictions that enable us to define point elasticity or that kind of demand curve itself, if he had not wished to work out a method of approximation that would, in many cases at least, prove manageable statistically. In fact, those restrictions which give rise to many objections become completely understandable only if we look at them from this standpoint. Take the concept of consumers' rent. It is true that not much has come from this particular suggestion. But unless it was meant to lead up to statistical evaluation of a quantified welfare, why should not Marshall have been content with mentioning the existence of such a surplus, a function of many variables, instead of courting the danger of misunderstanding and opposition by insisting, as Dupuit had done before him, on this kind of simplification that would reduce the number of independent variables to two? The same reasoning applies, of course, to his cost and supply functions and, among other things, explains his adherence to those long-run industrial supply curves that do not look well to the theorist, yet open up certain statistical possibilities [7] that are closed to more correct and more general models.

Marshall's conquests in the field of monetary theory could also be invoked in support of the thesis that the vision of a theoretical apparatus that would effectively grip statistical fact pervades all his work and actually is its most distinctive feature. Böhm-Bawerk's reasoning is no doubt quantitative. But the possibility of statistical measurement seems never to have occurred to him, and he did nothing to fit his theory for it. Walras' system, while not as hopeless as many of us believe it to be, presents difficulties formidable enough to deter. Only Marshall's teaching urges on. Never

[7] Those possibilities have been partially exploited by G. T. Jones in his work on Increasing Returns.

mind that it also cautions. We can do with that, too. Urging or cautioning, he is still the great teacher of us all.

Standing on the edge of the ravine in which we all vainly seek for a concrete highway, we behold him whenever we look back, serene, in Olympian repose, safe in the citadel of his beliefs, still telling us much that is worth our while to hear—nothing, however, that is more worth while to ponder over than this: 'The more I study economics the smaller appears the knowledge I have of it . . . and now at the end of half a century, I am conscious of more ignorance of it than I was at the beginning.' Yes, he was a great economist.

VILFREDO PARETO *
1848-1923

I<small>N A</small> volume devoted to Pareto's life and work,[1] Professor Bousquet relates that the obituary article devoted to Pareto in the socialist daily, *Avanti*, described him as the 'bourgeois Karl Marx.' I do not know that a man can rightly be called 'bourgeois' who never missed an opportunity to pour contempt on *la bourgeoisie ignorante et*

* Reprinted from the *Quarterly Journal of Economics*, vol. LXIII, no. 2, May 1949. Copyright 1948 by the President and Fellows of Harvard College.
[1] G. H. Bousquet, 'Vilfredo Pareto, sa vie et son œuvre' (in the *Collection d'études, de documents et de témoignages pour servir à l'histoire de notre temps*, Paris, Payot, 1928). Except for the mathematical parts of Pareto's work, this book, written in a vein of generous enthusiasm by a man who is an economist and sociologist in his own right and as far as possible removed from the state of mind of the disciple or biographer who basks in reflected glory, is herewith strongly recommended. Bousquet also wrote a *Précis de sociologie d'après Pareto*, introductions to the latter's *Systèmes Socialistes* and *Manuel d'économie politique*, and also a short English appraisal entitled, *The Work of Vilfredo Pareto*, 1928, besides reserving for him a place of honor in his *Essai sur l'évolution de la pensée économique*. Of other memorial appraisals it will suffice to mention what may be called the official one, Professor Alfonso de Pietri-Tonelli's address to the economic section of the Italian Association for the Advancement of Science, published in the *Revista di Politica Economia*, November and December 1934 and January 1935, and Professor Luigi Amoroso's article in *Econometrica*, January 1938.

lâche. But for the rest, the analogy conveys very well the impression that Pareto had made upon his countrymen: they had in fact raised him to an eminence that was unique among the economists and sociologists of his time. No other country erected a similar pedestal for his statue, and in the Anglo-American world both the man and the thinker have remained strangers to this day. There was, indeed, a short Pareto vogue in this country that followed upon the translation of his sociological treatise.[2] But it died out soon in an uncongenial atmosphere. Moreover, so far as the small circle of pure theorists is concerned, Pareto came to exert considerable influence on Anglo-American economics in the 1920's and 1930's, that is, after the publication of Professor Bowley's *Groundwork.* But both in England and the United States, Marshallian and post-Marshallian economics offered enough in the line in which Pareto excelled to prevent him from gaining much ground of his own even before other tendencies took away whatever he had gained.

This might seem surprising owing to the fact that several important developments in theoretical economics are now seen to stem from him. But it is not difficult to explain. Pareto was the product of a sector of the Franco-Italian civilization that is far removed from English and American currents of thought. Even within that sector his towering figure stood almost alone. Pareto cannot be pigeonholed. He paid court to no 'ism.' No creed or party can claim him as its own, although many creeds and parties appropriated fragments of the vast intellectual realm over which he held sway. He seems to have taken pleasure in running counter to ruling humors and slogans. Votaries of extreme laissez-faire may cull plenty of passages from his writings in support of their views. Yet there was nothing he despised so thoroughly as the 'pluto-democracy' or

[2] At Harvard, this vogue was represented by the eminent physiologist, the late Professor L. J. Henderson. See his *Pareto's General Sociology,* 1935. Some Harvard men will still remember his informal Pareto 'seminar' that practically consisted in a series of monologues by the professor. Sympathetic understanding and a profound sense of the unconventional greatness of Pareto's thought there struggled valiantly with inevitable professional handicaps.

'plutocratic demagogy' of liberalism. Socialists are under obligation to him for rendering, as we shall see, a very important service to socialist doctrine, and also for his protests against the anti-socialist measures that the Italian government took in 1898. Yet he was not only an anti-socialist but one of that type whose criticism derives sting from contempt. French Catholics might thank him for his attacks upon the persecution of the French clergy that was so unedifying a sequel to the Dreyfus affair. Yet he attacked the 'laicist' policies of the Combes ministry because he was a gentleman, and not because he believed either in the mission of the Catholic Church or in her teaching.

A gentleman of such independence and pugnacity who is in the habit of dealing vigorous blows right in the midst of arguments that might in themselves be agreeable to some party or another has little chance of being popular. By now he is a figure of the past. But even in the epoch of his prime the political and social slogans with which we are all familiar controlled official phraseology, the press, party programs, and popular literature including its economic sector. The wrapping in which he presented his strictly scientific results were then not much more popular than they would be now. One has only to imbue oneself with the spirit that pervades an American textbook and then open Pareto's *Manuel* in order to realize what I mean: the naïve lover of modern social creeds and slogans must feel himself driven with clubs from Pareto's threshold; he reads what he is firmly resolved never to admit to be true and he reads it together with a disconcerting wealth of practical examples. Therefore it seems that the problem is not to explain why Pareto did not exert influence more widely; the problem is rather to explain how he came to exert as much as he did.

Could we confine ourselves to Pareto's contributions to pure theory, there would be little need for glancing at the man and his social background and location. But into everything that was not a theorem in the pure logic of economics the whole man and all the forces that conditioned him entered so unmistakably that it is more necessary than it usually is in an appraisal of scientific performance to convey an idea of that man and of those forces. I shall make an attempt to do so first (i). Then I shall briefly survey Pareto's work in pure theory (ii). And I shall end up with a glance at his conception of society that has found so inadequate an expression in his *General Sociology* (iii).[3]

I. THE MAN

Pareto's father, the Genoese Marchese Raffaele Pareto, seems to have been a typical product of the Italian Risorgimento of the first half of the nineteenth century, an ardent adherent of Mazzini— perhaps more from national than from social reasons—an uncompromising enemy of all the governments that barred Italy's way toward national unity, and a revolutionary in this if in no other sense. Accordingly, he exiled himself to Paris where Vilfredo, the subject of this memoir, was born of a French mother: if General Galliéni once described himself as 'Francese ma anche Italiano,' Vilfredo Pareto might have described himself as 'Italiano ma anche Francese.' He was taken to Italy in 1858 and there went through the usual course of studies that issued in a Doctor's degree in engineering in 1869. He immediately embarked upon engineering and indus-

[3] There is a bibliography that cannot be very far from being complete by Messrs Rocca and Spinedi in the *Giornale degli Economisti*, 1924, but only the following items need be mentioned here: 'Considerazioni sui principi fondamentali dell' economia politica pura,' *Giornale degli Economisti*, 1892-3; *Cours d'économie politique professé à l'université de Lausanne*, 1896-7; *Résumé du cours donné à l'École des Hautes Études Sociales de Paris*, 1901-2; *Les systèmes socialistes*, 1902 (reprinted 1926); *Manuale di economia politica*, 1906 (reprinted 1919); *Manuel d'économie politique*, 1909 (reprinted 1927) (a translation of the preceding item which must, however, be listed separately because of the mathematical appendix that was completely redone); *Trattato di sociologia generale* (1916) French translation, 1919, English translation, under the title *Mind and Society*, 1935; 'L'économie mathématique' in the French *Encyclopédie des sciences mathématiques*, 1911 (the corresponding article in the original German edition of the Mathematical Encyclopedia is of negligible importance). There are several other books besides innumerable articles, but they do not, so far as I know them (Pareto published many articles in the daily press, most of which I do not know), contain anything of a scientific nature that is not contained in one or more of the publications mentioned.

trial management as a profession and after various other appointments rose to be manager general—we should say 'president'—of the Italian Iron Works. It was only in 1893 that he was appointed successor to Walras in the University of Lausanne, although he may be considered as a full-time economist a few years before that. Thus, the span during which he was primarily engaged in economic research extends from about 1892 to about 1912—practically all his later work is sociological in nature. He resigned his chair in 1906 and then retired to his home, a country place on the lake of Geneva, to grow in the course of a vigorous and fertile old age into the 'lone thinker of Céligny.'

Substantially, this suffices for our purpose: we have to underline a few of these facts rather than to add others. First, theorists will note that owing to his training as an engineer—and he seems to have cultivated theoretical aspects—he acquired at an early age command of mathematics on a professional level.[4] Second, it is worth while to notice that, to a degree quite unusual with scientific economists, Pareto was thoroughly familiar with industrial practice —familiar in a sense which is quite different from the kind of familiarity that may be acquired by the means available to the academic economist, the public servant, the politician. But, third, it was his passionate interest in the current issues of economic and general policy, presently to be commented on in another connection, which made him something of an economist long before he started his own creative work. Francesco Ferrara was then at the height of his fame and influence, and the frosts had not yet fallen upon a theoretical structure glorified by uncritical liberalism. His writings, especially his famous introductions (*prefazioni*) to the classics published in the *Biblioteca dell' economista*, served Pareto as well as, or better than, any of the university courses could have done that were avail-

---

[4] I feel unable to say precisely how much this amounted to. Pareto had to be told by Volterra that an expression of the form $Xdx + Ydy$ has always an infinity of integrating factors whereas with more than two variables no such factor *need* exist. (*Manuel*, p. 546n.) I wonder whether a real 'professional' could have overlooked this.

able in his student days. His way to Walras, however, was chalked
out later on by Maffeo Pantaleoni.

None of the facts above will account completely for Pareto's
vision of society and politics, or even for his attitudes to the practical problems of his age and country. Nor do I believe for a moment
that the deep pool of personality can ever be drained so as to show
what is at the bottom of it. But there is the patrician background
which, I am sure all who knew him will agree, meant much more
in his case than it usually does. In particular it prevented him from
becoming a brother in spirit to the men—and a fully accepted member of the various groups—with whom life threw him. It also prevented him from establishing *emotional* relations with the creations
of the bourgeois mind, such as the twins that are called democracy
and capitalism. Acting upon this background, his financial independence—a bare independence at first, something like affluence
later on [5]—helped to isolate him still further by offering the possibility of his isolating himself.

Still acting upon this background, his classical scholarship
worked the same way. I do not mean that part of it which he shared
with every educated person of his time, but that part which he conquered himself through incessant study of the Greek and Roman
classics during his sleepless nights. The ancient world is a museum,
not a laboratory of applied science, and he who trusts too much to
the wisdom to be gathered there is bound to stray from every group
of men that was in existence either in 1890 or 1920. Isolation was
made complete by the result of his participation in the debates on
the policies and politics of his country—so complete that he had
decided to emigrate to Switzerland even before he received the call
to Lausanne. And isolation had its effects—soothed only late in life
by a second marriage that brought domestic peace (see the dedication of the *Trattato*)—upon a fiery temperament that was not really
made to stand it.

[5] This relative affluence was due to an inheritance, not to his previous
activity as a business executive.

But why should he have left his country in wrathful exasperation—the country that he loved from the bottom of his heart and whose national rebirth he had not only yearned for but witnessed? The detached observer is all the more likely to ask this question because it will seem to him that the new national kingdom did not do so badly in the thirty years that preceded Pareto's emigration. Besides progressing economically at a considerable rate and growing out of financial disorders—*pace* our Keynesians—it took its first steps in social legislation and established itself successfully as one of what then were called the great powers. Looking at things in this light, our observer will develop a good deal of respect for a régime such as that of Agostino Depretis. And, considering the difficulties incident to the beginnings of the new national state, he will make allowances for the less exhilarating parts of the picture. But Pareto made no such allowances. He saw nothing but incompetence and corruption. He fought with impartial ferocity the governments that succeeded one another, and it was then that he became known as an ultraliberal—in the nineteenth-century sense of uncompromising advocate of laissez-faire—and that he helped to create, among the German New-Dealers of that period, the impression that marginal utility was just a wicked trick with which to thwart reformers.[6] Possibly this is all there is to say about Pareto's attitude in matters of economic policy and the strong traces it left upon his scientific writing before 1900. But even then there was something in that ultraliberalism of his that points in a direction exactly opposite to the creeds and slogans of official liberalism. He certainly was *antiétatiste,* but for political reasons rather than for purely economic ones: unlike the English classics, he did not fight against government activity *per se* but against the governments of parliamentary democracy, of the very parliamentary democracy that commanded

_____

[6] German critics received his *Cours* accordingly. In fact, the book contains very little that may be used for a different interpretation. It does, however, contain the remark that the virtues therein predicated of pure competition have no bearing upon the actual economic process, since pure competition does not actually prevail.

the fervent allegiance of the English classics. Viewed from this angle, his type of laissez-faire acquires a connotation that is entirely at variance with the laissez-faire of the English type. And once we realize this, the rest is easy to understand.

Toward the end of the nineteenth and during the first two decades of the twentieth century, an increasing number of Frenchmen and Italians began to voice dissatisfaction that varied from mere disappointment to violent disgust at the manner in which the *cotillon* of parliamentary democracy functioned and at the results it produced in France and Italy. Such sentiments were shared by men as different as E. Faguet and G. Sorel, and they were not confined to any one party. This is not the place to analyze let alone to pass judgment upon them. All that matters for us is their existence and the fact that the later Pareto stands out from this current of thought only because he himself stood out from his contemporaries and because he wrote a sociology that was—along with those of Sorel and Mosca—to rationalize it.

Englishmen and Americans, oblivious of the particular and historically unique circumstances that have developed in their minds an equally particular and unique attitude toward parliamentary democracy, have wondered about the possible meaning of Pareto's attitude toward Fascism. But this attitude is not problematical in the least. No theory is necessary in order to explain it. The events of 1914-22 had called him back to the arena of political debate. The masterly analyses he published on the origins of the First World War, on the miscarriage of Versailles, and on the futility of the League are among his strongest performances although they found no answering echo outside of Italy. But above all he witnessed with something like horror the social disorganization in Italy which it is necessary to have seen in order to believe. Attributing all the troubles of those years to the weakness of the political system of a decadent bourgeoisie, the student of Roman history may have thought of the formula by which, in republican Rome, the senate, in order to deal with an emergency, used to direct the consuls to appoint an officer of practically unlimited though temporary power,

the dictator: *videant consules ne quid detrimenti res publica capiat.*
But there was no such provision in the Italian constitution, and it
would not have done any good if there had been one. So the dictator
had to appoint himself. Beyond this and beyond approval of the
success with which Mussolini restored order, Pareto never went.
Mussolini honored himself by conferring senatorial rank on the man
who kept on preaching moderation and who stood throughout for
the freedom of the press and of academic teaching.[7] But to his last
day Pareto refused to embrace this 'ism' as he had refused to embrace any other. There is no point whatever in judging his action—
or, indeed, any action or sentiment of his—from the standpoint of
Anglo-American tradition.

Everything else is at the bottom of the pool.

II. THE THEORIST

Any appraisal of Pareto's contribution to economics must first
of all give due credit to a feat of leadership. He never taught in
Italy. The Faculty of Law in the University of Lausanne did not
make very favorable headquarters for a campaign of intellectual
conquest. The country house in Céligny looked like a *buen retiro.*
Yet he did what Walras had not been able to do: he formed a school
in the full sense of the word. An inner circle of eminent economists,
a wider circle of followers of less eminence, and beyond this a broad
fringe of more or less definite adherents emerged soon after 1900.
They co-operated in positive work. They cultivated personal contact.
They stood for one another in controversy. They recognized One
Master and One Doctrine.

This school was specifically Italian. As has been pointed out
already, there were but few foreign adherents, though individual
pieces of Paretian teaching eventually gained acceptance both in
England and in the United States. Nor did the Pareto school ever
dominate Italian economics. No school ever does dominate its own
country. Impressions to the contrary, e.g. the impression that the
Ricardo school ever dominated English economics, are due to noth-

[7] See on this, Bousquet, op. cit. pp. 182-94.

ing but unrealistic historiography. Several other Italian leaders, like
Einaudi, held their own ground entirely, and others, like Del
Vecchio, while recognizing Pareto's eminence and adopting this or
that of his doctrines, thought and wrote pretty much as they would
have done had Pareto never lived. Still, there remains the fact that
a school did emerge on the basis of a theoretical structure that was
inaccessible not only to the general reader but, in some of its most
original parts, also to students of economics, students moreover who
had never heard or seen the master.

But once we have duly recognized and thereupon discarded
this feat of leadership, we see a theorist who continued the work of
Walras. Nobody, of course, ever denied this, not even the most ardent disciple and, least of all, Pareto himself. Difference of opinion
on this point is inevitably confined to the extent to which he surpassed the great pioneer and to the relative mental statures of the
two men. There are several reasons why disciples will never agree
on this either with outsiders or among themselves. One of these
reasons must be noticed at once. Walras presented his immortal
theory in the garb of a political philosophy that is extra-scientific in
nature and, moreover, not to everyone's taste. I am afraid that there
is no better way of conveying what that philosophy was than to call
it the philosophy of petty-bourgeois radicalism. He felt called upon
to preach an *idéal social* that hails from the semi-socialist French
writers of the first half of the nineteenth century or, as we may say
with equal justice, from utilitarianism. He looked upon the nationalization of land as an essential item in his teaching, and he was a
monetary reformer whose plans have a strikingly modern ring. All
this was gall and wormwood to Pareto. It was just metaphysical
speculation and metaphysical speculation of a very unsympathetic
kind. Their common ground was confined to pure theory and specifically to Walras' equations of equilibrium. But in every other respect they were as different as two men can be, and even their
companionship in arms in the fight for mathematical economics
and Pareto's obligation to Walras in the matter of the Lausanne
professorship did not prevent their deap-seated mutual dislike from

asserting itself or even from spilling over in conversation with third persons. While their pure theories are cast in the same mould, their systems of thought taken as wholes and their visions of the social process are not. And all those economists who are not disposed to neglect a man's philosophy and practical recommendations completely, that is to say the majority of the profession, will, for this reason alone, consider the Paretian structure to be something completely different from that of Walras.

In any case—we are neglecting sociology for the moment—it was, with one exception, in pure theory alone that he made scientific history. Let us note this exception first. In the *Cours* and also in a separate memoir of 1896 Pareto published a highly original pioneer achievement in econometrics that first established his international reputation and, under the title of 'Pareto's Law,' created what may be fairly called a whole literature devoted to its critical discussion. Call N the number of income receivers who receive incomes higher than x, and A and m two constants; then Pareto's 'Law' asserts that

$$\log N = \log A + m \log x$$

Chapter 7 of the *Manuel* contains Pareto's most mature interpretation of this generalization. We must confine ourselves here to noticing the two classes of problems which it raises. There is, first, the question of fit. Numerous investigations have been made, some of which were held by their authors either to refute the Law completely or else to establish the superiority of other methods of describing the inequality of incomes. The reader will observe that the central issue turns on the approximate constancy of the m. However, by and large, the 'Law' has stood fire rather well as the fact that it is sometimes used by competent statisticians even now suffices to prove. But there is, second, the question of interpretation. Granted that up to quite recent times the distribution of incomes according to brackets has been remarkably stable, what are we to infer from this? This problem has never been attacked successfully. Most participants in the discussion, Pigou among them, have confined themselves to criticizing Pareto's own interpretation—which, to say the least, was in fact open to objection at first—and, like so many of our controversies, this one has petered out without yielding a definite result. Few if any economists seem to have realized the possibilities that such invariants hold out for the future of our science.[8] Viewed from this standpoint, Pareto's 'Law' is path-breaking in the literal sense even though in the end nothing whatever is left of its particular form.

I take this opportunity to dispose of another matter. In the *Manuel,* Pareto dealt with his 'Law' of Income Distribution in the chapter on Population. So far as the topics are concerned that are usually dealt with under this heading, this chapter does not contain much that would call for notice. But it contains a number of other things which, like the 'Law,' are not usually included in the theory of population, and it is these items which liven up this chapter and impart to it its freshness and originality. Pareto's theory of the *circulation of the élite* is an example (see below, section III). Most of them are sociological rather than economic in nature, and some of them bring out sharply, indeed almost naïvely, certain prejudices that sat so incongruously upon the great analyst of human prejudice.[9]

In the field of pure theory, properly so called, Pareto's thought developed slowly and in fact retained certain pre-Paretian features to the end. In addition to the early influences of Ferrara and of the English and French economists of the 'classic period,' he had Walras' equations of static equilibrium to start from—after having realized, not without considerable initial resistance, that they were

[8] In particular, nobody seems to have realized that the hunt for, and the interpretation of, invariants of this type might lay the foundations of an entirely novel type of theory.

[9] For instance, whatever we may think of his explanation of the phenomenon of feminism, we can hardly suppress a smile when we read the first sentence of this discussion (p. 400), which begins with the words, 'Le féminisme est une maladie. . .' a turn of phrase that does not indicate much objectivity or detachment. Both on Pareto's theory of population in the strict sense and on those sociological additions, I refer the reader to Professor J. J. Spengler's 'Pareto on Population,' *Quarterly Journal of Economics,* August and November 1944.

in fact the keys to everything else. He was further stimulated by all
the suggestions that no competent theorist could have helped receiving in the decade from 1885 to 1895.[10] Finally, he was acutely aware
of the technical shortcomings and other limitations of his immediate
predecessors. Thus his own theoretical work was cut out for him—
most of it, indeed, by Walras himself.[11] But his earlier work, such
as his 'Considerazioni sui principi fondamentali dell' economia politica pura' (Giornale degli Economisti, 1892-3), never went beyond
the range of the Walrasian signposts. This is also true, and em-
phatically so, of his Cours. Some economists who respected Pareto
but were not strictly Paretians have paid him the dubious compliment of calling the Cours his masterpiece. It is, indeed, a striking
performance enlivened throughout by a strong temperament that
imparts sparkle even to conventional passages. But Pareto was right
in refusing to sanction a reprint or a second edition. For, so far as
pure theory is concerned, there was nothing specifically Paretian
about it. It was only after 1897 that he rose to heights of his own.
The first major publications that testify to his progress are the
'Sunto di alcuni capitoli di un nuovo trattato di economia pura'
(Giornale degli Economisti, 1900) and the Résumé of his Paris
course.[12] The Manuale or rather, because of the appendix, the

[10] To some of these suggestions Pareto reacted in a negative, if not,
indeed, in a hostile manner. He never appreciated Marshall fully—mainly
because he objected on principle to partial analysis—and he seems never to
have seen all there was behind the primitive technique of the Austrians. But
he did appreciate Edgeworth and, many objections notwithstanding, Wicksteed. Much more than is commonly known he appreciated Irving Fisher,
not only the Mathematical Investigations but also, later on, the Nature of Capital and Income and the Rate of Interest. It was a revelation to me to hear
him bestow high praise on Capital and Income.

[11] Walras was perfectly aware of all the short cuts he had had to make
in order to finish what he himself realized was a provisory structure. He
never believed that such assumptions as those of constant coefficients of production, of timelessness of production, of absence of overhead costs, of equal
size of firms could or should stand forever. It cannot be averred that, in this
respect, Pareto was quite just to him. It was not only that Walras' was the
pioneer performance: Walras had also indicated what was to be done next.

[12] See above, note 3.

Manuel (1909), then marks the point of highest elevation that he reached.

The structure of the tower he erected on that spot is far from faultless. Many things that are essential in a comprehensive treatise received but scant attention. I do not mean merely that Pareto's work cannot stand comparison with Marshall's in those qualities that are ordinarily looked for in a 'manual.' Much more serious is it that important parts of the *theoretical* organon are inadequately thought out. Pareto's theory of money, for instance, is on the whole inferior to that of Walras. His theory of capital and interest derives all its merits from that of Walras. As regards interest he seems to have been content to rely for explanation on the fact that items of physical capital, hence their services, are not free goods. His theory of monopoly cannot, I believe, be salvaged by even the most generous interpretation.[13] In spite of all this, the adverse judgment arrived at by some critics is completely wrong. For it neglects not only many individual strong points but, much more important, the essence of the achievement. The most important of those strong points, the theories of value and of production, will be discussed presently. But first we must try to define that achievement itself of which these two theories were but applications.

The first idea that must occur, from a purely theoretical point of view, to anyone who has mastered Walras' system is to raise it to a still higher level of generality. When we follow Walras and, indeed, all the marginal utility theorists on their progress through the phenomena of exchange, production, and so on, we discover that they are trying to solve problems that in ultimate logic reduce to one only: *all* their problems—not only the problems of production—are problems in the transformation of economic quantities and formally alike, the differences consisting merely in the different restric-

---

[13] Some merit there was, however, in his inclusion of the theory of monopoly in the body of general theory. Also, his theory of international trade must not be reduced, as it mostly is, to a mere criticism of comparative costs. He sketched, although he did not elaborate, a theory of his own that was the first to apply to international trade the apparatus of general equilibrium. See v. Haberler, *Theory of International Trade*, 1936, p. 123.

tions to which economic action is subject in different fields. Suppose we decide to do what we do in all the sciences, that is, to separate out the common core of all economic problems and to build a theory of this common core once and for all. The point of view of 'mental economy' (E. Mach's *Denkökonomie*) will justify this endeavor to utilitarians. A theory of this kind will work with quite general indices, such as 'tastes' and 'obstacles,' and need not stop at the specifically economic meanings that we may assign to these words. We may transcend economics and rise to the conception of a system of undefined 'things' that are simply subject to certain restrictions and then try to develop a perfectly general mathematical *logic of systems*. Stretches of this road should be quite familiar to economists who have for generations used primitive devices, such as our venerable friend Crusoe, for the purpose of displaying certain features of economic logic. Pareto simply did the same on a much higher level and on a much broader front. But in these altitudes it is difficult to breathe and still more difficult to gain ground. Critics as competent as the late A. A. Young have been of the opinion that Pareto achieved nothing but 'arid generalizations.' But only the future can tell whether this is so. Meanwhile we should recognize the greatness of the attempt.

An example will show that such a 'rush for generality' may produce not only logical stones but also economic bread, though it suffers from the weakness that it still moves on a relatively low level of generality and, indeed, dates from the *Cours*. As everyone knows, Marx's work is an analysis of the capitalist process, no doubt geared to the purpose of showing that this process will issue in a socialist society but entirely free from any attempt at blocking out the economics of this society. And there are a number of Marxist and Neo-Marxist contributions to the latter problem that can be described only as complete failures. As everyone also knows by now, the service to socialist doctrine that Marxist theories have been unable to render has been rendered by E. Barone, whose famous paper on the subject ('Il Ministro della produzione nello stato colletivista,' *Giornale degli Economisti,* 1908) has been surpassed by modern writers only in secondary details. But the essential idea of Barone's argument is clearly indicated in the second volume of Pareto's *Cours* (p. 94) and in his *Manuel* (p. 362), namely the idea to lift, as it were, the logical core of the economic process above the ground of the institutional garb in which it is given to observation. The reader will observe how easily this idea suggests itself, as a special case, once we place ourselves on the standpoint of Pareto's general theory of tastes and obstacles, although it also suggested itself to Wieser.

In this special case, Pareto has nearly lost his claims to priority—at least among Anglo-American economists—although he had not only posited the problem but also pointed out the way to its solution. In other cases, he lost them completely because he confined himself to mere suggestions. Thus, assisted by hindsight, we may discern in the *Manuel* many pointers toward the later economic dynamics. However, none of them, such as his reference to a form of adaptation similar to a *courbe de poursuite* (dog-and-his-master problem, see e.g. p. 289) and to the presence of *vibration continuelle* (see e.g. p. 528), was put to any use other than the negative one of showing that the economic system's tendency toward a unique and stable 'solution' (i.e. a unique set of values that will satisfy its conditions) is a much more doubtful matter than the economists of that period, including Walras, supposed.[14] No positive use was made of these suggestions,[15] and no method was indicated for attacking these problems. I think therefore that we should not hesitate to describe Pareto's work as static theory, and that substantial justice is done if we add that he, more than others, was aware of its limitations and of the call of the problems beyond.[16]

[14] See e.g. his discussion of unstable equilibrium in the article in the *Encyclopédie des sciences mathématiques*.

[15] The jejune theory of crises (pp. 528-38) certainly does not qualify for being listed as an exception.

[16] Pareto himself (p. 147) divided the subject of pure economics into statics; a dynamics that studies successive equilibria and seems to me to denote comparative statics; and another dynamics that studies the *mouvement du phénomène économique* and seems to merge genuine dynamics with the problems of evolution in a manner that would have proved highly incon-

We now proceed to a brief discussion of Pareto's work in the fields of value and production keeping in mind that, from the standpoint adumbrated above, they really merge into a single theory.

Most modern theorists, although not all, will agree that the historical importance of the utility and marginal utility theory of Jevons, Menger, and Walras rests mainly upon the fact that it served as the ladder by which these economists climbed up to the conception of general economic equilibrium, although this conception was much more clearly perceived and much more fully developed by Walras than it was by either the Austrians or Jevons.[17] In other words, the utility and marginal utility theory was one of several possible avenues to the thing that really mattered and, besides offering an excellent method for demonstrating in an easily understandable way the relations that hold the economic system together and, in fact, make a unified system out of the mass of economic phenomena which departmentalize so easily, had no great importance in itself.

venient but for the fact that both remained, with Pareto, quite rudimentary. I know that the situation must look different to a disciple. But although the latter's attitude has its place, it cannot be adopted here.

[17] As Lord Keynes in his biographical essay on Alfred Marshall has pointed out, Marshall was also in full possession of that conception, and we have Keynes's word, as well as other indications, for believing that he arrived at this conception independently and earlier rather than later than Walras. This does not alter the fact, however, that he published nothing about it that antedates the relevant notes in the Appendix to the *Principles* (notes xiv and xxi of the fourth edition) which, moreover, cannot be described according to the ordinary rules of assigning priority as more than glimpses. We have, therefore, to conclude that Walras' priority is unchallengeable. But so is that of the Austrians and especially of Wieser. It is perfectly clear that it was only lack of mathematical skill and especially the inability to handle systems of simultaneous equations that prevented Menger from producing an exact system that would have been substantially similar to that of Walras. But I do not think that those historians are right who attribute the concept of general equilibrium already to Cournot. Chapter xi of the *Researches into the Mathematical Principles of the Theory of Wealth* contains nothing but recognition of the general interdependence of economic quantities, and neither there nor anywhere else does Cournot offer guidance toward the great attempt to make this conception explicit and fruitful. All the actual work in the *Researches* is either partial analysis or else, to some extent, aggregative analysis.

Or, to put it still differently, utility theory was an extremely useful heuristic hypothesis and nothing more.[18] But neither Walras nor the Austrians were of this opinion. On the contrary, for them the utility theory was nothing less than ultimate truth, the discovery of the key to all the secrets of pure economics. In consequence, they placed an emphasis upon it that in turn induced Pareto and the Paretians to place undue emphasis upon their renunciation of it. Authors in the English-speaking world, particularly Professors Allen and Hicks, followed suit and very generously congratulated Pareto on what to them also seemed a new departure of first-rate importance. In fact, there is a widespread opinion to the effect that this new departure constitutes Pareto's main contribution.

There are indications in the *Cours* that Pareto was not quite satisfied with the Walrasian theory of value from the first. But his amendments, either insignificant or not original, remained within the precincts of the principle itself. Of the insignificant amendments, we merely mention the introduction of the term *ophélimité* in the place of the term utility (*ophélimité élémentaire* for marginal utility or Walras' *rareté*) on the ground that the latter carried too many misleading associations. Of those that are not original with Pareto I mention the conception of utility and marginal utility as functions of all the commodities that the consuming unit possesses or consumes in an appropriately chosen period of time, instead of Walras' conception of total and marginal utility of every commodity as function of the quantity of that commodity alone. This obvious improvement is due to Edgeworth, but I confess to some doubt whether Edgeworth was fully aware of the theoretical difficulties this improvement would cause, for it turns the final degree of utility that was simply an ordinary differential coefficient with Jevons, Walras, and also with Marshall, into a partial differential coefficient and this

[18] I wish to make it quite clear, however, first, that I do not think that its heuristic value is as yet exhausted, and, second, that the statement in the text must be read with the proviso, 'so far as the purpose of establishing the determinateness and stability of static equilibrium is concerned.' There may be other uses for it and it is impossible to be sure that for such other purposes it might not be revived any moment.

greatly increases the mathematical difficulties we encounter when trying to prove the determinateness of the economic system even in its most simplified form.[19]

Before long, however, and certainly before 1900, the year in which he delivered his Paris lectures that made his change of standpoint publicly known, Pareto realized that, for his purposes at least, the concept of measurable utility (cardinal utility) might be safely abandoned [20] or that, in any case, it would have to be abandoned for reasons that were first stated exactly in the second part of Irving Fisher's *Mathematical Investigations into the Theory of Value and Price* (1892). To save the situation he appealed to the indifference and preference curves that had been first introduced by Edgeworth. But, whereas Edgeworth still started from a measurable total utility from which he deduced the definition of these lines, Pareto inverted the process. He took the indifference lines as the given thing to start from and showed that it was possible to arrive from them at the determination of economic equilibrium in pure competition and

[19] To be more exact: when we are trying to prove that there is one and only one set of values that will satisfy the equations of general equilibrium, so far as I can see everything is plain sailing so long as we adhere to the assumption that the marginal utility of every commodity depends only on the quantity of that commodity and so long as we do not admit any money but only a *numéraire*. The restrictions that are necessary even then in order to produce proof of determinateness seem to me quite bearable economically. It is the intrusion of those partial differential coefficients which creates the real difficulty.

[20] Gustav Cassel came to the same conclusion in 1899. He went even further than Pareto and claimed to be able to do without any utility concept at all. It is not possible to explain here why this claim was unjustified, and why his method of starting with market demand curves which he simply postulated is inadmissible. However, in order to appreciate that episode in the history of economic theory it is necessary to remember that at that time not only the utility theory itself but also all the theory of cost and distribution that was built upon it still met with great resistance. This resistance was, especially in Germany and Italy but also elsewhere, sometimes motivated by objections against operating with unmeasurable and unverifiable psychic magnitudes. And so the opposition to marginal utility theory from Pareto and others joined forces with (or at least added new vitality to) a common-run argument that had been repeated again and again by writers with whom Pareto would not have cared to find himself associated.

also to proceed to certain functions which might be identical with utility if it exists. In any case, it was possible to obtain (ordinal) *indices* of utility or what Pareto called index functions (*Manuale,* p. 540, note 1).

I wish to bring out two points quite clearly. The first is that Pareto, though he may have adapted an invention of Edgeworth's to his own use, imparted to the indifference varieties a meaning that they do not carry in Edgeworth's *Mathematical Psychics*. They are quite divested of any utility connotation, and what the concept of utility had done for the theory of economic equilibrium was now to be done by certain assumptions about the form of these indifference curves. The new idea was to replace utility postulates by postulates about observable behavior and thus to base economic theory on what seemed to Pareto to be more secure foundations. It might be urged of course that in spite of several attempts nobody has as yet succeeded in carrying out such observations and that it is difficult to indulge in the hope that we might construct them from objective data *in their whole extent* so as to derive a complete empirical indifference map. Let us call them, therefore, potentially empirical or, to misuse a Kantian term, 'referring to possible experience.' In any case, their introduction for a purpose entirely foreign to Edgeworth's might be called a truly original achievement were it not for the fact that this achievement had been, as Pareto recognized, foreshadowed in Fisher's work mentioned above.

The second point is that Pareto's own argument brings out the difficulty he experienced in disentangling himself entirely from the old utility theory. He always kept an eye on the cases in which it might be possible to speak of utility and even of cardinal utility, the existence of which—hence the question of integrability—continued to interest him very much. And his index functions bear after all a pretty close similarity to the old concept. In fact, as has been pointed out by Allen and Hicks, he never succeeded quite in disentangling himself entirely, and he continued to use concepts such as the Edgeworthian definitions of rivalry and complementarity that do not go well with his fundamental idea. This fundamental idea, let us add, was developed and defended as early as 1902 by P. Boninsegni.[21] By 1908, Enrico Barone, in the paper mentioned already, definitely went beyond Pareto by confining his fundamental assumptions in the matter of value theory to what he called the *fact* that, confronted with given prices of products and productive services, every individual distributes his receipts from the sale of his services between expenditures on consumption goods and saving in a certain unique manner 'of which we are not going to investigate the motives.' This, so he pointed out, does away with any concept of either utility or indifference functions. The rest of the story is too well known to detain us. I shall merely mention the papers of Johnson and Slutsky that for the time being remained practically unnoticed; the important reformulation of Bowley in his *Groundwork* that was more influential; and the work of Allen and Hicks, Georgescu-Roegen, Samuelson, and H. Wold. If we accept the present situation as 'provisionally final,' we must indeed salute either Fisher or Pareto as the patron saint of the modern theory of value.

But, still more definitely than patron saint of the modern theory of value is Pareto the patron saint of the 'New Welfare Economics.' The story of how, once more, he came to render a service to a cause with which he was—or would be—completely out of sympathy is not without its humor. From the very beginnings of economics, a loosely defined public welfare played a great role in the writings of economists. The familiar slogans of utilitarianism (Beccaria, Bentham) did something toward rationalizing the concept, and the utility theory of value seemed admirably qualified to implement it: in fact it was promptly harnessed to the task, e.g. in the field of taxation. The Fisher-Pareto theory of indifference varieties, destroying as it did the bases of arguments that worked with cardinal utility or even with interpersonal comparison of utility (satisfaction), should, so we might think at first blush, have done away with all this. But instead of drawing this conclusion—and in spite of his contempt for the political humanitarianism of our age—

[21] 'I fondamenti dell' economia pura,' *Giornale degli Economisti,* February 1902.

Pareto immediately went on to attack the problem of maxima of *collective* satisfaction afresh. The definitive formulation was left for Barone,[22] but the main idea is again Pareto's. He observed, first, that all changes imposed upon any given economic pattern may be said to increase welfare or collective satisfaction in a perfectly objective sense if those who gain in terms of *numéraire* could compensate those who lose in terms of *numéraire* and still have some gain left. This criterion will in fact salvage some though not all of the welfare judgments usually passed by economists.[23] Second, Pareto pointed out that welfare judgments that cannot be salvaged in this manner must be explicitly based on extra-economic, e.g. 'ethical,' considerations. And third, he showed (pp. 363-4) that the criterion may be used in order to establish that *l'état collectiviste* may improve upon the level of welfare that is practically attainable under perfect competition.[24] But, barring developments, these points are pretty much what the New Welfare Economics amounts to.

That part of Pareto's welfare economics which deals with the logic of production provides a convenient transition to his second

[22] See 'Il Ministro . . .' p. 276 (mentioned above, p. 124).

[23] The criterion, in strict logic, is independent of whether that compensation is actually made or not. In the latter case, we simply split the change imposed into two parts: into a change that improves collective satisfaction to which the criterion applies and a transfer from losers to gainers to which it does not apply. Even so, I do not wish to appear in the role of an advocate of the welfare judgments that the criterion protects from being invalidated by objections against the use of cardinal utility or of interpersonal comparison of states of satisfaction. There are other and much more important ones, especially the objection that these 'objective' welfare judgments neglect all but the immediate effects.

[24] The last sentence on p. 363 of the *Manuel* seems to me to anticipate substantially Professor Hotelling's argument in 'General Welfare in Relation to Problems of Taxation and of Railway and Public Utility Rates,' *Econometrica*, VI (1938). The practical application to railroads of the principle that welfare might be maximized by charging prices that will cover marginal cost even in the case of decreasing cost industries and by financing fixed costs (as Pareto said) in some other way is old. So far as I know, it is due to Launhardt, who inferred from this that investment in railroads should 'never' be left to private industry (*Mathematische Begründung der Volkswirtschaftslehre*, 1885, p. 294; and earlier writings).

great contribution to pure theory, his theory of production.[25] Approaching the problem from the side of the theory of choice and applying to the producer's case the general apparatus of indifference curves and derivative concepts (*lignes du plus grand profit, lignes de transformations complètes et incomplètes* etc.), he sketched out a comprehensive structure only parts of which are explicitly present in the literature of his time [26] and which may be said to constitute the foundation of the mathematical theory of production of our own age or, at all events, of its statics. In particular, its very generality leaves room for all the special cases that we may wish to treat without placing exclusive emphasis on any one of them: the 'obstacles' may be anything at first, and can then assume any of the forms that occur more commonly in practice—the factors that are required in fixed quantities irrespective of output, the factors that are required in technologically determined quantities per unit of output, the 'compensatory' factors, and so on, all take their places in a theoretically complete schema of possibilities. In appraising this achievement, we must keep in mind that Pareto was primarily concerned with generalizing and otherwise improving the work of his great predecessor. Again his work may be divided into a first part that culminated in the *Cours* and a second part that culminated in the *Manuel,* though some minor touches were added in the article in the *Encyclopédie des Sciences Mathématiques* (Volume 1, 1911).

Originally, Walras had expounded his theory of production on the assumption of fixed coefficients of production—fixed (average) inputs per units of output—not because he believed that this was the only or even a very important case but because he thought himself justified in adopting what he considered to be a simplification.[27] His reply to private criticisms that poured in on him was

[25] See in particular *Manuel,* chapter III, paragraphs 74-82, 100-105; chapter V, and paragraphs 77-107 of the Appendix.

[26] But if we leave out the word 'explicitly,' then a much greater part of Pareto's schema must be credited to some of his contemporaries, or even predecessors, and especially to Marshall.

[27] It is curious that the greatest of all theorists should have entertained that opinion. For, first, this simplification creates analytic difficulties that may

that 'the economists who will come after me are free to insert one by one all the complications they please. They and I, so I think, will then have done everything that it was our duty to do' (*édition définitive,* p. 479). So far as this goes Pareto cannot be said to have done more than take Walras' advice. In addition, when the *Cours* appeared, Walras had already introduced variable coefficients, on a suggestion of Barone's that reached him in 1894,[28] though without altering the argument of the fundamental section on production. In the same year (1894) appeared Wicksteed's *Essay on the Coordination of the Laws of Distribution.* Finally, variable coefficients of production were no novelty in any case after all that Jevons, Menger, and Marshall had said on the subject. Pareto's *Cours* added only an elegant formulation and a number of reasons—not all of them convincing—why the case of compensatory coefficients should not be treated as the only or the fundamental one either.

It is of course a mere matter of terminological taste whether or not we are to confine the phrase 'marginal productivity theory' to this case.[29] Pareto did so confine it and, in the years following upon

set us wondering whether in the end it is a simplification at all; and, second, it creates a gulf between theory and reality that is great enough to make it doubtful whether results obtained by means of it are of any use.

[28] This was done in a *Note* published in 1896 and reprinted in the third edition of the *Éléments.* In the fourth edition (1900) a full-fledged marginal productivity theory was presented in the 36th *leçon* in a form that was open to criticism on various counts and was later on revised for the final edition that was published posthumously in 1926. See on this and for a useful rendering of Pareto's later theory: H. Schultz, 'Marginal Productivity and the General Pricing Process,' *Journal of Political Economy,* October 1929.

[29] The main reason for doing so is a textbook tradition which takes into account only production functions that represent quantities of product as dependent on 'substitutional factors' alone and arrive at the theorem that, in perfect equilibrium of pure competition, the unit of each of the innumerable requisites of production earns a compensation that equals physical marginal productivity times the price of the product. But we do not leave the precincts of the marginal productivity argument if we admit 'limitational factors' or, more generally, restrictions upon the production function that will produce results at variance with that theorem. See e.g. A. Smithies, 'The Boundaries of the Production Function and the Utility Function,' *Explorations in Economics, Notes and Essays contributed in Honor of F. W. Taussig,* 1936.

the publication of the *Cours,* grew increasingly hostile to it, declaring it definitely 'erroneous.' He was evidently under the impression that he had refuted or, at any rate, outgrown it in the same sense in which he felt that he had refuted or outgrown the marginal utility theory. His brilliant theory of cost—which, among other things, withdraws from their dangerously exposed positions the textbook theorems that, in perfect equilibrium of pure competition, price should equal marginal cost and total receipts should at the same time equal total cost—permit us to test this claim.[30] So far as productive combinations depend on economic considerations—and, after all, it is the economic considerations which it is the economists' task to clear up—the difference, as compared with straight marginal productivity theory, is not great. But Pareto does teach us how to handle the deviations from it that technological and social restrictions impose. And, here as elsewhere, he does something else: he always points beyond himself.

III. THE SOCIOLOGIST

There is nothing surprising in the habit of economists to invade the sociological field. A large part of their work—practically the whole of what they have to say on institutions and on the forces that shape economic behavior—inevitably overlaps the sociologist's preserves. In consequence, a no-man's land or everyman's land has developed that might conveniently be called economic sociology. More or less important elements that hail from that land are to be found in practically every economic treatise or textbook. But beyond this many economists, and especially those who define economics proper rather strictly, have done sociological work. A. Smith's *Moral Sentiments* and Wieser's *Gesetz der Macht* are both outstanding

[30] We use this opportunity in order to advert to Pareto's conception of rent which arises in the cases where those two conditions (total cost = total receipts; price = marginal cost) are incompatible, and especially in the cases where transformation of savings into certain kinds of capital goods meets with difficulties. This theory of rent has experienced a renaissance in our days. It may help us toward an improved theory of friction. But it can hardly do more.

instances of a large genus. But few if any men in the list of great
economists have devoted so large a part of their energy as has Pareto
to what at first sight seems to be an extra-curricular activity, and
few if any owe so much of their international reputation to what
they have done in that field. But his achievement is not easy to characterize and to appraise. The enthusiastic applause of some and the
hostility of others are both understandable but neither can be taken
quite seriously because the non-scientific sources of both are pain-
fully obvious in most cases. Although several minor works and a
large number of newspaper articles would have to be considered in
order to give a satisfactory picture, we need not go beyond the
Systèmes socialistes, the *Manuel* (especially Chapters II and VII), and
the *Trattato di Sociologia Generale.*

Let us begin with two aspects of Pareto's sociology that are
perfectly obvious and the reverse of difficult to characterize. First,
although Pareto the economist touched upon a large number of extremely concrete and practical problems throughout his long life,
his purely scientific contribution is in the realm of the most abstract
economic logic. It is, therefore, quite understandable that he should
have experienced a wish and, in fact, a need to erect alongside his
pure theory another building that would shelter facts and reasonings
of a different kind, facts and reasonings that would do something
toward answering the question how the elements taken care of by
his economic theory might be expected to work out in practical life.
Second, we have seen that in his earlier days, at least as long as he
lived in Italy, he had taken a passionate interest in the debates on
questions of economic and general policy. The born thinker that he
was must have been struck by the impotence of the rational argument, and the question must have intruded upon him of what it
really is that determines political action and the fate of states and
civilizations. Again, it is quite understandable that, so soon as he had
settled down to a life of thought, this question should have emerged
from the sphere of easy and superficial answers that all of us are
prone to give when immersed in our daily work, and that he should
have attempted to raise it to the plane of scientific analysis. This

amounts to saying that primarily and fundamentally his sociology was a sociology of the political process. Of course, everything that man does or thinks or feels and all his cultural creations and his attitudes toward cultural creations are bound to come in somehow or other when we think about the political process which then becomes but a special case. But it was this special case which fascinated Pareto and for the sake of which he erected and adorned a much larger structure.

Next, still moving on ground that is relatively easy to survey, we shall consider his method. Pareto himself emphasized again and again that he simply applied the same 'logico-experimental' methods that had served him for the purposes of economic theory to the task of analyzing the 'experimentally' verifiable reality of other aspects of social life, allowing himself to be guided here as elsewhere by the example of the physical sciences. This was, of course, a complete delusion. It is easy to observe, for instance, that he made large and in part illegitimate use of psychological interpretations for which there is no analogy in the physical sciences and that his material, such as it was, was the product of observation and not of experiment—a difference which is fundamental from the standpoint of method. I am afraid that what he really meant to emphasize when trying to formulate his rules of procedure was simply the detachment of the philosopher who does not identify himself with any party, interest, or creed. The possibility of such detachment raises, of course, a very well-known fundamental difficulty and one that Pareto was the less qualified to overcome because he failed to see it. Actually he used two different analytic schemata: one that may be called a morphology of society and does invite the use of facts that are, potentially at least, amenable to observation as are the facts of anatomy or biology in a similar sense; and another that pertains to social psychology. Both schemata are indeed *illustrated* or even, to some extent, *verified* by historical and contemporaneous instances, but neither is *derived* from them by anything like a 'logico-experimental' method: both are reflexes of a highly personal vision of the social process that owes much to Pareto's background, practical experience—and resentments. The affinity of the morphological schema with Darwinian selection and of the socio-psychological schema with parts of the teaching of Tarde, Dürkheim, Lévy-Bruhl, and Th. Ribto is obvious. Still more so is the relation of both with the current of thought glanced at in the first section of this essay that issued in derogatory criticism of the doings of parliamentary democracy—the current that was anti-intellectualist, anti-utilitarian, anti-equalitarian and, *in the special sense defined by these terms,*[31] anti-liberal. But the force of the man created from these materials something that was nevertheless specifically his own.[32]

The morphological schema centers in the proposition that all societies consist of heterogeneous masses of members—individuals or families—and are structured according to the aptitudes of these members for the relevant social function: in a society of thieves, the *ex hypothesi* widely varying ability to steal would determine social rank, and hence influence upon the government of the society. Pareto seems to assume that these abilities, while capable of improvement and of decay, are substantially innate, though he makes little effort to establish this. Moreover, though distributed continuously in the population, they lead to the formation of classes, the 'higher' ones of which have and use the means of buttressing their position and of separating themselves from the lower strata. In consequence, there is in the lowest strata a tendency to accumulate superior ability that is prevented from rising, and in the topmost stratum, in the aristocracy or *élite,* a tendency to decumulate energy through disuse—with resulting tension and ultimate replacement of the ruling minority by

---

[31] This proviso is very necessary. There are other meanings of the word 'liberal,' one of which would describe Pareto's position much better than could any other term. Similarly, there is a sense in which he might be justly called a great humanitarian. But it is not the one which he applied to *individus dégénérés, d'intelligence et de volonté faibles* (*Manuel,* p. 130).

[32] It is highly instructive to observe how different the results are that different men arrive at not only from the same facts but also from the same intuitions. Graham Wallas was an orthodox English radical and a Fabian. But in *Human Nature in Politics* he drew a picture that was not in the least more flattering to the slogans of political democracy than was Pareto's.

another ruling minority that is drawn from the superior elements in the *couches inférieures*. This *circulation des élites* does not, however, affect the principle that it is always *some* minority which rules, and does not do anything to bring any given society nearer to the ideal of equality, though it does produce equalitarian philosophies or slogans in the course of the struggles that ensue. With a turn of phrase that recalls the first sentence of the *Communist Manifesto,* Pareto proclaimed that history is essentially a history *de la succession des aristocracies (Manuel,* p. 425). But his presentation of this part of his argument is so very sketchy and he leaves his readers with so much to interpolate that I am not at all sure that I have rendered justice to his thought. Nevertheless, I had to make the attempt. For some such argument is necessary in order to put his social psychology into its proper light.

The socio-psychological schema centers in the concept of the non-logical (not necessarily illogical) action. This concept recognizes the well-known fact—well known, in particular, to economists —that the great mass of our everyday actions is not the result of rational reasoning on rationally performed observations, but simply of habit, impulse, sense of duty, imitation, and so on, although many of them admit of satisfactory rationalization *ex post* either by the observer or the actor. So far there is nothing in Pareto's psycho-sociology that could be unfamiliar to anyone. What is unfamiliar, however, is his tremendous emphasis upon the additional facts that a great number of actions—and let us add at once, beliefs—are being rationalized, both by actors and by observers, in ways that will not stand up under scientific analysis and, more important, that some actions and beliefs are altogether incapable of being rationalized in any way that will. The importance of this second step for a sociology of the political process becomes obvious if we take a third one: Pareto maintained that the large majority of all the actions and beliefs that make up that process are of the type mentioned last. Take, as an instance on which we all agree, the idea of the Social Compact or, as an instance on which most of us agree, Rousseau's theory of the *volonté générale.* Only, according to Pareto, practically all the actions, principles, beliefs, and so on prevailing in the collective mind of electorates belong in the same category. And a large part of the *Trattato* consists in illustrating this, often amusingly, sometimes instructively.

It will serve our purpose to put this point strongly, more strongly than Pareto himself ever put it. The masses of thought and the conceptual structures that form the conscious surface of the social and in particular of the political process have no empirical validity whatever. They work with entities such as liberty, democracy, equality, that are as imaginary as were the gods and goddesses who fought for and against Greeks and Trojans in the *Iliad,* and are connected by reasonings that habitually violate the rules of logic. In other words, from a logical standpoint, they are nonsense unalloyed. This makes a political philosophy that is best described by its diametrical opposition to that of Jeremy Bentham. It should be observed, however, that this diagnosis of the political myths (Sorel) did not induce Pareto to overlook the function that this logical nonsense may fill in national life. After having gone through with an analysis that is severely positivist in nature, he refused to draw the conclusion that would seem the obvious one to the positivist. While political creeds and social religions—with Pareto there is very little difference between these two—contribute to dissolution in dissolving civilizations, they also contribute to effective organization and action in vital civilizations. This is a very curious attitude for a thorough-going positivist to take and will perhaps be cited at some future time as an outstanding example of the mentality of an epoch that destroyed one type of metaphysical beliefs while ushering in another. It reminds me of the advice which I have heard some psychoanalysts give to some of their patients, namely the advice to cultivate with a view to possible remedial effects a sort of synthetic belief in God. There is of course no contradiction between maintaining that social and political creeds have no empirical significance and admitting that some of them may make for social cohesion and efficiency. But the social philosopher who should thereupon undertake to advise the adoption of the latter would run into the same difficulty as our psychoanalyst: so long as his *analysis* is being accepted his advice must be ineffective, for no synthetic God can be trusted to help; so soon as his *advice* is accepted his analysis will have to be rejected.

That tissue of creations of our imagination Pareto called *dérivations*. The argument adumbrated in the preceding paragraph abundantly shows that they are not without importance as factors that help to shape the historical process. It was Pareto's opinion, however, that this importance is relatively small and that substantially these *dérivations* do no more than verbalize something more fundamental that comes much nearer to determining actual political behavior and the sum total of non-logical actions. Now if we defined this more fundamental something in terms of group interests, and if we then went on to define these group interests in terms of the social location of groups within a society's productive organization, we should be, to say the least, very near Karl Marx's view of the matter, and there is in this point actually a strong affinity which I think it important to emphasize. In fact, if we adopted this line of reasoning, there would be only two major points of difference left between Marxian and Paretian political sociology. On the one hand, Pareto introduced explicitly an element that is only implicitly present in the Marxist analysis: the importance for the explanation of an actual stretch of history, of the greater or smaller degree of social flexibility that a given society displays, or, in other words, the importance of the fact that there exists an optimum or vertical mobility and of resistance to it that will better than others guarantee what might be termed stability of political change. On the other hand, we need only recall our sketch of Pareto's social morphology in order to realize that with Pareto the historical process is not so much the result of the conflict of comprehensive social classes as it is the result of the conflict of their ruling minorities. It is submitted that, while both differences are to the credit of Paretian sociology, they do not amount to more than corrective improvements upon the Marxist schema. I might add the fact that property relations *per se* are much less in evidence with Pareto than they are with Marx, and that this also constitutes a claim to superiority of the Paretian analysis. But it will be readily seen, that this point is really implied in the other two.

Actually, however, Pareto did not follow up this line of analysis. With him the link between the tissue of delusions which he called *dérivations* and the objective determinants of actual behavior was supplied by what he called the *résidus*. I am conscious of the danger of being unfair if, for the sake of brevity, I define these *résidus* as impulses generally found to be present with human beings that revive, and not in a very inviting manner, the old psychology of 'instincts.' We need not discuss the list that Pareto drew up—and which contains such items as an instinct of combinations, the sexual impulse, and so on—especially as Pareto himself does not seem to have been very satisfied with it. It is sufficient to point out the obvious methodological objection to any such procedure; even if Pareto's *résidus* and the 'laws' of their association and persistence were much more satisfactorily analyzed than they are, they would still be labels rather than solutions of problems, and call for professional investigation of a kind for which Pareto lacked the equipment. It is therefore quite understandable that Pareto's work has exerted so little influence upon professional sociology and social psychology, and that professional sociologists and social-psychologists have but rarely displayed a sense of the greatness of the structure as a whole.[33]

But those and other shortcomings are not decisive. Pareto's work is more than a research program. Also, it is more than mere analysis. The fundamental principle that what individuals, groups, and nations actually do must find its explanation in something much deeper than the creeds and slogans that are used in order to verbalize action, conveys a lesson of which modern men—and none more than we economists—stand much in need. We are in the habit when discussing questions of policy of accepting at face value the slogans of our own and, indeed, of a by-gone time. We reason exactly as if the Benthamite creed of the eighteenth century had ever

[33] Professor Talcott Parsons' analysis of Paretian sociology stands almost alone in the Anglo-American sociological literature.

been valid. We refuse to realize that policies are politics and to admit
to ourselves what politics are. We cultivate the subnormal and do
our best to suppress whatever there is of strength and sparkle. In
conditions such as these, Pareto's message, however one-sided, is a
healthy antidote. It is not, like his economics, a technical achievement of the first order. It is something quite different. It is an
attempt to preach a sermon.

EUGEN VON BÖHM-BAWERK *
1851-1914

ND now this great master has left us. No one who has been close to him both personally and scientifically would be able to describe the feeling that lies heavy on all of us. No words can express what he has been to us, and few of us if any will have yet resigned ourselves to the realization that from now on there is to be an impenetrable wall separating us from him, from his advice, his encouragement, his critical guidance—and that the road ahead will have to be traversed without him.

I fear I shall find myself less adequate to the task of tracing the outlines of his scientific lifework than I should wish to be. Perhaps the time for this has not yet arrived. This gigantic *massif* of ideas is still too near to us, the dust clouds of controversy are still too dense. For he was not only a creative mind but also a fighter— and to his last moments a live, effective force in our science. His

* This article appeared originally under the title 'Das wissenschaftliche Lebenswerk Eugen von Böhm-Bawerks' in the *Zeitschrift für Volkswirtschaft, Sozialpolitik und Verwaltung,* vol. xxiii (1914), pp. 454-528. It was abridged and translated by Dr. Herbert K. Zassenhaus, who studied under Professor Schumpeter at Bonn and was later his research assistant at Harvard. He is now Associate Professor of Economics at Colgate University.

work belongs not to one generation, not to one nation, but to mankind. Only long after all of us have left the field will economists become aware of the true proportions of his genius and its full influence.

In one respect, perhaps, one who has been sincerely and personally devoted to him is least fitted for this task. And I should indeed deeply regret it if I should ever be capable of writing of his lifework in a spirit of cool objectivity, or if the reader of what follows could find in it anything but a tribute of loyal devotion and a mourning remembrance. As a personality of infinite richness, as a man to whom life offered much because he had so much to offer, and likewise as a thinker, Böhm-Bawerk is in no need of either the one or the other—he was great enough to stand unaided, and to withstand all criticism. But for us, any other attitude would be impossible.

Nevertheless, the attempt at a hurried sketch from so close a range also has its merits. Its justification lies in this, that though there is much of which the definitive significance cannot as yet be determined, there is also much else that is still fresh in our memory which will escape from the historian of our science into the twilight of the past. We have known the man, the concrete conditions of his work, the world for which he wrote, the manner in which his problems presented themselves to him, the material which he moulded. Of all this, those who were close to him know the most. Summits are lonely; fast spreads the void that separates the present of any science from even its recent past; and soon the wider circles of scientific colleagues will fail to make out distinctly much of the detail which nevertheless is indispensable for a more penetrating understanding.

I am to speak only of the scientist. But the silhouette of the man is everywhere the same—in all the fields comprehended by the wide orbit of his life, the intensive beat of his pulse left its mark. In all these fields we are met by the same brilliant personality, the same large and strong features—the statue appears cast of one metal at one pouring, no matter from what point we view it. As is well known, he was not only one of the most brilliant figures in the scientific life of his time, but also an example of that rarest of statesmen, a great minister of finance. His name is inseparably joined to fruitful legislation, to the best tradition of Austrian fiscal administration, and to the greatest successes and the most felicitous period of Austrian financial policy. And his political achievement bears the same imprint as his scientific work. As a scientist, he chose the most difficult task under the most difficult circumstances, without regard for applause or success. As a public servant, he stood up to the most difficult and thankless task of politics, the task of defending sound financial principles—difficult and thankless everywhere, even where well-informed public opinion protects the statesman, even where he has the benefit of support from a strong party organization, even where the public ideal is national and where therefore the watchword 'the state demands it' is always a victorious ally—but a task almost superhuman in Austria. It is the same high ability that saw him through to victory in politics as in scientific research; the same originality and constructive vigor; the same clear view of reality and of the possible; the same steady current of energy that measures up to any task and masters the obstacles of the day without reluctance, doubt, and loss of force; the same calm, and the same sharp scalpel—for the great controversialist was also a redoubtable debater to whom many an adversary paid the highest compliment that man can pay to man, that of shying from giving him battle. And in politics and scientific work the same character proved its mettle: the same self-control and intensiveness, the same high standard of duty which impressed itself on subordinates as well as on disciples, the same ability to see through men and things without the cold detachment of the pessimist, to fight without bitterness, to deny himself without weakness—to hold to a plan of life at once simple and grand. Thus his life was a completed whole, the expression of a personality at one with itself, never losing itself, everywhere proving its superiority by its own weight and without affectation—a work of art, its severe lines gilded by an infinite, tender, reserved, and highly personal charm.

I

Böhm-Bawerk's scientific lifework forms a uniform whole. As in a good play each line furthers the plot, so with Böhm-Bawerk every sentence is a cell in a living organism, written with a clearly outlined goal in mind. There is no waste of effort, no hesitation, no deviation, but a calm renunciation of secondary and merely momentary successes. Of pieces written on the spur of the moment, which play so large a part in the life of the ordinary writer—of work that is the product of an external stimulus, there is virtually nothing—only here and there a brief article for the daily press. And even these newspaper articles are characteristic. They always serve a specific, clear purpose; they are never mere literary or scientific play. The full superiority of the man, motivated by a great task and full of living creative power, is here revealed to us; the superiority of the clear, self-possessed mind which from a feeling of intellectual duty renounced many a passing distraction. And this integrated plan was carried out in full. Completed and perfect, his lifework lies before us. There cannot be any doubt about the nature of his message.

He knew as few did what he wanted to do, and this is why it is so easy to formulate. He was a theorist, born to see—and to explain —large relationships; to seize instinctively, but with a firm hand, on the threads of logical necessities; to experience the most intimate joy of analytical work. At the same time he was a creator, an architect of thought, to whom even the most varied series of small tasks, such as the course of scientific life offers to any man, could never give satisfaction. True, he was the greatest critic our science has ever had. But his critical work, prominent as it was in its brilliance, its scope, and its meticulousness, served only to clear the obstacles from his way, to support his real work; it was never a purpose in itself, and never more than a subordinate task.

As soon as this intellect became preoccupied with the socio-economic process—this happened when he was about twenty-four years old—he chose with quick resolution his point of departure: Carl Menger. He always felt himself to be the ally of Menger, and he never wanted to found a different scientific school. His path first led through the structure which Menger erected and then continued, through the terrain where the greatest unsolved problems of economics lay, to climb to new heights—where he finally combined his own new ideas with Menger's teachings into a coherent structure, into a comprehensive theory of the economic process. To the elaboration of this structure he gave his constant attention; to it he devoted all his brilliant gifts and his magnificent energy. Wrestling with this problem, he became one of the five or six great economists of all time. He gave us an all-embracing theory of the economic process—one of the great analyses of economic life on the scale of the Classics and of Marx—conceived on a Mengerian foundation, and developed from the point of view of the one problem whose solution seemed to him to be still missing. This was the problem of interest, of the net return to capital, the most difficult and the most important in economics. Its difficulty, though it is not easy to make clear to a wider public the intricacies in the explanation of so common a phenomenon, is attested to by the fact that the work of centuries did not produce a satisfactory solution. Its importance stems from the fact that nearly all of our insight into, and our whole attitude towards, the nature and meaning of capitalism depend on our view of the meaning and function of interest and profit. Before Böhm-Bawerk this was clearly understood only by Marx. For Marx's system is in its scientific core nothing but a theory of interest and profit—everything else follows more or less conclusively from it.

The scientific environment in which it was Böhm-Bawerk's lot to find himself is, next to his personal disposition, the second element in understanding his subjective achievement and its objective form. This environment was not favorable to the scientist of large views, to a man of the intellectual stamp of Ricardo, above all to a man whose natural disposition was that of the exact theorist. Menger's sturdy figure stood out alone from a pack of adversaries. An understanding of the aims of analytical research was wholly lacking. To understand this, one has to remember that economics is a very young discipline which has hardly outgrown its baby shoes; that it had experienced only *one* real flowering, and that not in Germany; that the analytic bent of mind with which nature endowed Böhm-Bawerk had never taken firm hold in Germany, had never ceased to appear foreign and thus unpopular, had indeed up to then never been really understood. One must remember that the interest of German economists had been fastened on social reform, on altogether practical questions, and on problems of administrative techniques, and that the purely scientific interest, so far as it existed at all, had concerned itself exclusively with economic history. For a theorist there was absolutely no place, and most economic specialists, lacking theoretical training, could not only not evaluate achievements of an analytic nature, viewing them with prejudice and disfavor, but were not even in a position to form an independent opinion about the logical consistency of a theorem, much less to grasp its significance or to judge the subjective intellectual performance of its author.

Only when keeping all this in mind, when familiar with all the pat phrases which met every attempt at abstract thought, can one understand the situation of theoretical minds and much of their behavior—something which would otherwise often have seemed strange to men of the exact sciences. This is what explains the mountains of controversy, the obstacles to every step on the road of any analysis, the necessity to begin at every new turn of the argument with the most elementary aspects of the matter in hand—for otherwise hardly a dozen readers would be able to follow—and this also explains the sacrifice of every refinement of detail. At that time— and indeed to some extent even now—every theorist was on his own, always in danger of misunderstanding; he himself had to fashion every brick for his structure, he could assume nothing in his readers but a disposition to often quite adventurous misconstruction. A happier future will soon have forgotten all this. And probably the exact scientist is already quite unable to imagine himself in the position of, say, a mathematician who, before attacking a problem in the calculus of variations, would be under the necessity of first wresting from his readers an agreement on the elements of arithmetic. To put this down, to impress it on people's minds for all the future, this is the task of the contemporary who is close enough to this period to understand it. It is an essential element in historical justice to all the great fighters and regenerators of economics, and a necessary condition for understanding them. He who judges the pioneers in the field too often forgets that they were the first, and that the judge stands on their shoulders.

Böhm-Bawerk's success was not quick in coming. For a long time he was less successful than colleagues whose achievements, when compared to his, could by no device of perspective be made more than barely visible. Indeed, before he submitted the solution of his chief problem, he had first to show to the scientific world what the nature of this problem was—to many, indeed, that there *was* a problem; he had to defend the foundations of his system in a protracted controversy; he found himself confronting opponents who considered methodologically impossible such things as the investigation in the abstract of an isolated group of facts. Nor was there a circle of like-minded students, nor for a long time the possibility of attracting around himself a group of scientists or of training his own disciples. All the more imposing is the result. He achieved it solely through the force of his written argument, without pursuing literary success, without appeal to public opinion, without a journalistic campaign, without academic politics—that is, without any of those means which, granting that they may occasionally be necessary and justifiable, fall short of the highest ideals of scholarly enterprise—and without causing bitterness or engaging in personal squabbles.

Quiet, fruitful teaching activity as the leader of an academic school became possible for him, however, only during the decade 1904-14, after he had served three times as Austrian Minister of Finance. For the scientific milieu of Innsbruck from 1880 to 1889 was too narrow to permit the training of disciples who would be inclined to make the special field of theoretical economics the object of their lifework. This was more especially the case in a Faculty of Law, among students oriented essentially toward the study of jurisprudence. And the period as *Honorarprofessor* in the University of Vienna was for him a time of practical activity which, though never occupying the full breadth of his mind, nevertheless largely neutralized his energy. Only after 1904 began that activity which will remain unforgettable to all of us—and that series of seminar discussions in the summer semesters.

II

I have written of Böhm-Bawerk's scientific goal and characterized it as an analysis of the general forms of the socio-economic process. Now, before entering on a discussion of his separate achievements, let us review briefly the way he carried out his task. In this fashion the unity of the plan and the imposing consistency of its realization will be thrown into sharp relief.

The over-all view of the socio-economic process which rose before his eye rests on principles that had the simplicity of the great fundamentals of physics. Like the latter, they could be developed in a few pages, if necessary in one. But nobody could do much with such an exposition, for—again, like the basic principles of physics— they acquire fruitfulness, and even their true meaning, only in the thicket of details of the empirical world. In the absence of a *communis opinio* in the economics of his time, Böhm-Bawerk found himself faced with the necessity of submitting to the public every assumption and method he used, every link in the chain of his argument, of fighting every step of the way for a clearing on which to build the structure of his system. Moreover: this system contained many difficult and controversial ideas, especially those relating to his main subject, the problem of interest and profit. Apart from the need for reinforcement of the fundamentals which he had inherited from Menger, there were more than a score of attempts at a theory of interest to be cleared away, an operation necessary not merely to gain an audience for himself, but also because proof of the inadequacy of these attempts, a substantial achievement in its own right, was a prerequisite for his own positive theory.

Even the simplest elementary concepts presented difficulties. For the creative scientist, definitions are a subordinate matter. New insights at first simply occur; they appear suddenly, no one knows whence they came or how they got there. Definitions become necessary only when applying them, and then of course when describing them. Involving himself in this latter task, Böhm-Bawerk ran into the ancient controversy over the concept of an economic good. His first publication, *Rechte und Verhältnisse vom Standpunkte der volkswirtschaftlichen Güterlehre* (Innsbruck, 1881), attacks this problem. Having solved it with characteristic care and clarity, he was confronted by the two main tasks which had to precede the actual construction of his system. The fundamental explanatory principle of any system of economics is always a theory of value. Economic theory concerns facts that are expressed in terms of value, and value is not only the prime mover of the economic cosmos, but also the form in which its phenomena are made comparable and measurable. The theorist's view of the economic world depends on his view of the phenomenon of value—and here a firm foundation was essential. The second preparatory task concerned the theory of interest and profit: the underbrush needed clearing away, and it had to be demonstrated that here was a large, unsolved problem.

As to the first of these two tasks: the problem was to develop a defense and elaboration of the Mengerian doctrines. And in 1886 there appeared in two papers (*Conrads Jahrbücher*, New Series, vol. XIII) that masterful exposition of the theory of value ('Grundzüge der Theorie des wirtschaftlichen Güterwertes'), which will perish only with our science. With this he paved the way to his positive theory, and won his place among the new founders of theoretical economics. Ever since, his name has been inseparably joined to the theory of marginal utility, so much so that followers as well as opponents began to speak of the 'Böhm-Bawerkian theory of value.' In these articles he had in fact made this theory his own, just as

Wieser had; for no mere disciple could have written them. Their original contributions are many; I mention only two. He gave to price theory its specifically Austrian form—in partial contrast to the form Menger's teaching assumed in other parts of the world. And he presented his own solution to the problem of imputation, differing from both Menger's and Wieser's, of which we shall have to speak again later on.

Böhm-Bawerk remained a watchful and powerful protector of the subjective theory of value, victoriously fighting many of its battles. This fact too is part of his lifework, which would otherwise have remained insecure in its foundations and incomplete in its details. And it is but the logical outcome of his personality that he would not permit any position to remain without reinforcement, that he felt compelled to allay by means of ever-renewed research, every possible theoretical doubt. No creative mind relishes the repeated discussion of matters that it has already settled to its own satisfaction. But we should be the poorer for not possessing the achievements of this controversy, which has no equal in economic literature and which is a veritable armory of analytical tools.

When the *Grundzüge* appeared, the foundation of the author's reputation had already been laid by the second preparatory work, which had been published as the first volume of his magnum opus, the *Geschichte und Kritik der Kapitalzinstheorien* (*Kapital und Kapitalzins,* vol. i, 1st ed., Innsbruck, 1884)—the greatest critical work in economics. It met recognition at once, but the overt expressions of applause and admiration from his professional colleagues, more and more frequent as time went on, are insignificant beside the unspoken homage to which the profound influence of this book still bears testimony. A monument of creative analysis and a milestone on the road of our science, this work presents a series of critiques of theories of interest, each a piece of theoretical cabinet work, each a work of art unequalled in its perfection. The book does not give descriptions of the social and historical milieu in which each theory originated. Nor are there any philosophical embroideries or synthetic substitutes for explanation. Even the history of thought in the field of its central topic takes second place. The author limits himself to one of many possible tasks: he concentrates on one theory of interest after another, considering in each case only its substantive content. This content he reformulates with masterful perfection, appraises its essentials with an unflinching eye, using only a few simple but decisive arguments. With a minimum of effort, following the straightest possible line, and with the most graceful elegance, he dispatches one theory after another; and—after having carefully exposed the cause of the disaster—he continues on his way without losing another word, or indeed without saying one word too many. There is no book from which one could learn better how to seize firmly on the essentials and how to ignore the irrelevant.

And then, everything having been so methodically and conscientiously prepared, there appeared, as the second volume of *Kapital und Kapitalzins, Die Positive Theorie des Kapitals* (preface dated November 1888; published 1889, English translation by Wm. Smart as early as 1891). As we have already remarked, this was, despite the suggestion of a narrower content in the title, a comprehensive analysis of the economic process, *the* work of his life, the most personal product of his efforts. Whatever views future generations may hold of the separate links in the chain of his thought, they can never fail to admire the magnificent design, the grandiose *élan* of the whole work. It is in any case quite certain that this was an effort to scale the greatest heights that economics permits, and that the achievement actually reached a level where only a few lofty peaks are to be found. A comparison with Marx has always forced itself upon me. This may seem strange, but if so only because Marx's name has always been surrounded by the heat of political passion, and because his system is animated by a very different temperament. His name cannot be separated from social movements and their phraseology, which reveal him and make him meaningful to a very wide public, but which also obscure his real scientific achievement. All that is absent from Böhm-Bawerk. He wanted to be nothing but a scientist. Not a leaf in his garden is stirred by political storms. None of his words mar the flow of his scientific thought. And again, he shuns the sociological background, which, considering the state of our discipline, would have reconciled to the underlying laborious intellectual work many who had little appreciation of it. His work offers no popular rostrum from which he could have spoken to the masses, no ornaments but the classic form of its lines and its inner faultlessness—the fruit of renouncing everything that led away from the core of the problem on which he had earnestly and steadily fixed his eye. Yet, however different were Marx and Böhm-Bawerk, their lives, their convictions, and therefore in many ways their work, the parallel between them as theorists is unmistakable. To begin with, they both—as scientists—had the same objective. Secondly, an analogous set of circumstances of time and of the state of their science, as well as an analogous conviction of the overwhelming importance of the problems of interest and profit, forced both of them to take specifically from this problem the orientation for their analyses of the socio-economic process. Each borrowed the basic idea for his analysis from others—Menger was for Böhm-Bawerk what Ricardo was for Marx. They worked with similar methods and proceeded in similar progression. And they each created an edifice, the grandeur of which can be expressed no better than by the observation that no criticism, regardless of how effective it may be against its concrete target, can detract from the significance of the whole.

But the first impression on the scientific world was less than that of the critical part of the work, and only slowly did the *Positive Theorie* strike roots in the soil of economic thought. This is partly in the nature of the case. So powerful an organism as Böhm-Bawerk's *Positive Theorie,* whose inner mechanism can be fully understood only after prolonged study, and which escaped the grasp of the nontheorist altogether, forced the expert, especially in 1889, to work himself into a completely novel world of ideas. For this reason it could not but remain quite inaccessible at first. Even today, many an admirer of the man ranks it second to other parts of his work, especially to the *Geschichte und Kritik;* and the judgment of many experts in the field is caught by mere subordinate details. At any rate, although the greatness of the book even now is not clear to far too many, it has become a standard work which cannot be by-passed by anyone who intends to do theoretical work. It belongs in the tool chest of any theorist, and it has become by far the most successful of the original contributions of our time.

The second edition (1902) was an unaltered reprint of the first. But during the years 1904-9, Böhm-Bawerk's entire strength was devoted to a renewed 'thinking through of the whole work.' After 'five years of strenuous work,' which left 'no fold' of his system untested (cf. preface to the third edition), he resubmitted it to the public without having had to change its fundamentals. Nevertheless, this edition is a new book: only a few sections are left entirely unrevised, nearly all of them have been expanded, and there are a number of important additions. Moreover, the years of self-criticism had made him want to discuss a number of subjects more thoroughly than it would be possible to do in the text. Hence, in addition to the two appendices, he added twelve 'excursuses.' Though originally amplifications of the text and critical notes, many of them are self-contained monographs. They make the book into a compendium of economic theory, and it may be said that in this fashion he was permitted to complete his lifework.

One final piece, however, was not added to the book, though he had long planned it. He gave it to us in his last article, 'Macht oder ökonomisches Gesetz?' He had often encountered the slogan that economic processes in general, and the distribution of the social product in particular, were determined not by purely economic value phenomena, but by the social power of classes. Only a slogan, but widely held—and in our field we are in no position to underestimate slogans. Moreover, there is certainly a real problem here, one on which he had to take a position if only to assure himself of the solidity of his own system. This he did and at the same time analyzed important questions of the theory of wages. For us, this paper has a significance also because of the many hints it contains of the direction in which further research should move, of those innumerable problems of detail whose contours lie as yet in the hazy stretches of the far future.

One more paper belongs to this integrated plan of work, outside which there are only a few publications that will be mentioned presently. It takes its inner meaning from the parallelism of his scientific efforts with those of Marx. This is his critique of Marx which he published under the title 'Zum Abschluss des Marxschen Systems,' after the appearance of the third volume of *Das Kapital*, as a contribution to a memorial volume in honor of Karl Knies (Berlin, 1896; Russian translation, St. Petersburg, 1897; English translation, London, 1898). Marx had innumerable critics and apologists—more than almost any other theorist, though Böhm-Bawerk has now perhaps a comparable number—but most of them suffer from one of two defects. Either their chief interest lies outside the scientific core of Marx's work, and they escape into matters that are irrelevant from the point of view of that core—matters historical, political, philosophical, et cetera—or they are not fully up to the author and his work. This is what gives Böhm-Bawerk's criticism its significance: it seizes upon the core and only the core of the matter, and every line shows the master; the greatness of the object of the critique measures the greatness of the critic. This is why this critique takes a prominent place in the panorama of Böhm-Bawerk's work; this is why it will never cease to be *the* critique of Marx in so far as the theoretical content of Marx's system is concerned. I cannot, however, consider it in further detail.

III

If we follow Ostwald's classification, Böhm-Bawerk will have to be designated a typical 'Classic.' This fits the style of his writing; it is direct, unadorned, reserved. The author lets the subject speak and does not distract us with his own fireworks. Precisely in this lies the undoubtedly strong esthetic appeal of the literary costume— it emphasizes the logical form of the underlying ideas, precisely but unobtrusively. Yet his style is very personal, and any sentence of his could be spotted no matter in what company it might appear, for all the regularity of his syntax. His sentences—beautifully hewn blocks of marble—are frequently long, but never tangled. The influence of

official and administrative language is faintly perceptible, even
juridical forms of style and expression. But this is never disturbing.
On the contrary, it turns out that the official language has its own
·qualities of style, which are in the proper hands not without their
effect. The expression and 'temperature' of his exposition are always
tailored to the occasion: thoughtful and cool in the development of
an argument, full of energy and pungency in the decisive passages
and in the résumé. The author refuses to obscure the structure of
his exposition, and the caesuras are sharply marked. Word play is
absent. And hardly ever is there a touch of that charming gaiety in
conversation—I know no better expression for it than 'playfulness'
—which was so much his own in personal contacts. But within the
bounds of the strictest reserve, expression frequently rises to rhetor-
ical effects, and often he found a happy turn of phrase and coined
an unforgettable word or expression.

IV

A few words will suffice to characterize his methodological
position. His method of work, a method which in his hands proved
its power so brilliantly, was determined by the nature of his problem
and by his individual disposition. The problem was to describe those
most general laws which manifest themselves in any economic system, regardless of time and nation. The existence of such laws,
always and everywhere, follows from the essence of economic activity, and from the objective necessities that condition this activity.
The tasks this problem poses are therefore predominantly analytical.
That is, there is no longer a special task of collecting facts—the
relevant basic facts of economic life are, as experience shows, simple
and familiar to us from practical experience, and they repeat themselves everywhere, if in many different forms. In any case, collecting
facts recedes before the task of the intellectual digestion of these
facts and of developing their implications. This cannot be done save
by mental isolation of the elements of experience of interest to us,
and by the abstraction of many irrelevant matters. The resulting
theory, it is true, is abstract, separated by the hiatus of many hy-

potheses from immediate reality, as any theory is; but it is as realistic and empirical as a theory of physics. When, of course, it is a matter of applying such a theory or of concrete detailed investigations, new systematically collected factual material is indispensable. But since Böhm-Bawerk's problem was that of drawing the large contours of the inner logic of the economic process, and since he was concerned neither with applications nor with detailed empirical investigations, his method was that of theoretical analysis, of exact speculation. And his personal disposition pointed in the same direction.

His interest was in problems and results, not in discussions of method. A born scientist, the methodological necessities of each group of problems in each actual case were so much a matter of course to him that general disquisitions on method were not to his taste. Only occasionally did he write about them. The essence of his opinion on the subject, so far as he expressed it in the first two places where he can be said to deal with methodology at all,[1] leaves no doubt: 'Write little or nothing on method, and instead work the more energetically with all available methods.' In a third publication he addressed words of methodological warning to a group of French sociologists, members of the Institut Internationale de Sociologie, on the occasion of his election as president of this Institute. They are published in the *Revue Internationale de Sociologie* (20ᵉ année, 1912) under the title, 'Quelques remarques peu neuves sur une vieille question.' Written with calm and modest earnestness and in beautiful form, they deserve attention elsewhere, too—particularly the weighty, infinitely appropriate warning that, if sociology does not soon find its Ricardo, it will inevitably produce its Fourier. And finally, there is a methodological section, on 'Die Aufgaben der Preïs-theorie,' added to the third edition of the *Positive Theorie,* where he takes issue with those German theorists who deny the possibility of a general price theory.

[1] (a) Preface to the first edition of the *Positive Theorie.* (b) 'Zur Literaturgeschichte der Staats-und Sozialwissenschaften,' *Conrads Jahrbücher,* vol. xx, 1890.

All these writings have a definite, defensive purpose; they are not written for their own sake, and they are not intended to be epistemological investigations. For these, the man concerned primarily with results would have no time. That he had no taste for those refinements of expression and form that are the joy of other minds can be explained, incidentally, from his position in the history of our science. He was one of those pioneers in the field to whom only the essence of their subject matters, who can and must leave the 'refinements' to the epigones. He was an architect, not an interior decorator, a pathbreaker of science, not a salon scientist. Thus he is not much agitated about whether one can really speak of cause and effect, or only of functional relationships. Thus he occasionally speaks of relatively small quantities where one can strictly speak only of infinitesimal quantities. Thus he uses the term marginal utility indifferently to designate both a differential coefficient and the product of this coefficient and a quantitative element. Thus he failed to define exhaustively the formal characteristics of the utility function, which with him appears as a discontinuous scale of utilities. And thus his price theory in particular compares to that of the men of Lausanne as the figure of an old Teuton compares to a courtier of Louis XV. Assumptions about the shape of functions he expressed in the form of tabulated numerical examples. But all this does not really matter. The future will do the necessary polishing. What was at stake for him were fundamental principles, and these he developed better and more effectively in his own way than he could have succeeded in doing otherwise. His theory of price is still the best we possess, the one that best answers all fundamental problems and all basic difficulties.

His position in respect to sociology is particularly characteristic in this connection. Following in part the necessity of cultivating the newly broken ground and in part the line of least resistance, economists had streamed into this field, and this bloodletting of scientific manpower explains much of German economics. Böhm-Bawerk was not pulled into the stream; he wanted to be nothing but an economist. And as an economist he feared for the progress of his science when he observed how sister disciplines, which were by method and content as far beneath economics as it in turn was beneath the natural sciences, robbed it of so much of its personnel and brought with them that journalistic style of writing which overgrows all disciplines that lack a well-trained body of expert opinion. He was too thorough to see full compensation in these stimuli, which could not but affect the field of economics too, and as a consequence he remained a lifelong stranger to the various sociological schools of his time. He was well aware that anyone who takes genuine achievement seriously must confine himself within a narrow field and endure the reproaches of the public for being a specialist, rather than flit weakly and nervously from one subject to another.

This is the place to mention the fact that he almost never participated in the discussion of questions of the day. He stayed aloof from any political position, and his work belongs to no party. In practice, he tackled many a current question, dealt with many a great practical problem, but as a scientist he wrote, so far as I know, only once about a 'practical' question (in three articles in the *Neue Freie Presse* for 6, 8, and 9 January 1914, on 'Unsere passive Handelsbilanz'). And here he shows himself a master of such discussions. 'The threat of money flows will in most cases have the effect which, in the event of its ineffectiveness, the actual money flows would produce.' 'The balance of payments commands, the balance of trade obeys, and not the other way round.' 'It is said, and it is probably true, that in this country many private persons live beyond their means. But it is certain that, for some time, very many of our public authorities have been living beyond theirs.' 'Financial policy has with us been the whipping boy of politics.' And so on. No one can deny the author either interest or understanding, or the greatest talent for this kind of work. Yet he remained outside the discussions of the day—why? These discussions, dominated by practical issues and limited by the horizon of the audience, cannot stand lengthier arguments, deeper research, more refined methods. They tie science down to the level of popular debate—to arguments that have remained the same for the last two hundred years. These discussions are directed toward 'instantaneous production,' a sort of production analogous to economic production without machines, and in their rush they leave no time for the theorist to catch his breath, no time to get down to real work—at best they can be mere applications of already existing knowledge. But they are fascinating, often fired by the heat of political passion; and thus it has come to pass that many economists give them their whole time, and most, a large part of it. This is one of the reasons why things go so slowly in our field. Böhm-Bawerk worked for future centuries—when what now seems to be 'playing intellectual games' can perhaps be expected to bear practical fruit—and he understood it was his duty, despite all temptations, to let the day go its way, and the people talk.

V

From our survey of his work, it becomes clear that the structure of his economics and the totality of his achievements and opinions can best be developed by a closer view of the *Positive Theorie*. This I shall now attempt.

Only a few of the problems of theoretical economics in the proper sense of the term are not taken up in this work. As I see it, the omitted problems are the following:

1. The basic process of socio-economic life can be demonstrated through the model of an isolated economy. Though there is a theory covering the relations of several economies with one another, it does not contribute toward our knowledge of the essence of the socio-economic process. Since Böhm-Bawerk's concern was with this essence, he always worked with an isolated economy; and a theory of international values cannot be found in the main body of his work, though a contribution to it is contained in the three articles of 1914 mentioned above.

2. These articles, too, have one of his few brief remarks on the problem of money, namely, the remark that there is an 'indestructible core' of truth in the quantity theory. However, he did not give us a theory of money. After having vanquished the primitive bullionist and mercantilist ideas, economics has with hardly any

opposition accepted the view that money—the economy's accounting medium—is only a veil, which covers up deep-seated processes without affecting their essential nature. Böhm-Bawerk agreed.

3. The *Positive Theorie* refrains from those specialized inquiries which are theoretically mere applications of price and distribution theory (incidence of taxation, theory of monopoly, theory of political intervention in the process of distribution, et cetera). But the article, 'Macht oder ökonomisches Gesetz?'—containing an investigation of whether strikes could permanently raise the level of real wages—is of this kind, and it should be pointed out that as an essay in applied economics it represents one of the first achievements of the Austrian school, a paradigm for research of its kind.

4. The *Positive Theorie* furthermore contains nothing on the problem of cycles. The reason becomes clear when we consider Böhm-Bawerk's single mention of this problem (in a review of v. Bergmann's *Geschichte der nationalökonomischen Krisentheorien,* in the *Zeitschrift für Volkswirtschaft,* 1896): he appears to have taken the view that economic crises are neither an endogenous nor a uniform economic phenomenon but rather the consequence of what are in principle accidental disturbances of the economic process.

5. A foreign growth in the body of economic theory, but one that has nevertheless been spreading ever since the time of the Physiocrats, is what is referred to as the 'population problem.' There is of course no room for it in the *Positive Theorie,* or in any of Böhm-Bawerk's other works. It may be of interest to note, however, that in a passing reference to it in the paper, 'Macht oder ökonomisches Gesetz?', Böhm-Bawerk puts himself, by implication, in the Malthusian ranks.

Except for these matters, however, the *Positive Theorie* is, as already pointed out, an exposition of the whole field of economic theory. Value, price, and distribution are the three peaks that serve as directing beacons; everything else has been grouped around them, among other things the theory of capital.

The sociological framework is only hinted at; again and again Böhm-Bawerk repeats that he investigates only the inner logic of the economic process. Yet he believes that the basic elements which are his concern are strong enough to make themselves felt in any real situation. The question of the precise limits of these elements, such as the problem of class structure and its economic functions, the influence of race differences, the origin of that rational calculus which is at the root of so much in modern economies, the genesis and social psychology of the phenomenon of the market—all these do not touch his problem and would to him have been but deviations from the main theme. Thus we find the elements of an economy classified simply in the categories of workers, landlords, capitalists, and entrepreneurs, distinguished from one another by, and only by, their economic functions. Disregarding their extra-economic relations, men matter for the purpose of this investigation only in so far as they are workers, capitalists, landlords, and entrepreneurs—they matter only, so to speak, as representatives of the logic of their respective positions.

Workers and landlords, to begin with, are characterized by the possession of the factors of production indicated in their designation, and by their economic functions. This point needs emphasis if the theory of distribution is not to be misunderstood: it is at bottom not the worker, and similarly—which is quite important—not the landlord, into whose lap the distributive process washes an income; labor and the land itself receive it. What is at issue therefore is, to use an American expression approvingly mentioned by Böhm-Bawerk in his last work, 'functional' not 'personal' distribution; and it would be a great mistake to look in his work for anything like a tendency to 'justify' the distribution of income.

Workers and landlords live on what their means of production produce. They do *not,* however, live on what they are at any given time engaged in producing—their current output is of course not yet ripe for consumption—but on products that have been produced *at some previous time.* To furnish this store of means of subsistence is the function of the capitalists—workers and landlords can be said then to live, always and everywhere, on advances made to them by the capitalists. This is true as much for the workers and

landlords of a modern capitalist economy as it is for primitive grub-
bers and hunters.

The figure of the entrepreneur is not prominent in Böhm-
Bawerk's theoretical canvas. His functions as a manager and specu-
lator are, it is true, mentioned; but most of the time he appears because of characteristics he possesses frequently but not necessarily:
those of a capitalist, of an industrialist working with his own capital.

Though the main features of the socio-economic process, as
Böhm-Bawerk conceives it, can now be made out, the function of
capital needs closer attention.

With this Böhm-Bawerk begins his *Positive Theorie*. The
very first thing he has to tell us—in the Introduction—is a warning
to distinguish between two radically different aspects of this problem, the confusion of which has been one of the most frequent mistakes of popular as well as of scientific discussion: the problem of
capital as a means of production, and the problem of capital as the
source of a net return. Nothing could be easier than to consider the
undoubted connection between the two as itself a theory of interest,
and simply to say: capital is indispensable in production and thus
'yields' a net return, just as the means of production 'cherry tree'
'yields' the product 'cherries.' And this is the seat of one of those
fundamental errors which Böhm-Bawerk, in a tireless and life-long
fight, succeeded in eliminating from scientific discussion, so that, in
this naïve form, it can no longer be found in the work of more than
one or two reputable economists. At the threshold of his work,
Böhm-Bawerk re-emphasizes this, and then turns to the theory of
capital as means of production. Though it is difficult to resist an
attempt to describe the logical beauty of his argument in detail, it
must suffice here to say that Böhm-Bawerk begins with an investigation of the nature of the productive process, and the charm of this
first section—which otherwise is a treatment of matters that are by
now little discussed and do not evoke great interest—lies in the fact
that it suggests the guiding motifs of what is to follow.

Production is the transformation of matter for the purpose of
creating things capable of satisfying our wants. This concept, not

unknown to the Classics, is the first bench mark in the course of his argument. The purpose is more perfectly achieved if labor is spent not directly on such 'transformations' as may result in immediately consumable objects, but first on nonconsumables with whose help final products can be produced more efficiently, in which case the same input of original factors produces a larger total result— that is, production proceeds in roundabout ways. This—and here is the second bench mark of the work—is the economic philosophy of tools, or generally of 'produced means of production,' and the definition of their productive function. This idea itself, again neither genuinely original nor complicated, has nevertheless been adequately formulated only by Böhm-Bawerk. He alone fully exploited its theoretical meaning, especially in the treatment of the time factor, which is the origin of nine-tenths of the fundamental difficulties that beset the analytic construction of the economic process.

This yields, as its most important by-product, a concept of the nature of 'capitalism.' The reality of which we think when using this term has of course been the subject of very different interpretations: not only scientific, political, and ethical, but different interpretations even within the realm of science, flowing from sociology, social psychology, analysis of culture, and history. But for pure economics, and thus for Böhm-Bawerk, only the question of the purely economic characteristics of capitalism matters. His answer is: capitalist production is 'roundabout' production; its opposite is direct production—production without produced means of production, e.g. primitive hunting. And accordingly, capital is 'nothing but the total of the intermediate products which are generated in the various stages of the roundabout method of production.' This is in fact a theory, not a mere definition, and it is important to understand it. It does not, of course, deny the fact that a modern economy is significantly different from economic systems of the past. It does not deny either that the economic process in a socialist economy—where production, according to this definition, would nowadays also be 'capitalist'—would be very different. But it does say that all those characteristics which both science and social criticism have attached to the phenomenon of capitalism have nothing to do with the economic essence of the capitalist process of production, that especially private property in the means of production in general and in capital goods in particular, the system of wage labor, production for a market, et cetera, are irrelevant for the essence of what constitutes a capitalist process. The most important implication of this view is that a net return to capital is *generated* also in a socialist economy, though of course it will not there accrue to private persons—a matter that is, in any case, of secondary importance from the point of view of functional distribution. Almost every productive process is, therefore, 'capitalist'—it can only be a matter of more or less.

At this point Böhm-Bawerk's argument pauses to consider the 'controversy over the concept of capital.' For his own definition of capital, his view of the capitalist process of production was decisive; though, starting from the same conception, he could have called something else capital, namely, the supply of consumption goods— the economy's subsistence fund, which is a necessary complement to roundabout methods of production and which acquires its significance for the problem of interest from the productivity of these roundabout methods.

In Book II, on 'Capital as a Means of Production,' we are led to the result already announced in the first section of the first book, that the services of land and labor are the elemental, original factors of production, and that therefore capital, which in an economic sense consists of these two, cannot be an independent factor. Again, the proposition as such is simple, even self-evident. Again, it has been presented before, in its most pregnant form by Sir William Petty. But nobody took it seriously; nobody recognized the analytic tasks in which it could have served as a useful tool; in short, nobody recognized its theoretical usefulness or the possibility of systematically exploiting it, of gaining considerable insight and analytical simplification with its help. Rather, the history of economic thought shows three main deviations from it: the Physiocratic proposition that eventually all economic goods spring from the lap of nature; the Classical thesis of the exclusive productivity of labor; and lastly the proclaiming, in part by the Classics, more by their epigones, of capital as the third independent power of production. None of these deviations as such was 'wrong'—in their own way they were perfectly correct—but they led to either useless or naïve conclusions. What matters is not the 'correctness' of such fundamental hypothetical propositions; the merit of a theorist consists in his ability to make an effective choice of his point of departure from any number of possible, equally unquestionable, heuristic alternatives. It was Böhm-Bawerk's achievement to bring order into these things and to have visualized, chosen, and developed that hypothesis which enables us best to negotiate all the shallows and which yields the best crop of insights and outlooks. Especially the theory of distribution received its characteristic features from the complete parallelism of land and labor services plus their juxtaposition with capital.

The next step consists in the decisive use of the idea of roundabout production in the treatment of the time factor. Roundabout production yields a larger final product than direct production, but only in the farther future is it 'time consuming.' This combination of these two factors, this particular introduction of the time factor and this conception of the characteristics of constant capital, are entirely original. To do justice to the analytic advance it represents one does well to revert briefly to the Ricardo-Marx view. Ricardo, like Marx, focused the problem on the influence the differences in the length of the period of production in different industries had on his (labor) theory of value. Both attempt—in otherwise different ways, as the problem indeed may present itself in different forms—to show the fundamental insignificance of this influence, to suppress as much as possible of what then becomes fatal to both of them. The great synthesis of these two elements, this disengagement and combination of time and added returns, alone makes possible a consistent theory of the role of time in production, free from *tours de force,* and an illumination of its peculiar double role. This leads deep into the understanding of the economic process and very close to the problem of the net return on capital.

This net return must be, according to Böhm-Bawerk, the result of the influence on the formation of value of the increased technical productivity of roundabout production on the one hand, and of the consequent postponement of its results on the other. The question is then only, *how*. Hence the necessity for investigating the principles of value into which those two facts will have to be fitted.

This is in fact the next step. But first some other matters have to be settled. As the most immediate development of this principle of the productivity-increasing effects of roundaboutness, Böhm-Bawerk presents the proposition that further extensions of the period of production will yield further but decreasing additions to the final product. And to make it possible to speak of a definite period of production in the case of goods in whose production increasing quantities of labor are used, the concept of an 'average period of production' is constructed. A number of interesting implications could be mentioned here—e.g. an important generalization of the concept of roundabout production, and the rich discussion originating here— but this we must pass by, as well as the 'Theory of Capital Formation,' or rather that more external part of it which is dealt with in the last section of the second book. Let us emphasize only its core: one saves consumers' goods, thereby saving means of production, thereby in turn producing capital goods—a view that eventually anchors the formation of capital in the process of saving, without however (an attractive and frequent error of the old analysis) inferring anything from this about the theory of interest.

VI

Let us turn now to the second of the two pillars that support Böhm-Bawerk's structure—the theory of value and price (Book III), which presents as complete a chain of thought as the one we have just left. We shall later consider the superstructure that rests on the two.

The general relation of goods to the satisfaction of wants which has been called utility—not without the danger of misunderstanding—can be reduced to what has importance for our economic behavior, which we designate as value (use value) when a certain quantity of a certain commodity becomes the recognized condition of a satisfaction that would otherwise have to be foregone. Whether this is the case is determined, given the general utility relationship, by the size of that 'certain quantity' in relation to our wants: for value to emerge, relative scarcity has to be added to utility. With the aid of a distinction between want categories (or want directions) and want intensities, and under careful consideration of the factor of substitutability, Böhm-Bawerk arrives (in Menger's sense, and in a way similar to Wieser's) at the law of decreasing marginal utility with increasing 'coverage' of wants within each category—i.e. with increasing quantities of the commodity in the possession of an individual—and at a solution of the old value antinomy, the *contradiction économique*. Böhm-Bawerk formulated the result in this proposition: 'The magnitude of the value of a commodity depends on the importance of that concrete want, or partial want, which, among the wants covered by the available total quantity of the commodity concerned, is the least important.'

Böhm-Bawerk then turns to a number of elaborations of this general proposition, a number of special problems concerning the magnitude of subjective value, for the solution of which he employs a fundamental principle (calling it the 'passe partout' for all the difficulties of the theory of value): 'One has to look in a twofold manner at the economic position of the individual from whose point of view a commodity is to be evaluated. First, imagining the good to be added to the stock of goods in the possession of the individual, one observes how far down in the scale of concrete wants satisfaction can be carried. Second, one imagines that the good is to be taken away from the individual's stock of goods, and again one gauges how far down the scale satisfaction can still reach. It will then become apparent that now a certain layer of wants, namely the lowest layer, must remain unsatisfied: this lowest layer indicates the marginal utility which decides the value of the commodity.' And after developing this proposition for a number of special cases, Böhm-Bawerk takes on the important case of the value of freely augmentable commodities. According to the 'passe partout,' we value such goods also in proportion to the decrease in satisfaction their loss would occasion. Now in this case, this decrease is given as the loss of satisfaction suffered by foregoing the purchase of that quantity of goods that could have been purchased had the commodity at first considered not been lost. The goods foregone are not necessarily of the same kind as those lost, but usually different goods. In this case, therefore, we value according to the 'substitute utility'—and here a very important principle is discovered.

Its first application is to the case of freely reproducible commodities, that is, from the point of view of the economy as a whole, of nearly all commodities. And this case is merged with admirable logic with the case of goods capable of more than one use. From here in turn we are led to the solution of the problem of the difference between 'value in use' and 'value in exchange.'

This clears the ground for the treatment of the value of 'complementary commodites' (Menger), i.e. commodities that produce satisfaction only in combination with others. The value of a group of complementary commodities is determined by the marginal utility they jointly create, and the problem is to derive from this the value of the individual members of the group. For this, Böhm-Bawerk's rule is as follows: '. . . of the total value of the whole group—which is determined by the marginal utility of the joint employment—the replaceable members are given their previously fixed value,[2] and the remainder—which varies according to the amount of the marginal utility—is imputed to the nonreplaceable members as their individual value.' This proposition announces a fundamental principle of modern theory which has found innumerable applications in all directions, especially under the name of the 'principle of substitution,' which Marshall gave it.

Another application of this theory is the next step to a height from which a wide view into the innermost working of an economy is gained. Means of production are also complementary goods. But

[2] Determined from their substitute utility.

their values are not directly determined: we value them only because they somehow or other lead to consumers' goods, and their value can thus, from the point of view of the subjective theory of value, be derived only from the value of these consumers' goods. But many factors of production are always involved in the production of a single consumers' good, and their productive contributions are seemingly indistinguishably intermixed. In fact, before Menger, one economist after another thought it impossible to speak of distinguishable shares of the means of production in the value of the final product, with the result that further progress seemed impossible along this route, and the idea of subjective value appeared to be unusable. The theory of the value of complementary commodities solves this seemingly hopeless problem. It enables us to speak of a determinate 'productive contribution' (Wieser) of such means of production and to find for each of them a uniquely determined marginal utility, derived from its possibilities of productive application—that marginal utility which has become, under the names marginal productivity, final productivity, *prodittività marginale, productivité finale,* the basic concept of the modern theory of distribution and the fundamental principle of our explanation of the nature and magnitude of the incomes of economic groups.

In applying this 'theory of imputation' (Wieser), which owes to Böhm-Bawerk one of its most perfect formulations, we arrive at the law of costs as a special case of the law of marginal utility. As a consequence of the theory of imputation, the phenomenon of cost becomes a reflex of subjective value, and the law of the equality of the cost and the value of a product is derived from the theory of value—never in our science has there been a more beautifully closed chain of logic.

But all this so far still refers only to the world of values. That all of its forms express themselves also in the mechanism of the exchange economy can be shown only by a corresponding theory of price. Böhm-Bawerk therefore turns to price theory, developing the implications of the law of value for the behavior of buyers and sellers, and his investigation culminates in that celebrated proposition (for the case of bilateral competition) which has since become 'historic': 'The level of price is determined and limited by the level of the subjective valuations of the two marginal pairs'—i.e. on the one hand by the valuations of the 'last' buyer admitted to purchase and of the seller who is the 'most capable of exchanging' among the ones already excluded from the exchange, and on the other hand by the valuations of the seller 'least capable of exchanging' among those still admitted to the exchange and of the 'first' excluded buyer.

All this is developed first for the situation with given quantities of exchangeable commodities with the conclusion that, since the forces operating on the supply side of the market are the same as those operating on the demand side, the old 'law of demand and supply' turns out to be simply a corollary of the law of marginal utility. This is then extended to the case of the formation of the prices of commodities whose available quantities can be varied by production. Confronting the difficulties that arise here, as everywhere when one attempts to follow the operation of a basic principle through the maze of reality, Böhm-Bawerk does not leave the reader behind at a single point. He clears all the chief obstacles from the road, one by one, and the chain of solutions he presents will for a long time form the basis for further theoretical work.

The conclusion—bringing out the parallelism of value theory and price theory, and at the same time the logical unity of this step— is the presentation of the law of costs, this time in the guise of price. It follows first that prices, determined in the play of all subjective valuations, will, in equilibrium and with free competition, tend to equal unit costs. This is no longer a postulate, but a corollary of the law of marginal utility, so that the law of costs which played so important a part with the Classics acquires its true meaning and above all its strict proof only in the framework of the subjective theory of value. It also follows how superficial is that version which declares that subjective valuations determine the oscillations of prices, and costs their long-run centers of gravity: subjective valuations determine both the oscillations and the centers of gravity, although the latter can be characterized further as also showing the validity of the cost principle—which, however, is no longer an independent principle. It follows, finally, that the extent to which costs can be 'intermediate causes' of price movements in particular cases is explicable from the marginal utility principle. And in the end there is unfolded the panorama of the economic process in which, under the pressure of subjective valuations, the means of production of the economy are forced into their various uses.

The fundamental principles for the understanding of wages, ground rents, and profits now drop into our laps all by themselves. The ultimate, original means of production are the services of land and labor. All commodities, consumers' as well as capital goods, ultimately reduce to them. Directly or indirectly—the latter through the medium of capital goods—the value of the product must be reflected back to land and labor, the services of which thus acquire their values and, in the market and under free competition, their corresponding prices, that is, their wages and rent. According to Böhm-Bawerk, therefore, wages are—with provisos to be added later —the expression in terms of prices of the marginal product of labor; labor is compensated according to its 'productive contribution,' or as we may also say, according to its marginal importance for the socio-economic process. The same could be said of ground rents, though Böhm-Bawerk speaks here only of labor. Under the stated assumptions, the total national product would resolve itself into wages and rents. With almost dramatic suddenness we are thus presented with a solution of these ancient problems, which in point of correctness, simplicity, and fruitfulness, towers above all older achievements.

This result is the abacus,[3] so to speak, of the second pillar of the building, to stay within my earlier metaphor. But for the operation of other factors, there would be neither profit nor interest. Here we should imagine the whole argument of the *Kritik und Geschichte* inserted in the text, an argument that was designed to show the inadequacy of all previous attempts to fit profit and interest into this picture. But this I must forego, and it must suffice to say that

[3] The upper member of the capital of a column, supporting the architrave. [Ed.]

Böhm-Bawerk pointed to two circumstances that interfered with the equality between revenue and cost.

The one he summarizes under the heading of 'frictions.' Stoppages occur in the flow of the means of production which cause a temporary, sometimes prolonged, deviation of the prices of consumers' goods from the norm set by the law of costs, and these are the source of profits, but also of losses, to entrepreneurs. Böhm-Bawerk thus accepts that form of the explanation of entrepreneurial profit which runs in terms of imperfections in the mechanism of markets; from these imperfections the position of the entrepreneur enables him to derive a decided benefit—at the same time he is instrumental in removing them.

The second cause of disturbance is the passage of time, and that is the 'fold' in which, according to Böhm-Bawerk, we shall have to look for an explanation of the phenomenon of interest. Thus we enter that superstructure, built upon the foundations so far delineated, which is his most personal achievement and which distinguishes him, essentially, from those who were otherwise nearest to him—the superstructure that contains his solution for the most difficult and most profound problem of theoretical economies, and whose powerful façade impresses both friend and foe. It gives the sum total of his system a characteristic imprint, for our view of the net return from capital, as we saw above, colors our view of practically all other problems, branches out into all the streams of economic discussion, and even beyond into the broad field of social vision.

VII

This theory of interest has been called an exchange and agio theory. Its foundation is the thesis that present goods are valued higher than those which become available in the future though otherwise in all respects the same, serving to provide for the same categories and intensities of wants. What is at issue here is therefore the introduction of a new fact, a widening of the factual basis of economics. But this fact is not outside the principle of value; it is rather the discovery of a particular property of our valuations—occasionally 'anticipated' before Böhm-Bawerk, and emphasized systematically only by Jevons. With Böhm-Bawerk the theory of value absorbs this fact organically, adjusts itself to it, and never destroys the continuity of the argument or the unity of the fundamental construction. Rather, with him, the theory of interest also follows from the marginal utility principle. A decisive feature of this theory of interest is, as he himself expressed it (*Geschichte und Kritik*), the transmission of the effects of all the more remote determinants of the rate of return to capital through the common medium of a difference in value between present and future commodities. That is, interest is simply the price expression of this value difference, from which it is derived by way of the subjective theory of value and price; and it is a second problem, one step removed, to find the causes of this difference in value. In this step are found the remaining essential traits of his theory. It belongs to the third of the three groups of theories of interest Böhm-Bawerk describes in the summary of the first volume of his great work. The first group—the 'productivity theories'—comes to grief because of a confusion of what has ever since Böhm-Bawerk been called 'physical' productivity with 'value' productivity; the second group—the 'exploitation' theories—fails to show why the forces of competition will not wash the 'exploitative' gain away; the third group of theories looks for the origin of interest in the realm of value itself. And since the rate of interest is a price phenomenon, it *must* have its origin here. To this group belongs the agio theory; it is κατ' ἐξοχήν the value theory of interest. It is only the influence of the lapse of time on subjective valuations that produces the force which carries a part of the stream of commodities into the hands of the capitalists in the following manner.

All provision for the satisfaction of our wants implies, strictly speaking, taking account of the future, and all economic activity is therefore—and, according to Böhm-Bawerk's conception of the nature of capitalism, the more so the more that activity is 'capitalist' —under the influence of wants we shall experience only in the future, but which we can imagine already in the present; and on the other hand, it is under the influence of the objective necessities we shall meet only in the future but which we can predict already in the present. Therefore future goods are objects—the most important objects in fact—of our economic behavior and our valuations. Obviously, these valuations can be understood with the aid of the same principle of marginal utility. To this must be added the following facts (which are, however, in principle of no further interest): that we have to do with imagined rather than felt needs (always remembering that the former are just as commensurable as the latter); that we have to do not with the present relation between needs and provision for needs but with that relation at the relevant future point of time; and that future satisfactions always have to be multiplied by a certain coefficient which expresses the probability of the expected utility (a 'risk premium').

Now Böhm-Bawerk, introducing a fact of fundamental importance for the analysis of value, holds that present goods possess a higher subjective value than future goods of equal quantity and kind.

First, because either there is the hope of a more ample provision for wants in the future, or—when this is not the case—the possession of present goods permits provision both for alternative present as well as for future wants (especially in a money economy where a 'saving' of such provisions is always possible at little expense). Thus the value of present goods is at least equal to that of future goods, and a general 'value agio' of present over future goods is always present in the economy.

Second, because we generally underestimate future wants. Future wants do not easily enter our consciousness to their full extent; imagined wants do not possess the same sharp-edged reality as those actually felt; and, finally, provision beyond a certain time range will not be undertaken at all by the typical individual. These psychological factors reinforce one another and a 'prospective underestimation of future enjoyment' is the result—a second reason for the existence of a value agio in favor of present goods.

Third, because 'time-consuming' roundabout production is more efficient, that is, a given quantity of original means of production yields a larger *physical* product when applied first to the production of intermediate products (e.g. tools) and then to the production of consumers' goods, than when they are applied entirely to the direct production of consumers' goods. Old quantities of the means of production (i.e. those applied earlier in roundabout production) will therefore everywhere show a technical superiority over young means of production (i.e. those applied later)—save where a new invention or the like has in the meantime made the method using the 'old' means of production obsolete.

Here arises the question, absent in the first two reasons for the agio, whether this third factor causes not only a larger quantity but also a larger value of the output of 'time consuming' roundaboutness. Böhm-Bawerk's answer is in the affirmative. For according to the law of roundabout production, a quantity of present means of production will yield, when applied to such roundabout production, at all future points of time larger quantities of product than would an equally large quantity applied at any of these future points to direct production. It will also yield a larger product than an equal quantity applied later for shorter periods of time, since the productivity of means of production is the greater the more roundabout their use. Now, since of two quantities of the same commodity available to an individual at the same time, the larger is the more valuable, the value productivity (and not only the physical productivity) of a quantity of means of production that is available earlier in time must—under our assumptions and according to Böhm-Bawerk—always be greater than that of an equal quantity available later in time—no matter for what common point of time the two are to produce. Further, the undertaking of time-consuming roundabout methods implies that one can wait for their expected larger and more valuable yield, that is, that a subsistence fund of consumers' goods adequate to sustain whoever is engaged in the roundabout production is in fact available in the present. Thus the achievement of 'surplus value' from roundabout production is dependent on the existence of this fund of present consumers' goods, and, according to the general principles of the theory of imputation, this 'surplus value' is transferred to it. Therefore, here is another—the third and most important—reason for a value agio in favor of present and against future consumers' goods.

The thesis of the physical surplus productivity of roundabout production, as well as the thesis that it furnishes a separate third reason for the agio of present over future goods, independent of the other two, has been very much contested and there has grown up a whole 'literature on the third reason' (the reaction to which is to be found in the third edition and in the excursuses). Without entering into a discussion of this problem, we shall point out only how the third reason (independent in principle for Böhm-Bawerk) is, according to him, related to the other two. It is, of course, clear that the social fund of means of production will press most insistently into those occupations in which the highest marginal utility is attainable, and that this general theorem applies to the choice between productive results that emerge at different points of time in the future. The third reason would point to an infinitely long roundabout process, for any further extension of the period of production would, under our assumptions, promise a further increase—although at a constantly decreasing rate—of the quantity as well as of the value of the product. According to reasons number one and two, however, these constantly increasing quantities of value must be valued with an increasing prospective discount—and this mutual interaction between the first two and the third reasons will fix the length of the period of production that will yield the highest (present) value result. The effects of the three reasons are thus not additive for any one individual, either of the first two being capable of offsetting the third.

All these 'reasons' take effect in very different degree with different individuals—the value agio, though a common psychological fact with all individuals, operates differently within wide limits in the case of different individuals. But precisely this fact makes the exchange between individuals of present for future goods pos-

sible, by creating the necessary differences in their valuations. A
market for present and future goods is generated, and the theory
of the 'marginal pairs' determines a uniform objective price agio for
them—and thus is originated the rate of interest—in Böhm-Bawerk's
elegant formula, an agio in the exchange of present for future goods.
Like every price, this agio has a double levelling effect. First, even
those who otherwise would underestimate future goods less than
the market agio indicates will adjust themselves to it. Second—and
this is a highly interesting turn—'the magnitude of the agio which
present goods acquire over future goods at differently remote future
points of time will become proportional to the length of the separating interval,' while the individual underestimation of the future
could very well occur discontinuously and irregularly, so that, for
example, the difference between present enjoyment and enjoyment
one year hence could be very large, while that between enjoyments
one and two years hence could be hardly noticeable.

This, then, is *in nuce* the celebrated Böhm-Bawerkian theory
of interest. But he was not satisfied with an *aperçu;* he pursued his
ideas throughout the depth and width of the capitalist organism. Let
us follow him in all brevity. There are in the main two problems—
to demonstrate that the empirically ascertainable sources of interest
on capital really spring from the rock described above, and to derive
the level and the laws of motion of the rate of interest from this
theoretical basis.

The case of the rate of interest on loans presents no difficulty.
The definition of a loan as an exchange of present for future goods
furnishes everything we could wish for. Besides, it is clear that anyone who seeks a consumers' loan must value present goods higher
than future goods, so that a rate of interest would emerge even if the
lender did not undervalue future goods. It is clear, further, that for
anyone who seeks a producers' loan the prospect of a future net
profit establishes such an agio, so that the result is the same here, too.
But the problem of the great social fact of a rate of return to capital
and of the basis on which in a capitalist economy the upper classes
stand—indeed of the economic structure of capitalist society—lies

precisely in the explanation of such a net profit, of its regular emergence in the stream of the economy. And this net return on capital, which originates in the hands of the entrepreneur, is now to be explained by relating it to the basic schema.

It is the fruit of Böhm-Bawerk's pre-eminent skill that for this case, too, the principle of explanation can be formulated so easily that it is almost self-evident: the entrepreneur purchases means of production which in part consist of services of labor and land, in part are reducible to these two. The services of land and labor are potential consumers' goods and owe their value to this quality. But they are only future consumers' goods, the value of which must be less than the value of an equal quantity of present consumers' goods. The services of land and labor will be bought from their owners at their present value, and their future products will then be sold at *their* value at that future sales date. Thus a value increment arises as soon as the present means of production have begun in the hands of the entrepreneur to grow toward their consumptive maturity—and this value increment is the basis of the net return to the entrepreneur's capital. The application of this result to individual empirical cases is not always easy. Many of these problems—especially the difficulty resulting from multiple employability of the same producers' goods in processes with different periods of production—are solved by Böhm-Bawerk with that infinite care which will make his book an invaluable guide even for the remotest future of our science.

The next step is the demonstration that these value relationships will always lead to a price agio. This price agio will appear in an exchange transaction between workers and landowners on the one hand and capital-owning entrepreneurs on the other, as a discount from the money value of the full future marginal product of the original means of production. Or, if we separate the capitalist from the entrepreneurial function and consider the entrepreneur as a mere intermediary between the owners of original means of production and the capitalists, it will appear in the exchange transaction between the capitalists and the workers and landowners, repre-

sented, so to speak, by the entrepreneurs, as a price agio on the subsistence fund advanced by the former, in other words, in the direct
form of an interest rate. Here we meet the capitalists in their essential role as merchants of present goods—perhaps an unfamiliar view
at first sight, but one that penetrates, to an extraordinary depth, the
nature of the economic process. In both forms, which merely cover
the same core, the agio is shown to be inevitable. We shall now demonstrate its necessity in the second form, which must be reducible
to the first.

On this 'market for the means of subsistence,' then, capitalists
confront workers and landlords. The available quantities of the
means of subsistence and of the services of labor and land are, at any
one time, given. (Some further remarks about the first half of this
assumption are to be added later on.) To the capitalists the value in
use of their consumers' goods matters little—they cannot consume
more than a small part of them in any case. We can thus neglect
their undervaluation of future goods; if it does exist, our agio must
occur *a fortiori*. To the workers and landowners, the valuation of
their labor and land services derived from their potential use in direct
production (in so far as they themselves can undertake capitalist
production, they assume the separable function of capitalists) does,
strictly speaking, enter as the lower limit below which they would
not trade; but under modern conditions this limit lies in a faraway
haze. In these circumstances, the capitalists will be willing to trade
even at a very small agio, asymptotically approaching zero. The
workers and landowners, for whom, in accordance with the law of
roundabout production, any excess above the return from direct production depends on their having available means of subsistence, will
be willing to trade even if they would be left with only a very small
part, asymptotically approaching zero, of this surplus return. The
end result will depend on the intensity of this demand by the workers and landowners for the means of subsistence at that point of the
extension of the period of production which the given subsistence
fund permits. And here it is quite generally true that, however large
this fund, it is always limited. But equally, it would always be pos-

sible, by extension of the period of production beyond the length permitted by a given fund, to achieve larger surplus returns. Therefore, there would—assuming any practicable size of the fund—remain an active demand for further quantities of the means of subsistence, if there were no agio; and this demand could not be satisfied. Since any limited subsistence fund leaves this demand unsatisfied, the outcome is that all demands that are still active at a given price have the effect of raising this price. From this it follows that the price of present goods must always rise above parity with that of future goods, and that thus an agio, that is, a rate of interest, must always emerge—which is what was to be proved.

Conversely, it will be seen at once that, if there were no interest, an unlimited expansion of the period of production would become profitable; obviously a scarcity of present goods would follow, which in turn would lead to direct production and hence to the re-emergence of interest. From this the true function of interest in the economy becomes clear. It is, so to speak, the brake, or governor, which prevents individuals from exceeding the economically admissible lengthening of the period of production, and enforces provision for present wants—which, in effect, brings their pressure to the attention of entrepreneurs. And this is why it reflects the relative intensity with which in every economy future and present interests make themselves felt and thus also a people's intelligence and moral strength—the higher these are, the lower will be the rate of interest. This is why the rate of interest mirrors the cultural level of a nation; for the higher this level, the larger will be the available stock of consumers' goods, the longer will be the period of production, the smaller will be, according to the law of roundaboutness, the surplus return which further extension of the period of production would yield, and thus the lower will be the rate of interest. And here we have Böhm-Bawerk's law of the decreasing rate of interest, his solution to this ancient problem which had tried the best minds of our science and found them wanting.

Our proof shows further that, because only an agio on present goods puts the relative demands of present and future into proper balance with one another, the values of present and future goods cannot stand at par even in a socialist community, that the value phenomenon which is the basis of the rate of interest cannot be absent even there and hence demands the attention of a central planning board. From this it follows that even in a socialist society workers cannot simply receive their product, since workers producing present goods produce less than those who are employed on the production of future goods. Thus, whatever the community decides to do with the quantity of goods corresponding to that value agio, it would never accrue to the workers as a *wage* (but only as a profit) even though it were divided equally among them. This could very well have practical consequences whenever, for example, the community had occasion to become conscious of the economic value of its members to itself; in such a case it could assess the value of a worker only at the discounted value of his productivity, and since all workers equally able to work must obviously be evaluated equally, a 'surplus value' must even here emerge which would appear as an income *sui generis*. Theoretically more important, however, is the result—to use a terminology that has become accepted in treatments of this topic—that the rate of interest is a purely economic and not a historical or legal concept. Two corrections of the idea of exploitation are now also in order: first, one can speak of 'exploitation' as a cause of profit only in the sense in which such exploitation would occur also in a socialist state; second, there is exploitation not only of labor, but also of land. For moral and political judgment this is of course irrelevant, since the socialist state would use its 'exploitative gains' in a different way; but it is all the more important for our insight into the nature of the matter.

Thus, a whole logical chain of valuable results of Böhm-Bawerk's theory falls into our laps, and it would not be difficult to add more links. In this connection, I should point out only that our proof has also advanced us to the second stage on the way to a complete theory of wages and ground rent. In the theory of value and price, we conceived of wages and rent as the result of the marginal productivities of the two original factors of production. What we can now add—and here Böhm-Bawerk's wage and rent theories branch off from those of the economists otherwise closest to him— can be formulated as follows: wages and rent are the price expressions of the marginal products of labor and land times their quantities, discounted to the present [4]—a proposition that, far from being a deviation from the idea of marginal productivity, is clearly rather a sharpening of it in a certain important direction.

At this point I should mention a further elegant development which, flowing from the same basic idea, enables us to conceive of the phenomenon of ground rent, among other things, as a special case of a general theory and to deepen our understanding of it—the theory of interest from durable goods and of capitalization. Goods that admit of more than one use can be conceived of as bundles of services. It is their individual services that satisfy our wants and that are directly valued, while the value of the good itself is merely the sum of these values; at any point of time, therefore, this value is the sum of the values of the services not yet 'taken from' it. When the services become available only periodically, distributed over time, the valuation of those further in the future is subject to the principle of the undervaluation of future goods and must be arrived at by a process of discounting to the present. A process familiar from economic practice is thus, in an exceedingly simple way, fitted into the frame of a large principle. And from this follows the explanation of the formation of values and prices of such commodities—i.e. of capitalization—and the explanation of why commodities that yield an infinite series of services, as for instance agricultural land, yet have a finite value. And only this analysis yields a strict proof that ground rent is a net return. For what we observe directly is only the physical yield of the soil, which is the same thing as a gross income. Traditional rent theory, ever since the days of the Physiocrats, deals with this aspect of the matter only. Thus, Böhm-Bawerk could say that economic analysis had not at all penetrated to the economic essence of the problem, the problem of a net income. If, for instance,

---

[4] This theory of wages has been further developed by F. W. Taussig, one of Böhm-Bawerk's most distinguished comrades-in-arms.

a quarry yields for a hundred years a return of 1000 crowns a year and then becomes worthless, its owner could not, if it were not for discounting, consume any part of this sum or he would have to eat up his 'capital.' Only from the point of view of the theory here outlined does the rent appear as a net income. We need hardly show in detail how very much superior this whole construction is—with regard to explanatory value as well as depth—to that of Ricardo, how far constructively, not only critically, it goes beyond Ricardo.

We are now in a position to see how the phenomenon of interest, enveloping all other branches of net income, spreads into all economic processes, penetrates all valuations, is, in short, omnipresent. And one recognizes that the net return on caiptal is not simply an income parallel to wages and ground rent, but stands, so to speak, opposed to the latter. This aspect, which was at the time wholly novel and represented an essential step forward, has since been carefully elaborated upon in many quarters and has been brought to a systematic development in the works of Irving Fisher and F. A. Fetter.

We now approach the last step of the stairway that takes us to the top of Böhm-Bawerk's edifice. He was the first to realize fully the significance of the length of the period of production in its twofold aspect—the aspect of productivity and that of the lapse of time. He gave both aspects their exact content and their places in the foundation of the system of marginal utility analysis. He further made the length of the period of production into a determinant of economic equilibrium, thus giving a sharply distinct meaning to the concepts of 'productivity,' 'economic period,' 'flow of goods'; and he brought into the realm of analysis a rich multitude of relationships in economic life which are as yet far from exhausted. But few of his colleagues have so far followed him on these tortuous paths, and the voluminous discussion of his lifework has been so preoccupied with the first stages of his journey that the wealth of results of precisely the kind that the opponents of the marginal utility theory have always reproached it with failing to achieve—in comparison with, say, the Marxian system—has not yet been made accessible to a wider public. And few have realized the genius of his achievement on this very point. The fundamental idea, however, is extraordinarily simple.

The introduction and the exact treatment of the factor of the length of the period of production proceeds by way of its connection with the magnitude of the subsistence fund—which we took for granted a while back. This magnitude is determined when we realize that the subsistence fund provided by the capitalists simply equals the total stock of economic wealth—excepting of course the services of labor and land, and excepting also that small quantity that is consumed by the economy's spendthrifts, in emergencies, et cetera. This stock always has a well-defined size—absent in the old 'wages fund'—which achieves its independent explanation from the theory of capital formation and can be considered as a datum of the theory of distribution. Hence, since the number of workers and the quantity of land are data in any case, we have a new basis for the establishment of objective quantitative relationships—a considerable enrichment of our theory. But how is it possible that the total wealth of an economy consists of 'means of subsistence,' when there obviously must also be produced means of production? Well, the stream of means of subsistence flows of course continuously, and not all stocks necessary for a given period have to be available at its beginning, stored up somewhere. In the latter case the matter would be clear. But nothing essential is changed if all the numerous ongoing processes of production are not at the same productive stage at the same time but rather are staggered according to the degree of 'ripeness' of their product, so that the means of subsistence of the whole period are, at any point of time, in part already being consumed—with intermediate products like raw materials, machinery, et cetera, ready to take their place—and are in part yet to be produced. In this case it is quite possible to say that the total subsistence fund of the period equals the stock of all then existing goods, and that it is contrasted only with the original means of production. It is clear, further, that the subsistence fund, thus defined, is the larger the more distant the aims of production we admit to our range of vision. And finally, since the stream of goods flows continuously and all stages of the productive process are being worked on simultaneously—an assumption not always strictly correct but made here for brevity's sake, and in any case immaterial to the principle involved—it is clear that this stock needs to be sufficient for only one-half of the period of production.

Now a relationship between the two great data—the subsistence fund and the available quantities of land and labor services—has been established through the link of the 'period of production.' This link is now no longer—as it was with the Classics—rigid, but flexible; and we also are in possession of the law of its 'flexibility': the length which the period of production finally assumes depends, first, on the magnitude of the two data and, second, on the choice of the capitalist-entrepreneurs which in turn is oriented toward the largest possible profits. Objective quantitative relationships and subjective forces are combined to form a harmonious whole. Thus we can determine absolutely and relative to one another the length of the period of production, the rate of interest, wages, and rent.

Böhm-Bawerk does not present this result in its full generality but—neglecting rent—only for cases of wages and interest.[5] The reason for this lies in the technical complications, nearly unmanageable without the use of higher mathematics, which this problem raises. But this does not alter the nature of the problem, and we shall likewise be content with the simple case.

The solution is easily formulated: that wage rate will be established which will make most profitable for the entrepreneur-capitalists that period of production which just uses up the total available labor force of the economy at the wage rate mentioned and absorbs the total subsistence fund for its compensation.

In fact, if a random wage rate were tentatively established in the market, the result would be that, given a productivity scale of varying degrees of roundaboutness, one and only one period of production would be the most profitable for the entrepreneur-capitalists.

---

[5] The general problem was later, following Böhm-Bawerk, treated by Wicksell.

It will then be chosen, and with it a definite rate of interest will be determined. If, with this arrangement, the total quantity of labor and land services and the total subsistence fund just exchange against one another, equilibrium has been reached, and its condition, stated above, has been fulfilled. If not, the unemployed quantities of land and labor services and of means of subsistence will depress the rates of wages or the rate of interest or both, thus making a different period of production profitable until the equilibrium condition is fulfilled.

In this fashion the law of interest was discovered: the rate of interest must equal the rate of surplus return of the last extension of the period of production admissible under all the conditions just mentioned. Imagining that this last just possible extension is concentrated in single enterprises, we can conceive of their owners as the 'marginal buyers' in the subsistence-fund market, and consider the law of the level of interest as a special case of the general law of price.

Furthermore, the correct relationship between interest and wages (and rent), as well as the manner of their mutual determination, has thus been established, and a wealth of practical applications has been opened up. To illustrate the fruitfulness of the point of view thus gained, a few may be indicated. First, we obtain a precise insight into the effects of variations of the size of the subsistence fund and of the labor force, as well as of changes in the productivity scale of varying degrees of roundaboutness—changes that will, of course, continually occur as the result of technical progress; second, a solution of the problem of how an improvement in the quality of labor affects interest and wages; further, the knowledge that a rise of wages produces at first a fall in the rate of interest, then a lengthening of the period of production, and finally a rise again of the rate of interest but not to its initial level; and similarly, that a fall of wages will shorten the period of production, raise the rate of interest, increase the demand for labor and thus raise wages, but again to less than their former level. There is in addition the conclusion that the distribution of the subsistence fund among the capitalists is immaterial to the level of the rate of interest, and also that the distinction between fixed and circulating capital has a different and much less significant meaning than that given it by the Classics. The laws of the variation not only of the absolute level of wages but also of the relative share of workers in the social product can, given certain conditions, be derived. But this is not the place to elaborate on all this.

Thus with the simplest means a great victory was won. The theory of the socio-economic process is, in Böhm-Bawerk's pages, unfolded for the first time as an organic whole of valuations and 'objective' facts. Nowhere do we find the stature of the master so clearly illumined by the rays of genius as in the last section of his work. Nowhere did he show so distinctly what theory, in his hands, could achieve. It is striking with what sureness and correctness he employs essentially mathematical forms of thought, though never using a single symbol or adopting mathematical techniques. For these techniques were unfamiliar to him. Those forms of thought he had never learned. Quite unconsciously, with the unerring feeling of the born scientist for the logical necessities and the logical symmetry of his material, he discovered them himself.

To this sense of logical exactness and beauty he joined an equally strong instinct for the concrete and for what was practically important. Never slipping on his path, he knew how to direct his steps where concrete problems awaited solution, and his work is one great chart of treasures to be salvaged by the use of his methods. Through the introduction of appropriate empirical data into his theoretical frame, he brought the prospect of a concrete quantitative description of the phenomena of a capitalist economy if not into the realm of actual possibility, at any rate into the realm of serious hope. I do not know whether he himself ever thought of this possibility. So far as I know, he never expressed himself to this effect. But this possibility will one day become a reality, and his work above all will have led us to it.

To say that his work is immortal is to express a triviality. For a long time to come, the memory of the great fighter will be colored by the contending parties' hates and favors. But among the great achievements of which our science can be proud his was one of the greatest. Whatever the future will do to it or make of it, the traces of his work will never perish. Whatever will be the path taken by that section of our science which was his own most personal concern, his spirit will never cease to be heard:

> *Tratto t'ho qui con ingegno e con arte;*
> *lo tuo piacere omai prendi per duce.*

FRANK WILLIAM TAUSSIG *¹

1859-1940

I. EARLY YEARS (1859-1880)

WHATEVER we may think about the relative importance of nature and nurture or, more properly, of heredity and environment in the formation of eminent men, there cannot be any doubt that in Taussig's case the two combined in a most happy alliance. Still more than we should in other cases, therefore, we feel that, in drawing the picture of the man, the citizen, the scholar, the teacher, and

* Reprinted from the *Quarterly Journal of Economics,* vol. LV, no. 3, May 1941. Copyright 1941 by the President and Fellows of Harvard College.

¹ In gathering material for this memoir, we have received aid from many friends and relatives of Taussig. In particular we wish to acknowledge gratefully the co-operation of Taussig's sister, Mrs. Alfred Brandeis, Taussig's son, Mr. William G. Taussig, and Taussig's friend and classmate, Mr. Charles C. Burlingham. Dr. Paul M. Sweezy has been good enough to compile materials on Taussig from the Publications of the Class of '79. Most of the data about Taussig's father are from his article, 'My Father's Business Career,' in the *Harvard Business Review,* 1940.

For a bibliography of Taussig's writings, we beg to refer to the appendix of the volume, *Explorations in Economics, Notes and Essays Contributed in Honor of F. W. Taussig,* 1936.

[The "we" in this note refers to Professors Arthur H. Cole, Edward S. Mason and Joseph A. Schumpeter. These three constituted the committee appointed to prepare the obituary article for the *Quarterly Journal.*]

the public servant—all of which was Taussig—we must adopt the biographer's practice and first of all describe both his parental home and the two excellent people who created it.

Frank William's father—William Taussig—was born in Prague in 1826. Evidently not liking the surroundings on which the strife between Czechs and Germans was then beginning to cast ever-deepening shadows, the clever, energetic, and well-educated young man decided in 1846 to emigrate to the United States, where, first in New York and then in St. Louis, he found employment in the chemical trade. This was the beginning of a remarkably success-ful and (then) typical American career. After a few years, he aban-doned the crude chemicals of the wholesaler's shop and pursued the finer chemicals of the St. Louis medical school, took his degree, and established a practice at Carondelet—now South St. Louis—visiting his patients on horseback with his medicines and pistols in his sad-dle.[2] Steadily rising in the community, he became mayor, judge in the county court, and finally its presiding justice. The practice of medicine was reasonably successful but the Civil War brought un-bearable strain in that border state. So Taussig, a strong unionist and anti-slavery man, eventually accepted the position of district collector of federal taxes (1865) under the revenue acts of 1862 and 1864, and with the perquisites—since those collectors worked on a percentage basis and either received nothing at all or, if they had enough patience and energy to go to Washington and to insist, quite a sum [3]—he started his fourth career, that of banking. The Traders' National Bank of St. Louis, of which Taussig was a vice-president, was only moderately successful. However, among its customers was a bridge company organized for the purpose of building a bridge across the Mississippi. Taussig joined in the latter venture and suc-

---

[2] The pistols seem to have been very necessary at the time. The son was fond of telling how, when they ceased to be so, his father, by way of celebrating the fact, invited his wife to come out with him 'in order to shoot them off together.'

[3] The son recalled that his father did go to Washington and there, his accounts by his side, day after day sat on the steps of the Treasury until he got a hearing and the money that was due him.

cessively became treasurer and general manager. And this was the beginning of his fifth career, the one that was to bring prominence and prosperity. The enterprise was a success from the outset and eventually developed into the Terminal Railroad Association of St. Louis, which constructed the Union Station for all the roads entering St. Louis and by its own locomotives hauled the westbound traffic from East St. Louis to the terminal. It was Taussig's energy and resourcefulness [4] that triumphed over all the obstacles that city magnates and railroad boards put in the way of the scheme. When everything had been done and all the fighting was over, he was in due course elected president, a quiet and dignified position from which he retired in 1896, at the mature age of seventy. Still busy with all sorts of civic activities, universally popular, admired and respected, he lived until 1913.

The mother, Adele Wuerpel, was the daughter of a Protestant teacher in a village on the Rhine, who was dismissed during the revolution of 1848 and thereupon emigrated with his family. Taussig was married to her in 1857. The marriage was a very happy one. She must have been a charming woman—able and gentle, good looking and good natured, gay and affectionate, a comfort in adversity, a delightful companion in success. She had a fine mezzo-soprano voice and shared her husband's love for music. No problems seem ever to have arisen in the *foyer* warmed by her steady radiance. It is very easy to visualize the kind of home which, first in modest and then in ample circumstances, she created for her husband and her three children—the subject of this memoir, a younger brother who predeceased him, and a sister who survives him—all of whom were unreservedly attached to her. It was a home that was sufficient unto itself, sustaining a family that was very conscious of a corporate existence. No wonder that Frank William emerged from that home

[4] How he impressed a shrewd judge of business ability may be inferred from the following anecdote. The bridge company bought its steel cylinders from the Carnegie works. Some trouble arose about the deliveries, and Taussig went to Pittsburgh in order to straighten out the matter with Andrew Carnegie himself. Whatever his point was, he carried it victoriously—with the result that Carnegie offered him a partnership.

a confirmed family man to whom family life and family responsibility were essentials in the scheme of things.

As we should expect, he enjoyed a happy childhood. Moreover, as his sister observes, 'there was never any doubt of his being advanced in school and in his studies; and the large physical frame that we knew was early indicated. I remember him as a big boy. I also remember that he was never without a book in his hand, either for study or diversion, and that nothing distracted him while reading unless he was directly appealed to. It was his habit to work and study in the family living room. . . As to schools, it was public school, I am sure, until he was about eleven years old. After that he went to a school called Smith Academy. . . There was always much music in our family. Such artists as Rubinstein and Winiawski we were allowed to meet, and Theodore Thomas was at our house whenever he came to St. Louis. Frank must have begun his violin lessons quite early. The foremost violinist of our day in St. Louis was an intimate friend of the family and his teacher, and Frank was well advanced as a violinist when he went to college; and there he played quite regularly in a string quartet and was a member of the Pierian as well. Music was one of the joys and recreations of his life. . . There was no travelling . . . except summer jaunts.'[5]

In 1871 began Frank Taussig's lifelong friendship with Mr. Charles C. Burlingham, when they were classmates at Smith Academy. Together they entered Washington University and together they migrated, in 1876, to Harvard. The Dean, Charles F. Dunbar, proved his good sense by admitting them without examination to the exalted rank of sophomores, although they had expected to take entrance tests for the freshman class. Taussig, pitching his camp in what to Burlingham seemed to be a 'palatial' suite on Oxford Street, proved himself a brilliant scholar. He took every course in economics —political economy as it was then—and a lot of history, and in 1879 was graduated with 'highest honors' in the latter field. He gave one of the 'commencement parts,' the subject of the thesis being 'The

---

[5] Letter from Mrs. Alfred Brandeis to Professor Mason.

new empire in Germany,' and was elected to Phi Beta Kappa. But he was no recluse, though records are available to show that in 1878-9 he took out of the library a prodigious number of books, mainly on history and philosophy. He played on his class baseball team, rowed on one of the six-oared crews in the scratch races, joined half a dozen students' clubs and societies, and formed friendships in all sets. And there was, of course, his violin.

After the B.A. came the European tour. With another lifelong friend, Mr. E. C. Felton,[6] he sailed in September 1879. 'After spending a few weeks together in London, we separated,' wrote Taussig shortly afterwards. 'I went to Germany, and spent a winter, from October until March, at the University of Berlin, studying Roman Law and Political Economy.[7] In March, I left Germany, and rejoined Felton in Italy. We spent two months together in Italy and then went to Paris by the way of Geneva. In Paris, in May, we again separated, Felton going to England, on his way home, while I traveled in different parts of Europe chiefly in Austria and Switzerland.'[8] Some articles in the New York *Nation* published during the travels in Europe, testify, if testimony be needed, to the seriousness of the young man.

When he returned to Harvard, in September 1880, he did so in order to enter the Law School. He had not definitely committed himself to economics as a profession. The law still meant as much or more to him. But he was offered and he accepted the position of secretary to President Eliot—a laborious, though not a full-time job, which introduced him to the arcana of university administration and

[6] Son of S. M. Felton, the founder of the Pennsylvania Steel Works.

[7] It is worth mentioning that this inevitably implied contact with those principles of—shall we say?—conservative reform that were espoused by the Verein für Sozialpolitik. Taussig always acknowledged the influence of, and to the end retained his feelings of sympathy and respect for, Adolph Wagner. We do not know whether they actually met.

[8] From the publications of the Class of '79, *Secretary's Report,* Commencement 1882. In the report, Commencement 1885, Felton adds his own comments, testifying to the fact that they enjoyed themselves 'hugely' in London.

university politics [9]—and thus entered upon the service that was to
be central to his life for the sixty years that followed.

II. ASCENT (1881-1900)

His secretarial duties interfered for a time with Taussig's plan
to study law, but they left him enough surplus energy to work for
the Ph.D. in economics. The special subject he selected was the
history of American tariff legislation, a choice that was as indicative
of the importance, in his mental pattern, of the historical component as it was of the paramount importance, in the hierarchy
of his scientific interests, of the great questions of economic policy.
It is necessary here—and it will be necessary later on—to stress both
points. No doubt Taussig was an eminent theorist and a very great
teacher of theory. The institutionalist opposition that later on arose
against the type of theory he taught, seems however to have overlooked that a great part of his work was on institutional lines and
that, in important respects, it would have been more correct to claim
him as leader than it was to consider him an opponent. To him,
economics always remained political economy. His early training
and his general equipment were not only as much historical as they
were theoretical; they were primarily historical. The practical problem in its historical, legal, political, in short, in its institutional aspects
attracted him much more than any theoretical refinements ever did.
And nobody who knew him can have failed to admire his ability to
see problems in their sociological settings and in their historical per-
spectives.[10]

[9] Among the first fruits of this training was the fourteen-page report
on "The University 1879-1882,' published by Taussig in the *Report* of the
Class of '79, Commencement 1883.

[10] His knowledge of American history was in fact on a professional
level. In 1884 he gave, in the absence of Professor A. B. Hart, a course in
American history. Precisely because it was professional, however, that knowledge did not extend—not at the same level, at least—much beyond this
country. As we have seen, he studied Roman law and he had done much general reading. But neither ancient nor medieval history was ever a living reality
for him.

It was, then, in a thoroughly historical spirit that he approached his chosen subject: international trade. The prize essay of 1882 on 'Protection to young industries as applied in the United States,' which served as Ph.D. thesis and in 1883 was published as a book—and a successful book it was, for a second edition was required in 1884—contained very little theory, but excelled in factual analysis. Incidentally, there is another aspect to this performance that is too characteristic to be passed by, an aspect which foreshadowed his future eminence in the field of tariff policy. It is that balance and maturity of judgment which constitutes so important an element in his greatness as an economist and which in that book, written when Taussig was only twenty-three, shows to an extent that is quite astonishing. As much on grounds of political morality as on grounds of economic expediency, Taussig never was in sympathy with the tariff legislation of this country. He was far indeed from being a protectionist in the ordinary sense of the term. But he was not a free trader either. He frankly recognized whatever seemed to him to be tenable in the protectionist arguments—particularly, but not exclusively, the infant industry argument—and never tried to minimize it as economists who sympathize with free trade are in the habit of doing. This was not his way. He approached that problem, as he did any other, in a spirit that was both practical and judicial.

For another decade or more, his creative work followed the line thus auspiciously opened. The book on *Protection to Young Industries* was followed by the *History of the Present Tariff*, 1860-1883 (1885), and both developed into that classic, *The Tariff History of the United States* (1888, with various subsequent editions extending to the eighth in 1931), which established his reputation as the first American authority in that field and which, as a politico-economic analysis, has in fact no superior in any field. Most of the articles which he wrote at that time also deal with tariff problems, but the other public issues of those years did not fail to attract the attention of his active mind, and regarding two of them Taussig made significant contributions. The economic and political aspects of the silver question seem to have stirred him deeply. Mastering the subject with his usual thoroughness, he started in 1890 numerous publications in that area, and in 1891 produced his book *The Silver Situation in the United States,* which became the standard work of the anti-silver school and exerted strong influence all over the civilized world. Also in 1891 he published in *The Quarterly Journal of Economics* a 'Contribution to the Theory of Railroad Rates.' This paper, alone of all that he did until 1893, indicates leanings toward purely theoretical reasoning, and even that was concerned with an 'applied' problem. His writings do display, to be sure, full command of the analytic apparatus of economics such as it was at the time. But though he readily used it, he does not seem to have entertained any particularly deep interest in it until he was well over thirty.

In view of this fact, considerable biographical interest attaches to the preface he wrote in 1884 for the translation of Emile de Laveleye's *Elements of Political Economy.*[11] This preface is probably the only source for the methodological views that Taussig held at that time, and it usefully supplements what we know from other sources respecting his views on economic policy in general. Also it is highly characteristic of the man. Most of us would in such a preface confine ourselves to compliments and commendations or else refuse to write it at all. Not so Taussig. Compliments are there of course. But they are confined to a chaste minimum and, for the rest, he does not avoid showing, though always courteously, dissent and criticism. He points out what seem to him to be mistakes. He frankly says so when he feels that a certain view of Laveleye's is 'not authoritative.' He commends Laveleye because the latter less completely than others 'had broken loose from what may be called the classic system.' He gives guarded assent to his author's criticisms of laissez-faire and to his advocacy of government interference, although in Taussig's view

[11] He also wrote a supplementary chapter which, significantly enough, dealt exclusively with practical questions. It is entitled 'Economic Questions in the United States,' and its fourteen pages are devoted to a treatment of the tariff, internal taxation, money, silver (here arguing against Laveleye's bimetalist views as strongly as it is possible to argue against a man's views in that man's own book), and American shipping and navigation laws.

humanitarian sentiments seemed to have 'carried Laveleye too far.' 'Concreteness' and 'attention to the actual facts' are approved, but in at least one passage, Laveleye's argument is criticized—all too justly, of course—because of lack of 'incisiveness.'

So far as Taussig's own published work is concerned, the first signs of a theorist's interest in theory appear in 1893. Two papers that he contributed to the *Publications of the American Economic Association* for that year, the 'Interpretation of Ricardo' and 'Value and Distribution as Treated by Professor Marshall,' define his moorings with curious finality. The first tells us succinctly that, to Taussig, Ricardo was the greatest of all economists; and from this 'interpretation' of that eminent theorist, one can deduce why—then and throughout Taussig's life—this was so, Ricardo's only rival being Böhm-Bawerk.[12] There is a fundamental affinity in the mental patterns of those three great men that made Taussig enter into and appreciate the viewpoints—the theoretic styles, as it were—and the contributions of the other two as he entered into and appreciated the viewpoints and contributions of no other theorist. The second paper with equal clearness states the terms on which he, there and then, concluded his alliance with Marshallian teaching, adopting it as one of the main sources of his own classroom work. To this we shall have to return later.

For the moment, we will merely note that two further papers, published in the *Proceedings of the American Economic Association* in 1894, sound the note that was to dominate Taussig's creative work in theory. 'The Relation between Interest and Profits' and 'The Wages Fund at the Hands of the German Economists' are chips from the work he was then doing on the subject of *Wages and Capital* and paved the way toward the body of doctrine which he published in 1896 in a book bearing the latter title. An article on 'The Quantity Theory of Money,' that appeared in the *Proceedings* in

[12] Taussig once said as much to Professor Schumpeter. Since the latter happened to be an Austrian and a pupil of Böhm-Bawerk, friendliness may have had a share in prompting that statement. But in view of the line which Taussig took in his theoretical work, that share cannot have been great.

the following year, completed the groundwork of what might specifically be called Taussigian theory.

But let us return to Taussig's career at the University. The years from 1881 to 1896 were obviously strenuous ones—especially if one adds to his more strictly professional activities his membership on the editorial board of the *Civil Service Record,* his contribution of articles to the *Boston Herald,* the *Advertiser,* and the *Nation,* and his participation in the proceedings of the Cobden Club and the Massachusetts Reform Club. Undoubtedly they were more strenuous than was good for a man who, though powerfully built and healthy, was yet not of that strength that knows not fatigue. There was not much opportunity for relaxation or diversion, although he does seem to have found time to keep up his interest in music.

In the meanwhile—or, specifically, in March 1882—he had been appointed instructor in political economy for 1882-3; and the importance of this appointment was greatly enhanced by the absence, during that academic year, of the only full professor of economics, Charles F. Dunbar. Among other things, this meant that the introductory course (the present Economics A) was entrusted to the young man.

We have now met, for the second time, the name of that excellent man who cannot be omitted from any biography of Taussig.[13] Dunbar was not only the teacher who first introduced him to the science of which he was to become an outstanding leader. Dunbar's formative influence went much further than that fact in itself implies. If we compare some of his essays with Taussig's earlier work on the tariff, we cannot fail to observe that, in tone, spirit, and approach there is considerable affinity between the two. 'It was Professor Dunbar who cast Frank's horoscope and picked him for his own. He had been editor of the *Boston Daily Advertiser* and had retired to a farm when President Eliot persuaded him to become Professor of Political Economy, which up to that time had been

[13] See Taussig's tribute, 'Charles Franklin Dunbar,' in the *Harvard Monthly,* 1900.

taught by Professor Francis (Fanny) Bowen as a branch of moral philosophy.' [14] Since Taussig had assisted in one of Dunbar's courses, it is safe to assume that the latter's recommendation counted for much in Taussig's appointment to an instructorship.

Evidently prospects looked less bright after Dunbar's return. Any really able and energetic young man on the lowest rung of the Harvard ladder then seems to have faced—as he does now—a difficult choice between dwelling, for an indefinite time, in a position not altogether satisfactory, and the more alluring chances of other careers open to him.[15] Taussig provisionally solved the problem, after receiving the Ph.D. degree in June 1883, by accepting, in September of that year, a part-time appointment as instructor (to give a half course in tariff legislation) and by entering the Harvard Law School 'with the intention of taking the regular three years' course, and of practicing after I got through the school.' [16] That arrangement lasted until he obtained the LL.B. in June 1886. Some months before that, however, Harvard had thought better of the matter and, upon his refusal to accept a full-time instructorship, had appointed him Assistant Professor of Political Economy for five years.

From a purely worldly standpoint, the excursion into jurisprudence had therefore been a loss—in the sense that it had been a precautionary measure which eventually proved to have been unnecessary. Yet it is incumbent upon us to emphasize the contribution that the legal training made to Taussig's mental equipment. It is a

[14] From Mr. Burlingham's tribute to the memory of Taussig in the *Harvard Alumni Bulletin,* 30 November, 1940. In that respect, Francis Bowen (1811-90), therefore, enjoys the distinction of having been in a boat with Adam Smith. He was in fact something of a polyhistorian which, however, at his time unavoidably meant that he did not go very deeply into any of the subjects covered by that wide term. His *Principles* (1856; new edition under the title of *American Political Economy,* 1870), though not without merit, was hardly up to the level of those of the English classics whose teaching he rejected.

[15] Subordinate positions at Harvard were, however, more satisfactory then owing to the fact that it was much easier for a young man to conquer what is so difficult to conquer now, a course of his own.

[16] From the *Report* of the Class of '79, Commencement 1885.

debatable question how much a modern economist has to gain from such an expenditure of time and energy that might be sorely needed in the conquest of his own territory. In Taussig's youth the balance of advantage and disadvantage was different. Economics had no techniques which it takes years to learn. All-round competence was a possible goal and a reasonable ideal to cherish. Moreover, legal training then was perhaps the best available means by which the economist might make his mind 'work to gauge.' Finally, the kind of facts, familiarity with which jurisprudence conveys, are certainly relevant to the economist's pursuits. Especially if Roman law be included in the study, as it was in Taussig's case, the gain in the institutional line of approach must always be considerable. Now Taussig's was exactly the type of mind that would exploit those advantages to the full. The legal stamp was, in fact, on his work, both on his teaching and on his research, for anyone to see whose eyes are open for such implications.

He entered upon his duties—which really were those of a full professor—in the autumn of 1886. The half course on tariff legislation went on,[17] the general introductory course was handed over to him,[18] and his famous 'Ec 11' (as it later became) started on its illustrious career.[19] Other courses were added from time to time.[20]

[17] That course, later generalized into International Trade, was given as a half course in the academic years (ending in June of) 1884-94, 1896, 1897, 1901, 1906, 1913-17, 1920, 1921, 1923, and 1925-27. This was a graduate course. An undergraduate course in International Trade, also a half course, was given in 1921, 1922, and 1924.

[18] Taussig conducted the course now known as Economics A (then 'Polecon I') in the academic years (ending in June of) 1887-94, 1896-1901, 1904-9, and 1911-15. In addition he co-operated as special lecturer in 1922-28.

[19] This, a course in advanced theory, was given in the academic years (ending June of) 1887-94, 1897-1900, 1904-9, 1911-17, and 1920-35—an imposing record.

[20] We take the opportunity to list them here:
There were the '20' (reading) courses, 1891-1900, 1907-9, 1911, 1912, 1915-17, and 1920-35. In 1900 this was a half-course.
Then there was a course entitled 'Investigations in economic questions' (really selected problems in economic theory and policy), 1889, 1896 (half

Promotion to full professor followed in due course (1892), and in 1901 the newly established Henry Lee Professorship was conferred upon him. It was not until then that he wrote: 'I may hope to live in Cambridge and work for Harvard until I die.' [21] Practically, however, the appointment of 1886 not only was decisive but there are unmistakable symptoms that Taussig felt it to be so. He settled down. In the class report for 1890, he states with an accent of finality that since 1886, he had 'lived the uneventful life of a college teacher': is there merely contentment in this turn of phrase or also something like a gentle sigh? And, as a further sign of that deep attachment to Harvard that was to remain unshaken to the distant close, we may quote the sentence that follows: 'I was so fortunate as to be appointed just in time to take part in the celebration of the two hundred and fiftieth anniversary of the founding of the University, and, being then the youngest member of the Faculty, seem to have a better chance than any other member of taking part in the three-hundredth anniversary when that time comes around.'

On June 29, 1888, he was married at Exeter, N.H., to Miss Edith Thomas Guild of Boston. Their son, William Guild Taussig, was born in 1889. During the summer of that year he built the house (2 Scott Street) on what was then known as the Norton estate, hoping 'to live here in peace and quiet for many years to come.' [22] The eldest daughter, Mary Guild (later married to Gerald

course), and 1899 (half course);

A half course in Railway Transportation, 1891-94, and 1896;

A half course in Banking, 1896;

A half course in Taxation, 1897, 1898, 1900, and 1901; and

Finally, the undergraduate half course in Theory (Economics 1, as it was later), 1901, 1904, 1906, 1908, 1916, 1917, and 1930-35. Students considered this to be the crack undergraduate course.

[21] *Class Report,* Commencement 1895.

[22] That house, so well known to all Harvard men, remained his home till practically the close of his life. (It was only in the autumn of 1940 that he rented it and moved to his eldest daughter's [Mrs. Henderson's] house on Francis Avenue.) Domestic arrangements were later on completed by a family settlement that gave him the use of the spacious summer home in Cotuit, Mass., beautifully situated on the sea.

C. Henderson), was born in 1892, a second daughter, Catherine Crombie (now the wife of Dr. Redvers Opie), in 1896, and a third, Helen Brooks (for some years now an M.D. and pediatrician at Johns Hopkins Hospital, Baltimore), in 1898.

Besides his teaching and research, his multifarious activities flowed on in a swift steady stream: he currently wrote articles, threw himself into the fight against free silver, served as a member of the Cambridge School Committee (1893-94), as a member of the Governor's commission on the Massachusetts tax laws, as a delegate from the Boston Merchants' Association to the Indianapolis Monetary Convention, and so on. He did his part in the administrative work of the University, which labor, however, never was one of his major interests.[23] In 1888 he was elected a member of the American Academy of Arts and Sciences and in 1895, American Correspondent of the British Economic Association (Royal Economic Society).[24] These things, that might be important in the life of a lesser man, are here mentioned merely to round off the picture for those numerous friends and pupils who may be interested in every detail. For them,

---

[23] Here we will insert a conspectus of Taussig's official activities within the Harvard administration:

COMMITTEES OF THE FACULTY

Special students	1890/91-1891/92
Admission from other colleges	1892/93-1893/94
Instruction	1895/96-1900/01
Commencement parts	1896/97-1900/01
Bowdoin prizes (chairman)	1899/00-1900/01
Instruction and degrees at Radcliffe	1906/07-1908/09
(chairman)	1908/09

DEPARTMENT OF ECONOMICS

Chairman 1892/93-1893/94; 1895/96; 1898/99-1900/01; 1910/11-1911/12

DIVISION OF HISTORY, GOVERNMENT, AND ECONOMICS

Chairman	1896/97-1897/98

[24] In the class report, Commencement 1895, he wrote: 'I am told that the position as correspondent has caused me to be regarded in some quarters as a stubborn and traitorous enemy to American prosperity, but I am content to accept it as an honorable appointment from a body of distinguished men of science'—an interesting as well as amusing passage.

we will add that the sabbatical year 1894-95 was spent abroad—two months of it in Capri and two others in Rome—during which he added to his professional equipment by acquiring a reading knowledge of Italian.

Plenty of work awaited him on his return. The department was growing rapidly and the introductory course numbered over five hundred students. He found the lectures to these five hundred men a serious tax on his strength but also a great source of satisfaction, since they gave him an 'inspiring opportunity of reaching the great mass of undergraduates.' But what proved an even greater source of satisfaction and a still more inspiring opportunity for service, was his appointment to the editorial chair of the *Quarterly Journal of Economics* (1896), a position which he had temporarily filled during an absence of Dunbar in 1889-90 and which from 1896 he was to fill until 1935. Of this, more later on.[25] For the rest, another quotation from the class reports (1895) will fittingly conclude our survey of those years:

> In University politics, I am a firm advocate of the short-ening of the College course to three years [!], and of the modification of the admission requirements in such manner as no longer to give Greek any preference . . . among the subjects that may be offered by candidates. . . In politics I am a disgusted independent, awaiting the appearance of a new party that shall stand squarely on the platform of a moderated tariff, sound money, and, above all, civil service reform and honest government.

III. THE AUTUMN OF LIFE (1901-1919)

Taussig did not feel old at forty-two. There was nothing cramped or galling or hectic in his life. His reputation stood high. To a large extent, he had filled the measure of his ambition. In spite of all this and of perfect physical health, he suddenly found himself

---

[25] Further editorial work was involved in his being elected, also in 1896, chairman of the Publication Committee of the American Economic Association.

unable to work. We speak of nervous breakdown in such cases, which indeed are more frequent in the academic profession than one would infer from the general conditions of a professor's life. He took leave and went abroad for two years, relaxing completely and spending one winter at Meran in the Austrian Alps, another on the Italian Riviera, and the summer between (1902) in Switzerland. Catastrophe was thus avoided, and in the fall of 1903 he was able to resume his teaching and the editorship of the *Quarterly Journal.* Later on, he accepted election to the office of President of the American Economic Association, which he held in both 1904 and 1905.[26] But that was all: the years from 1901 to 1905 are a blank in the history of his achievements.

By the end of 1905 he was his old self again, at least as a teacher and a scholar. (In other respects he had to nurse his strength for the rest of his life.) It was then that he fully developed those methods and fully acquired that mastery of the high art of instruction that established his world-wide fame as a teacher. In his research, he went on with his work in the field of his first choice, international trade, and most of the papers that he wrote during those years belong to that field. The fruits of these labors were then harvested in that rich book which is an arsenal of industrial fact and a masterpiece of analysis, *Some Aspects of the Tariff Question,* first published in 1915 (third enlarged edition, 1931).

Also in 1915, Taussig delivered a course of lectures at Brown University which he published under the title of *Inventors and Money Makers.*[27] So far as we know, this book was the first tangible result of a type of research which had always interested him and for which he was quite exceptionally qualified. The general area may be called economic sociology or the sociology of economic activ-

[26] At that time he was also elected Fellow of the British Academy and of the Accademia dei Lincei. Other honors that were conferred upon him during the whole period now under survey also testify to his established reputation. He received the Litt.D. from Brown University in 1914, and, though *nemo propheta in sua patria,* from Harvard in 1916.

[27] In passing we should note here that he also gave a series of lectures at the University of California summer school in 1916.

ity. The study of institutions is a part of it. The study of individual or group-wise behavior within the institutional setting is another. And in this broad field a realistic analysis of the type and behavior of the entrepreneur constituted one of the most important groups of problems to which Taussig devoted increasing attention as time went on.

From 1905 to 1911, however, the bulk of his energies went into the composition of his *Principles of Economics*—'the result of many years of teaching and reflection.' The work, in two volumes, appeared in 1911. It was an immediate success and became, as it deserved to be, one of the most widely used textbooks of economics.[28] Neither intent nor achievement, however, is adequately expressed by that phrase. To be sure, it was an excellent pedagogic performance, embodying as it did the mature wisdom of a supremely able teacher. Moreover, Taussig took it upon himself to teach more than facts and methods. He taught an attitude and a spirit. He fully accepted for himself a tradition which at least some of us have become disposed to question—the tradition that attributes to the economist the right and duty to shape and to judge public policies, to lead public opinion, to define the desirable ends. Of that duty he had the highest possible opinion, and he meant to fulfill it with that sense of responsibility that was innate in his strong character. Like Marshall, he taught the gospel of his time without ever going beyond it or displaying a sense of its relativity. But he taught it impressively and at its highest. He thus joined the long file of great economists, headed by Adam Smith, who believed that teaching economics meant teaching humanity.

But this was not all. Rightly or wrongly, a textbook is generally thought of as a conveyor of material not one's own. Any systematic survey of the whole field must, of course, contain such material. But Taussig's treatise consists, to an extent that is quite exceptional, of material he had mined himself, and systematizes pri-

[28] Third edition, revised in order to take account of war effects, 1921. Japanese translation, 1924. Fourth edition, largely rewritten, 1939. The dedication reads: *Patri Dilecto Filius Gratus.*

marily the results of his own thought. This is obviously true of the
fourth book or section, which is one of the best things ever written
on international trade. To a lesser extent, it is also true of many
individual points in the third book (money and banking), in the
sixth (labor), the seventh (problems of economic organization such
as railroads, industrial combinations, public ownership and control,
and socialism), and the eighth (taxation).

The first book ('The Organization of Production': Wealth
and Labor, Division of Labor, Large-Scale Production, and so on),
besides introducing the whole subject of economics on traditional
lines, sounds, in the chapter on capital, a personal note which then
dominates the second and fifth books (Value and Exchange; and
Distribution). These books present Taussig's individual version of
that system which we now call classical and which marks the transi-
tional stage lying between the teaching of the old classics (Smith-
Ricardo-Mill) and the theoretical work of our own epoch. He built
his structure on the foundations laid in *Wages and Capital,* which
he had steadily developed during the intervening years—the most
important stepping stones appearing in his papers on 'Capital, Interest, and Diminishing Returns' (*Quarterly Journal of Economics,*
1908) and 'Outlines of a Theory of Wages' (*Proceedings of the
American Economic Association,* 1910). With much of what he
said the modern theorist will be unable to agree. What matters here
is that he conquered a place in the front rank of the group that
boasts of such names as Marshall and Wicksell.

The work that gave final form to the *Principles* was done in
an atmosphere of sorrow. Mrs. Taussig's health had given cause for
anxiety for some time. In 1909-10 he took a year's leave of absence,
which they spent in Saranac, N.Y., and there she died on April 15,
1910.

Research and teaching, however, went on unfalteringly. One
more quotation from the class reports, Commencement 1914, will
round off the picture of those years—which, indeed, remained unchanged until 1917: 'My life during the past seven years has been
quiet, the winters at work in Cambridge, the summers spent at our

house at Cotuit. I continue to conduct nearly the same courses as in previous years, and give a large part of my energy to Economics I, the first course in the subject, and now the largest elective course on the College list. It is the policy of our department, and indeed of the College in general, not to put the much frequented general courses into the hands of young instructors, but to keep them under the older and more experienced members of the teaching staff.' And Taussig goes on to state that in the spring of 1912 he took a brief journey to Europe as representative of the Boston Chamber of Commerce at an International Congress of Chambers of Commerce in Brussels, and then acted as chairman of the Program Committee for the Congress held in Boston, September 1912.

Early in 1917, however, he embarked upon a new career that was as distinguished as it was short. Nature had fashioned him for public service and in a wider sense he was a great public servant all his life. But for about two years and a half he now became one in the narrow sense of the term by accepting the chairmanship of the newly created United States Tariff Commission.

To head a new public agency, to shape its spirit and its routine, to create the nucleus of a tradition, is one of the most difficult of all the tasks that can be encountered in public administration. That is so in any country, but it is particularly so in this one where the 'old stagers' of bureaucratic work on whose experience any new agency can draw, are so rare. Not to fail at such a task in American administrative conditions amounts to proving beyond doubt an individual's exceptional force of personality. For the semi-scientific and semi-judicial functions of that body, Taussig was, of course, the right man and he was by all accounts an unqualified success. His idea of the proper function of the Commission was to stress the fact-finding aspect of its duties and to proceed by cautious steps from research to recommendations that he hoped would in time tend to supplant the ex parte statements on which legislative action in the tariff area was being based. Thus the Tariff Commission undertook, under his leadership, a systematic study of all the important commodities listed in the Tariff Act so as to be able to furnish reliable information to Congress whenever an occasion for revision should arise. Another project envisaged a revision of the customs administrative laws, which were an inheritance from the stage-coach days of 1799, and almost unbelievably cumbersome. The recommendations of the Commission were subsequently adopted, practically in their entirety. Another report dealt with the question of free ports and free zones and still another with reciprocity and commercial treaties, both of which were not only excellent pieces of work but exerted considerable influence in shaping the policy of the country. These reports were to a large extent his personal work and expressive of his personal views. Open-minded and receptive to all reasonable points of view as he was, his outstanding authority naturally made him the leader of his group in a sense that is not usually implied in an official position of this nature. We cannot do better than quote the addition made to the *Third Annual Report* of the Commission, which was formulated soon after his resignation:

> In the resignation of Dr. F. W. Taussig, which took effect August 1, 1919, the commission sustained an irreparable loss. For many years his knowledge of the tariff history and the tariff policies of the United States has surpassed that of any other living man. His books and numerous papers on these subjects form a collection of ably interpreted information to which students and lawmakers have long turned for guidance. At the same time his work and his views have manifested none of the narrowsightedness of the specialist, for the reason that his wide learning in other fields and his acquaintance with business affairs and business men have enabled him to see in the proper perspective the significance of tariff policies and the details of tariff measures. He has combined in high degree the vision of the educator and of the theorist with the sane judgment and common sense of the practical business man. To these qualities he adds a forceful personality and great energy. His selection by the President as the chairman of the Tariff Commission gave universal satisfaction and inspired in all quarters confidence in the fairness, accuracy, and usefulness of the commission's work. At no little personal sacrifice during

more than two years, his wisdom was of indispensable aid in shaping its organization, initiating and planning its investigations, guiding its counsels, and directing its activities.

With the country's entry into the war, Taussig's responsibilities were soon extended beyond the work with the Tariff Commission itself. He became a member of the Price Fixing Committee of the War Industries Board and for a time served with the Milling Division of the Food Administration and with the latter's sub-committee on the meat-packing industry. The burden soon became too great for him and he had to retrench. At the request of President Wilson, however, he retained his membership on the Price Fixing Committee together with the chairmanship of his own Commission.

President Wilson fully realized the value of the co-operation of so able, public spirited, and disinterested an advisor. Their relation was such that, as early as January 1918, Taussig felt able to submit to the President his views on subjects far beyond his official duties, especially with respect to the war aims of this country. Thus it was almost a matter of course that he was invited to join the Advisory Committee on the Peace. Naturally enough, too, the sub-committee of the latter on tariffs and commercial treaties was his special assignment, but he attended the meetings of, and acted as draftsman to, the general committee on economic provisions. He also lent his aid and gave advice on other matters, foreign and domestic.

He had gone to Paris deeply resolved to stand for justice and fairness and in a frame of mind completely free from vindictiveness. There is no doubt that on many individual points that came within his official competence, he was actually able to assert decisive and beneficial influence, smothering dexterously many an unreasonable demand.[29] But precisely how far that influence went we shall never know. Nor shall we ever know exactly what he thought and felt

[29] Many of the smaller questions concerning tariffs and treaties were, in fact, on English suggestion, left to him as an arbiter to decide, though some concessions to unreasonable demands seem to have been made against his advice.

about the more portentous clauses of the Treaty beyond what he told the Unitarian Society of Boston in a lecture entitled, 'A Human Story of the Peace Conference.' [30] In his delightful and almost chatty letters which he wrote home during those months, he confined himself to his daily preoccupations and observations. Part of what he did and thought might perhaps be reconstructed from intimate conversations. But he never expatiated on his share in that work and he was always severely reserved in his critical comments. Some of us may regret this but it was highly characteristic of the man. In whatever he did or said he was actuated by a deep sense of responsibility. He never 'let down' anyone with whom he had co-operated.

Before returning in June 1919, he had handed in his resignation from the Tariff Commission, which actually took effect in August. He served, however, on the President's Industrial Conference, 1919-20, and until 1926 on the Sugar Equalization Board.[31]

IV. THE GRAND OLD MAN (1920-1940)

At sixty, Taussig returned to Harvard, to his teaching, and to his research, with fame and authority still enhanced and with almost youthful zest, evidently resolved to carry out his early vow 'to live in Cambridge and to work for Harvard' to the end.

Again his life flowed on in the old channels. His days were well filled with work that was pleasure, interrupted by short brisk walks and, in the summers in Cotuit, by long hours of swimming and sun-bathing. In the evenings he enjoyed an occasional concert and still more company, mostly men's company of primarily academic description—company that his strong personality good-naturedly dominated to the point of imparting to his dinner parties some of the flavor of the classroom. His delightful and generous nature showing through a coating of dignified reserve, he then became the beloved leader who lives in our memory with all his

[30] An abstract of this lecture appeared in the *Christian Register,* 1920.

[31] For completeness' sake, we here record that he was made Commander of the Belgian Order of the Crown and Chevalier of the Legion of Honor.

shining virtues and with all his lovable little mannerisms.[32] In 1918, he had married Miss Laura Fisher, whose kindliness, for over a decade to come, brightened his home and cheered the youngsters who came to pay their respects to the great scholar in admiration, affection, and awe.

Within his professional activities, the editing of the *Quarterly Journal of Economics* more than ever occupied a prominent place. Both because of what the *Journal* meant to him and because of what he meant to the *Journal,* it is appropriate to stay for a moment in order to define his service and success. From 1896 to 1936— with but a few short interruptions, except for the two years of breakdown—he devoted himself with unflagging zeal to reading and judging manuscripts, inviting contributions, offering suggestions for improvement. Until Professor A. E. Monroe joined in the task in 1929, moreover, he worked with little help other than secretarial. His success was striking. No doubt is possible concerning the level at which he kept the *Journal* or concerning its contribution to the development of scientific economics all over the world.

Such successes are rare. In fact it would not be easy to think of another instance in our field of an editor's attaining Taussig's standard. To define the secret of his achievement in that line is to define his personality, in which strength and broadmindedness had formed so happy an alliance. He led the *Journal* with a firm hand and did not allow himself to be hampered by committees. He occasionally sought advice, but he always decided for himself pretty much independently of such counsel. A man who will do that and who holds his opinions strongly is apt to be narrow and dictatorial. But he was neither. He knew quality when he saw it and he insisted

[32] We shall mention here that he received honorary degrees from Northwestern University (LL.D. 1920), from the University of Michigan (LL.D. 1927), from the University of Bonn (Ph.D. 1928), and from the University of Cambridge (Litt.D. 1933). The last gave him the greatest pleasure. He crossed to England in order to receive it and thoroughly enjoyed both his stay in general and the ceremony in particular—the dignity of which was relieved by the pleasant jokes of the Orator. In 1920, he was elected President of the Harvard chapter of Phi Beta Kappa.

on having it. But it was quite immaterial to him whether or not he liked an author's methods or results. A striking instance of this is his treatment of mathematical contributions. His own attitude to mathematical economic theory was one of skepticism, if not of dislike. Yet he welcomed to the *Journal* the papers of Henry L. Moore and in the last year of his editorship he cheerfully accepted one of the most technical pieces of work ever done in that line. Nor was this all. In a singularly felicitous manner, he faced the problem that articles on matters of current interest present to any editor of a scientific periodical. He wished, of course, to keep the *Journal* in contact with the problems of the time. But he favored contributions on problems that lent themselves to treatment in the light of general principles, and he tried to get, and as a rule did get, contributions that were in one way or another of permanent interest. In the matter of reviews, he preferred review articles on carefully chosen books, thus avoiding another of the difficulties that beset an editor's path.

The exacting editor who set standards instead of accepting them thus became a teacher of the profession. But it is as the teacher of students at Harvard that we think of him when we look back upon the years now under review. All along we have emphasized that his heart and soul were in that work in which he had no equal. He had—admittedly—not only his equals but also superiors in the formation of schools of thought, although he himself formed one in the field of international trade and although the influence of his general vision of the economic problem is recognizable far and wide; he had, however, no equal in this or any other country as a master of the art of teaching. It is now time to try to define his method.

We have seen that he taught a wide variety of subjects. He also acted as tutor [33] and he was an effective and stimulating lecturer. But his world-fame as a teacher is associated with the teaching of theory, to which he confined himself from 1928, and espe-

[33] From 1925-26 to 1931-32, Taussig held conferences with a few honor students, the rule being one conference per student. The College Catalogue describes him as tutor from 1927-28 until 1934-35.

cially with his favorite (graduate) course, 'Ec 11'—a course that shaped the minds of many American scholars and was widely copied in American colleges and universities. And his personal success here was achieved by the method of class discussion. Both this method and the material he chose were ideally adapted to the situation of scientific economics as he found it and as he helped to shape it.

He was one of the first to realize that economic theory, like the theoretical part of any other subject, is not a storehouse of recipes or a philosophy, but a tool with which to analyze the economic patterns of real life. Hence the teacher's task consists in imparting a certain way of looking at facts, a habit of mind, an art of formulating the questions which we are to address to the facts. But it is not enough to understand the tool; the student must learn to handle it. Taussig's way of achieving this end was what he himself liked to call the Socratic method. At each meeting of the class, he started discussion on a particular problem which he admirably knew how to make interesting, and allowed his students to fight it out, guiding proceedings with a good-natured firmness that never has had and never will have its like. Returning from a meeting of his course, he once told a friend, 'I am not pleased with my performance today. I talked too much myself.'

In choosing his material, his practice was to steer a middle course between the doctrines of the past and the doctrines of the future. In his time, what is usually referred to as 'classical economics' (the views and methods of the leading English economists between 1776 and 1848) was slowly passing out of the picture. Nevertheless, while substantially teaching more modern theory, primarily Marshallian, he always kept the classical background in view. Again, in his time new tendencies were asserting themselves that have by now produced a different type of economics. Their development he followed cautiously and not further than he felt the ground to be safe. This policy had much to do with his tremendous success as a teacher. He avoided refinements that would have interested a few only, and at the same time resolutely steered away from what was becoming definitely obsolete.

It is not enough to say that students loved him and that he spoke with the authority of wisdom and experience. Far beyond what such a statement conveys, he succeeded in impressing something of his breadth of spirit and his high sense of public duty upon everyone who came near him.

As before, the fruits of his research in his last decades divided themselves into three groups. First, we may note that among the nearly sixty publications which may be credited to him from 1920 to 1934, the great majority pertained to problems of international trade. Results of his work with the Tariff Commission and the problems of the war and postwar periods loom large, of course—those experiences in fact not only offering opportunities for interesting applications and verifications of his views (which, by the way, were much more successful than detractors of 'classic' doctrine are in the habit of admitting), but also occasioning new progress.[34] A book of collected essays, *Free Trade, the Tariff and Reciprocity,* appeared in 1920;[35] and he bade farewell to teaching the subject, though by no means to his interest in it, by the publication of a masterpiece, his *International Trade,* in 1927.[36]

That treatise contains several novelties, which cannot be discussed here, but in the main sums up, with unsurpassable clarity and force, most of Taussig's work and teaching in the field. In order to appreciate at its proper value the imposing fabric of that work, it is first of all necessary to reduce, to its true dimensions, the importance of what to the modern theorist always proves a stumbling block. The pure theory of international trade is no doubt in a process of radical reconstruction which is bound to do away with most of the tools that Taussig used. He even started from a labor-quantity theory of value which he found useful in clearing up certain basic problems but which cannot be upheld except by means of a number of auxiliary hypotheses of a most dangerous nature. This stamps

[34] See, in particular, his important article on 'International Trade under Depreciated Paper' (*Quarterly Journal of Economics,* 1917).

[35] French translation, 1924.

[36] German translation, 1929; Japanese translation, 1930.

him as a 'classic' in the eyes of many people. But techniques as such never interested him greatly. He implemented his scientific vision with whatever instrument he found at hand and if the latter was Ricardian, its user was, in some respects, far ahead of his time— witness, for instance, his grandiose plan for an international allocation of raw materials. His success with the practical problems that really interested him was astonishing. And critics should marvel at what obsolete tools can do in the hands of a master rather than at the reluctance of the master to part with obsolete tools.

The theory is, however, not the whole of the achievement. It is not even the main part of it. Disregarding the wide horizons, the profound wisdom, the shrewd appraisal of political implications that were his, and confining ourselves to the purely scientific aspect of his performance, we cannot fail to admire the way in which he worked himself, and led his numerous pupils to work, in the spirit of econometrics: the 'theory' is followed by the 'facts' or, as he chose to put it, by 'problems of verification'; and here time-series analysis, though of an unsophisticated kind, comes into its own. But he goes much beyond the usual haunts of the econometrician. He makes his analysis an instrument of economic history and thus leads toward a future that is full of promise, in which theoretical illiteracy will no longer be a badge of honor for the economic historian to carry, nor historical illiteracy a badge of honor for the theorist.

Second, he set up another landmark by his work on the *Origin of American Business Leaders* published in 1932 (Dr. C. S. Joslyn collaborating). We have noticed Taussig's growing interest in what we have termed economic sociology. Individual behavior or motivation was what attracted him first. He then shifted to another approach. He was among those few economists who realize that the method by which a society chooses its leaders in what, for its particular structure, is the fundamental social function—such as, for instance, was the function of the warrior in feudal society—is one of the most important things about a society, most important for its performance as well as for its fate. And he made a bold and original attempt at coming to grips with this problem by collecting, through a questionnaire, extensive information concerning the problem of what the role of the self-made man, or else of his heir, in American industry really was. Whatever we may think of the merits of the methods Taussig used in drawing inferences from the material assembled, we cannot escape the fact that, viewed under the wide aspect which gives to the venture its true meaning, this study was pioneer work and a stroke of genius.

Third, two contributions should be mentioned that issued forth from his theoretical workshop. The one, 'A Contribution to the Study of Cost Curves' (*Quarterly Journal of Economics,* 1923), deserves to be remembered because of the importance which the subject has more recently acquired. It was a result of work done at the Tariff Commission and presented a theory of a 'bulk-line cost curve.' This particular theory, to be sure, did not prove successful, but, again, it was a lead. The second paper, 'Is Market Price Determinate?' (also the *Journal,* 1921), gave another impetus to scientific thought. As far as we know, Taussig was the first to face the fact that economic theory, if it is to be made quantitatively operational, will sooner or later have to work with ranges rather than with points, with zones of finite breadth rather than with functions in the ordinary sense. This lead has not been followed so far, for the excellent reason that it calls for an entirely new technique. One day, however, Taussig's 'penumbra'—a most felicitous term of his—will get its due.

But the day was at hand when the 'inevitable'—as he called it —began to cast its shadow. No major performance dates from any of the years after 1932. In the classroom he still did excellent work. But slowly he became aware of a danger of losing his grip. To a man of his character—to one whose life was his work—it must have been a severe pang. But he did not hesitate. He resigned his chair in 1935 and the editorship of the *Journal* in 1936.[37] Aferwards he

---

[37] The title of Henry Lee Professor Emeritus was conferred upon him. For 1936-7 he was elected President of the Harvard Alumni Association. His pupils and friends presented him, in celebration of his seventy-seventh birthday, with a volume of essays entitled *Explorations in Economics* (1936).

wrote of his retirement, 'My colleagues and friends said they were sorry, and their kind words made me hope that I had succeeded in carrying out what had long been my intention—to retire when people might still say with some show of frankness "it is a pity" and not to wait until they could say with complete frankness "it is time."'

It was fortunate, especially when the *Journal* had gone out of his life, that there was a duty awaiting him on which he had set his heart. His *Principles of Economics* had long been a matter of great concern to him. The revisions in the third edition (1921) had been done in a hurry and had never satisfied him. 'In view of the enormous economic and social changes of the period since 1914, the treatment of hardly any subject could be quite the same.'[38] And he bent his remaining strength to the exacting task of revising, partly rewriting the whole, and of recasting completely the third book (money and banking) and the fifth book (distribution). Securing able collaborators, he succeeded in this last revision, and in March 1939, he was able to write his prefatory benediction. The general framework, the vision and approach were not changed. Nor was the fundament of the theoretical structure.

And wisely so. Taussig's work as an economist has its historic place. From that place it can never vanish. It would not have done to obliterate its strong features by a nondescript eclecticism. Those features stand out impressively if we look at them in the light of the evolution of American economics. In the beginning there were the old masters of practical wisdom—Hamilton and others like him— but, as was natural in an environment where men had other things to do than to philosophize, no home-grown scientific economics flourished. There were protectionist Smithians of the Daniel Raymond type and, later on, such original but undisciplined thinkers as Henry Carey. After the Civil War or thereabouts, things began to move forward, slowly at first and then more quickly. More than any other man's, Taussig's name is associated with the development that wrought the change. But in his formative years, he, like every-

[38] From the preface to the fourth edition.

one else who appreciated serious thinking, had first to learn the English lesson in the form that Mill had imparted to it. Like Marshall, he got the elements from Mill. No keen mind, however, can read Mill without seeing the greater figure of Ricardo looking over his shoulder. And *there* was the kindred spirit whose guidance Taussig felt able to accept, not in a spirit of receptive imitation but in one of creative allegiance. The same difficulties that presented themselves to others who started with the Ricardian apparatus— Marx among them—must have presented themselves to him. And as he struggled with the famous fourth section of Ricardo's first chapter, he hit upon Böhm-Bawerk's work—which no doubt helped him to elaborate a theory of capital that at the same time was a theory of wages. Like Marshall, whose path was different but fundamentally parallel, he did not take kindly to the utility analysis—only still less so. But he felt no difficulty in going on to develop his theory of wages to the point which the phrase 'discounted marginal productivity of labor' indicates. This point once reached, the affinity between the English and the American Marshall becomes still more obvious. Both succeeded in building up an organon of analysis that was classic in the sense in which that term applies to the theoretical physics of the 1890's—in the sense that conveys beauty and simplicity of lines as well as technical limitation. Both made that organon serve a great historical vision and an ardent desire to solve the burning questions of their day. Both were right in respecting one another as they did and right in not surrendering any point to one another.

Completion of the new edition of the *Principles* left a great void in Taussig's life which he incessantly strove, yet was unable, to fill. It was not given to him to rest in idleness. He never ceased to feel that there was still work for him to do. In fact, there was. Few men's last messages are so much worth having as his would have been. But he was rapidly becoming incapable of sustained exertion and nothing—except the sketch of his father's life on which we have drawn—came of the painful efforts he kept on making. He was one of those men who ought to die in harness and for whom *Nunc dimittis* will never ring true.

To the end, however, he was free from the common discomforts of old age to a quite unusual degree. He enjoyed perfect eyesight, perfect hearing, unimpaired power to walk and to swim. He had no personal worries on his mind and he was happy in the circle of his family which for the last time gathered round him in Cotuit during the summer of 1940. At the usual time, the beginning of the academic year, he returned to Cambridge. There he suffered a seizure which left him unconscious for over a week. Without regaining consciousness he passed away, peacefully and painlessly, on November 11, 1940.

IRVING FISHER
1867-1947

IRVING FISHER'S ECONOMETRICS *

THE great American who has departed from us was much more than an economist. But the vast realm over which he held sway and the intellectual climate of the epoch that nourished his thought have been admirably surveyed in *Econometrica*,[1] and I shall confine myself to Fisher's purely scientific work in our field. This will restrict our subject. But it will not lower it—at least, it could do so only through my own fault. For whatever else Fisher may have been—social philosopher, economic engineer, passionate crusader in many causes that he believed to be essential to the welfare of humanity,

* Reprinted from *Econometrica*, Journal of the Econometric Society, vol. 16, no. 3, July 1948. Copyright 1948 by the Econometric Society.

[1] See Max Sasuly, 'Irving Fisher and Social Science,' *Econometrica*, vol. 15, October 1947, pp. 255-78. For other appraisals of the man and his work and for the external facts of his career, the reader is in addition referred to the 'Memorials' by Professors R. B. Westerfield and P. H. Douglas published in the *American Economic Review*, vol. 37, September 1947, pp. 656-63.

teacher, inventor, businessman—I venture to predict that his name will stand in history principally as the name of this country's greatest scientific economist.

I shall restrict my task still further. Mr. Sasuly, who has been a close collaborator of Fisher's, has presented a vivid and adequate picture of his statistical work and in particular has set forth the historical importance of *The Making of Index Numbers* and of Fisher's most original contribution to statistical method, the Distributed Lag. I am not going to repeat what he has written. It is the theorist only, not the statistician, who will be considered in what is to follow. Nevertheless, the statistician cannot be entirely eliminated even from the section of Fisher's activities with which I propose to deal. For throughout and from the start, Fisher aimed at a theory that would be statistically operative, in other words, at not merely quantitative but also numerical results. His work as a whole fits ideally the program of 'the advancement of economic theory in its relation to statistics and mathematics' and of the 'unification of the theoretical-quantitative and the empirical-quantitative approach.' [2] Considering the date of his first book, we must look upon him as the most important of the pioneers of econometrics since William Petty. It is this which I should answer were I asked to press into a single sentence the reasons I have for applying the epithet 'great' so unhesitatingly to his work. Substantially, this work is contained within the covers of six books, the *Mathematical Investigations, Appreciation and Interest, Capital and Income, The Theory of Interest, The Purchasing Power of Money,* and *Booms and Depressions*.[3]

[2] Section 1 of the constitution of the Econometric Society.
[3] *Mathematical Investigations in the Theory of Value and Prices* (his Ph.D. thesis; 1892, reprint 1926); 'Appreciation and Interest,' *Publications of the American Economic Association*, Third Series, vol. XI, No. 4, August 1896; *The Nature of Capital and Income* (1906); *The Rate of Interest* (1907), here considered in its later form, *The Theory of Interest* (1930); *The Purchasing Power of Money* (1911, revised ed., with H. G. Brown, 1913); *Booms and Depressions* (1932). We shall not consider books addressed to the general public (notably, *The Money Illusion*, 1928; *Stable Money*, 1934; and 100 *Percent Money* (1935); or such pedagogical masterpieces as his *Brief Introduction to the Infinitesimal Calculus* and his *Elementary Principles of Eco-*

II

I am sure that Ragnar Frisch surprised his audience when, at the American Statistical Association's testimonial dinner to Irving Fisher, he described the *Mathematical Investigations* as a work of 'monumental importance.'[4] For although the reprint of 1926 and other circumstances have prevented this work from vanishing from the list of great performances, full justice has never been done to it by the economic profession at large. Usually, even competent theorists see Fisher's chief merit in having presented, as early as 1892, a succinct and elegant version of Walras' theory of value and price and in having illustrated it by means of ingenious mechanical models. It is therefore necessary to remind the reader of what the book's contribution really consisted in.

Before trying to define this contribution, we must attend to another duty. This is the place to do justice to Fisher personally. For this purpose, we must not confine ourselves to those points in his work that were *objectively* novel but we must take account also of all that was *subjectively* novel in it, that is, of all that he found out himself in ignorance of other work that anticipated his. We do this in other cases—e.g. in the cases of Ricardo or Marshall—and it is only by so doing that we may hope to get a true conception of the intellectual stature of some of the greatest figures of our science. Applying this principle to Fisher's *Mathematical Investigations,* we discover that the usual evaluation is inadequate even so far as it goes. In a history of analytic economics, no name other than Walras' should be associated with the equations of general equilibrium. But for our purpose it is pertinent to recall Fisher's statement (Preface of 1892) that he found the equations of chapter iv, §10—which do not give the whole of the Walrasian system but do give its core— in 1890 'when he had read no mathematical economist except Jevons.' Moreover, it was 'three days after Part ii was finished' that

nomics. But a few out of a great number of papers will be mentioned as occasions arise.

[4] See *Econometrica,* vol. 15, April 1947, p. 72.

he 'received and saw for the first time Professor Edgeworth's *Mathe-matical Psychics,*' and, though the indifference varieties, preference directions, et cetera rightly stand in Edgeworth's name and in no-body's else, we also have a right to recall this statement of Fisher when trying to form an idea of the mental powers of our departed friend. He had Jevons' work and that of Auspitz and Lieben to start from and to help him. But *subjectively* he did much more than reformulate, simplify, and illustrate Walras.

Wholly his own, however, was his performance in the field of what, for want of a better expression, I must call utility theory—unless the reader will allow me to use my own term, Economic Po-tential. I find it extraordinarily difficult to say what I want to say about this performance and not only for lack of space. The present state in that field renders it all but impossible to state my remarks so as to avoid misunderstanding. Above all, Fisher's contribution was curiously Janus-faced. Let us look at the two faces separately.

The one reminds us of Pareto. Eight years (at least) before the latter's renunciation of utility as a psychic entity (not to say quantity), Fisher, in Part II of the *Mathematical Investigations,* anticipated in substance the line of argument that then runs on from Pareto to Barone, Johnson, Slutsky, Allen and Hicks, Geor-gescu, and finally to Samuelson. Both Jevons' final utility and Edge-worth's indifference varieties were foisted upon Bentham's (or Bec-caria's) calculus of pleasure and pain, and Edgeworth had gone out of his way not only to do obeisance to Utilitarianism but also to emphasize this lineage by introducing Fechner's 'just perceivable increments of pleasure.' Fisher felt that 'utility must be capable of a definition which shall connect it with its positive or objective com-modity relations' (Preface, p. vi). But in Part II he went further than this. After exploring trails that open up so soon as the utility of each commodity is treated as a function of the quantities of all commodities, he ended up with results (incompletely restated in §8 of chapter IV) that go far toward the suggestion to do without any kind of utility at all: what is left is a concept that lacks any psychological connotation and contains the germs of all the pieces of apparatus that were to emerge in Pareto's wake. Though Fisher did not use the term, he really was the ancestor of the logic of choice. Even details—such as the question of integrability—that were to play a role in later discussions, are to be found in these pages.

But there is the other face which reminds us of Frisch. Before taking the road at the logical endpoint of which lies Samuelson's consistency postulate or, as some might put it, the proof that utility is both an inadmissible and a redundant construct, Fisher, with unsurpassable simplicity and brilliance, supplied the theory of the measurement of this nonexistent and superfluous thing by defining its unit ('util') under the restriction that the utility of any one or at least of one commodity depends on its own quantity only and is independent of the quantities of other commodities.[5] This restriction may be inadmissible. The defects of the method indicated may be as numerous as were the defects of Columbus' flagship if judged by comparison with a modern liner. Nevertheless, it was one of the greatest performances of nascent econometrics. I hope that the readers of *Econometrica* are familiar with the further developments that are mainly associated with the name of Frisch. But I wish to return to the question: how was it possible for a man who was able to write Part II of *Mathematical Investigations* to conceive of measuring marginal utility as a justifiable goal of econometric research? Did he turn out the concept by one door—as he undoubtedly did in Part II—only in order to let it in by another? The answer seems to be this.[6] Actually, he turned out psychological utility completely—

----

[5] The reader knows how Fisher followed this up by the most striking of all his pedagogical masterpieces, the paper on 'Measuring Marginal Utility' that he contributed to *Economic Essays in Honor of John B. Clark,* 1927. The method for carrying out actual measurements may not be statistically satisfactory. But it illustrates the idea to perfection and it also does something else: it indicates a possibility of relaxing on the condition of independence, a possibility that was developed in another connection, by A. Wald ('The Approximate Determination of Indifference Surfaces by Means of Engel Curves,' *Econometrica,* vol. 8, April 1940, pp. 97-116). On the relation of Frisch's well-known work to Fisher's, see the former's Introduction to his *New Methods of Measuring Marginal Utility,* 1932.

[6] It is in part supplied by Frisch's axiomatics in 'Sur un Problème d'économie pure' (*Norsk Matematisk Forenings Skrifter* 16, 1926) which

also in Part 1—without ever letting it in again although, just like Pareto, he did retain turns of phrase that tend to obliterate this. But, unlike Pareto, he realized that a meaningful problem of measurement occurs also within the logic of choice or, to put it differently, that cardinal utility and psychological utility are not as closely wedded as most of us seem still to believe. We may wish to measure heat without wishing—or being able—to measure the sensation of heat. I am aware, of course, that the whole idea is under a cloud just now and that hardly anyone is interested in it. But it will come back.

III

The Walrasian system presents behavior (or maximizing) equations that embody theorems of the logic of choice, the choices being made subject to restrictions, part of which enter into the behavior equations and another part of which are contained in the system's balance equations. This system is very general and admits of different interpretations, in other words, may be made to produce different 'theories' according to the manner in which we conceptualize the phenomena of which it is to serve as a model. In order to have a unique meaning [7] it must, therefore, be supplemented by something which is, in the strict logical sense, nothing more than a

goes far beyond Fisher. It is curious, however, that neither Fisher nor Frisch went further into a matter in which both were evidently deeply interested. Fisher, in particular, considering his partiality for mechanical analogies, might have been expected to grapple, however tentatively, with the problems that arise from the fact that the relations that enter any satisfactory theory of utility, in addition to being nonholonom (containing equations between differentials of the commodity co-ordinates that need not be integrable: this Fisher was the first to point out) are sure to be rheonom (to contain time explicitly).

[7] This uniqueness of meaning has, of course, nothing to do with the uniqueness of the set of values that satisfies it, i.e. with the question whether or not the system is uniquely determined that has attracted so much attention of late. The theorists of Fisher's formative age, and he himself, were in the habit of taking this latter question rather lightly. Still less than about the question of the existence of a unique set of solutions, they bothered about the question whether there is in the system a tendency to evolve toward this set, if it exist.

semantic code but which, for the economist, involves his whole vision of the structure of the economic universe that he is to analyze, and prejudges many of the results that will emerge from his analysis. But concepts imply *relations* and since theory, so far as it consists in setting up rational schemata, is essentially a theory of an economic calculus, we may, instead of saying that the Walrasian system presupposes the solution of a problem of conceptualization, also say that it presupposes a schema of economic accounting. We know from experience, old and recent, that this conceptualization or schema of accounting centers in the themes of capital values and income values. This is why Walras included in his *Éléments d'économie politique pure* a few paragraphs that might have been entitled: elementary principles of accounting. And this is also why Irving Fisher supplemented the *Investigations* by a volume on the *Nature of Capital and Income*. So far as I can make out, this volume too was only moderately successful. Most people saw nothing in it but a continuation of the time-honored discussion of those two concepts of which they had every right to be tired. A few, Pareto among them, admired it greatly, however.[8]

In the first place, Fisher accomplished a task that was long overdue. I do not know whether others are as impressed as I am by the historical fact that economists habitually neglect to avail themselves of obvious opportunites and to take the obvious line. The fate of D. Bernoulli's suggestive tract is a case in point. Economists' failure to join forces with engineers is another. But nothing is more illustrative of that attitude than is the neglect by nineteenth-century economists of the opportunities to learn from accounting and actuarial practice and in turn to try to rationalize it from the standpoint of economic theory. Attempts to do both are of comparatively recent origin and the more important of them, though no doubt subconsciously, follow Fisher's example. The response from accountants was only in part favorable, Professor Canning's

---

[8] I do not know whether Pareto ever expressed his high opinion of the book in print. But he did express it in conversation.

work being the outstanding instance. Others criticized. But never mind. The essential thing is that Fisher broke the ice.

In the second place, Fisher's performance in this field may be likened to his performance in the field of index-number theory. When he entered the latter, about a century and a half had elapsed since Carli or nearly two centuries since Fleetwood. A huge amount of work had gone into the subject. Fisher's contribution was systematization on the one hand, and rationalization on the other, i.e. the setting up of a number of criteria that index numbers ought to satisfy. He proceeded similarly in matters of capital and income. Proceeding from the purposes these concepts were actually intended to serve, he deduced rationally a set of definitions of Wealth, Property, Services, Capital, Income that was new by virtue of the very fact that it fitted a rational schema. The result was not to everyone's taste. Again it is the exemplary procedure which matters and which, among other things, produced the modern emphasis upon the distinction of funds and flows. It also produced the definition: earned income = realized income less depreciation, or plus appreciation, of capital (p. 238) which, each term taken in Fisher's sense, is associated with the much-discussed proposition that savings are no proper object of income taxation or that the taxation of savings spells double taxation.[9]

[9] We shall not expect that a conceptual arrangement that yields so unpopular a result commended itself to economists. All the more important is it to emphasize that Fisher made a strong case for it (see especially chapter xiv, §10). Also the unpopular result is inescapable if we accept his psychic-income concept (the idea of which and term for which are due to F. A. Fetter), and Fisher has invariably won out, by virtue of his impeccable logic, in the controversies that arose on the subject. But it is for me a source of wonder how he can have believed—as he evidently did—that this logic would convert anyone who wishes to see savings taxed or be needed by anyone who does not. Views on taxation are ideological rationalizations of interests and resentments, and even if they were more than that, we should certainly make the question of whether or not to tax savings dependent upon considerations (such as remedial effects of taxation of savings in a depression and remedial effects of an exemption of savings in an inflation) other than the logical implications of a definition. I mention this because belief in reason—formal logic even—was so characteristic of this modern Parsifal. This bent of his

In the third place, the work cleared the ground for advance upon the theory of interest. The principle involved is, of course, Böhm-Bawerk's or, if you prefer, Jevons'. But one needs only to observe, and to purify analytically, the discounting processes of business practice in order to arrive at the conception of the relation between capital and income values that the book elaborates. This relation in turn suggests the idea that interest is not a return to a particular class of means of production but the result of that discounting process which is applicable—as a matter of logical principle— to all. That, e.g. the 'rent of land' should not be co-ordinated with 'interest of capital' had been seen though it had not been stated in so many words by Marshall whose concept of quasi-rent points in this direction. It had been stated explicitly by Fetter. But it was Fisher who carried out all implications and erected on this basis a structure of his own.

IV

Thus, as *The Nature of Capital and Income* was, in a sense, a companion volume to the *Investigations,* so *The Rate of Interest* (1907) was the outcome of both and, of course, of *Appreciation and Interest.* In its revised form to which alone the following comments refer [10]—published under the title of *The Theory of Interest* in 1930—the book is a wonderful performance, the peak achievement, so far as perfection within its own frame is concerned, of the literature of interest.[11] First, but much the least, the work is a pedagogical

mind, together with his habit of taking slogans, programs, policies, institutions (such as the League of Nations) at face value, made him, perhaps a bad adviser in the nation's or the world's affairs. But it also made him still more lovable than a more worldly Fisher would have been.

[10] This is not to say that the specialist can dispense with the older book altogether. The sketch of the history of the theory of appreciation and interest in the appendix to chapter v of *The Rate of Interest,* and the appendix to section 3 of this chapter, for instance, are left out in the later work.

[11] The reader will understand and appreciate it, if, throughout the section, I speak from the standpoint of the body of thought that culminates in Fisher's masterpiece, and if I refrain from saying what might be said against it from my own standpoint. In return, so I hope, the reader will do

masterpiece. It teaches us, as does no other work I know, how to satisfy the requirements of both the specialist and the general reader without banishing mathematics to footnotes or appendices, and how to lead on the layman from firmly laid foundations to the most important results by judicious summaries and telling illustrations. Second, the work is explicitly econometric in parts. The difference this makes can be made to stand out by comparing it to any other work on the theory of interest. Third and above all, the work is an almost complete theory of the capitalist process as a whole, with all the interdependences displayed that exist between the rate of interest and all the other elements of the economic system. And yet this interplay of innumerable factors is powerfully marshalled around two pillars of explanation: Impatience (time discount) and Investment Opportunity (marginal rate of return over cost).[12] The book is dedicated 'to the Memory of John Rae and of Eugen von Böhm-Bawerk, who laid the foundations upon which I have endeavored to build.' Quite so. But not everyone would have said it. Nor would everyone have disclaimed originality in fundamentals. Let us pause to pay our respects to Fisher's character but at the same time recog-

me the favor of not interpreting what he will read as a disavowal of what I have myself written on the subject.

[12] Lord Keynes stated explicitly (*General Theory,* pp. 140-41) that Fishes 'uses his rate of return over cost in the same sense and for precisely the same purpose as I employ the marginal efficiency of capital.' I think that this statement should be allowed to stand in spite of the protests of some of Keynes's disciples. More important is it, however, that Keynes *himself* also accepted (ibid. pp. 165-6) the time-discount factor, i.e. the whole of Fisher's theory. The time discount he identified with his own propensity to save (therefore also with his propensity to consume) in nearly the same way in which he identified his marginal efficiency of capital with Fisher's marginal rate of return over cost. Only as an amendment and on the ground that it is 'impossible to deduce the rate of interest merely from a knowledge of these two factors' [in the short run?], he introduced *in addition* liquidity preference. In itself, this does not make a great deal of difference. But actually it *was* to make a great deal owing to the increasing emphasis that Keynes and his followers were to put upon this element of the case. It then came to serve the purpose of making the rate of interest a function of the quantity of money, an arrangement that Fisher always repudiated. One reason for this difference is that Fisher's was not an underemployment model.

nize the originality of the structure which he erected on those foundations.

The core of the work is Part III, which carries out, with admirable neatness, the program enshrined in the propositions that the theory of interest is really identical with the whole of the theory of 'value and distribution' and that interest is not a separate branch of income in addition to wages, rents, and profits but only an aspect of all income streams. Part II goes over the same ground for the benefit of the nonmathematical reader. Part I links the argument to the conceptual apparatus developed in *Nature of Capital and Income*. Part IV is a receptacle for impedimenta that would have hampered the troops on the march and contains, among other things, the important Chapter xv—which, rather than Chapter xxi, is the real summary of the book's argument—the strikingly original Chapter xvi—'Relation of Discovery and Invention to Interest Rates'— in which Fisher broke new ground, and Chapter xix which presents the result of no less original statistical work as stated already.[13] Splendid wheat, all of this, with very little chaff in between.[14]

Fisher's interest analysis is essentially income analysis in the sense that the principle of choice between alternatively available income streams is made the pivot on which economic analysis in general is to turn. This income analysis is couched in real terms, basically, and treats the monetary element as a vehicle of the shifting of receipts in time rather than under the liquid-asset aspect. Anyone who wishes to do so can, however, insert the latter and for the rest we should be further along if we had chosen Fisher's work as the

[13] As pioneer work this chapter retains its historical importance irrespective of what we think of its methods in the light of later developments of statistical theory. Moreover, it contains suggestions for the construction of dynamic models (see below, section vi) some of which have not been exploited as yet.

[14] The criticism of Böhm-Bawerk's teaching on the 'technical superiority of present goods' in §6 of chapter xx must, I fear, be classed with the chaff. By that time it should have been clear that, whatever may be said about Böhm-Bawerk's technique, there was no real difference between him and Fisher in fundamentals. Other criticisms, however, e.g. that of waiting considered as a cost (p. 487), constitute brilliant pieces of reasoning.

basis of our own. This, however, has not been done to any great
extent.

V

A comprehensive system of economic theory, then, had been
partly worked out and partly sketched out in *The Rate of Interest*.
In particular, all the essentials of a theory of money were there.
However, like most great system builders, Fisher felt the impulse
to treat the problems of money with all the pomp and circumstance
of a central theme. This he did in his *Purchasing Power of Money*.
Again, let us first notice the work's most obvious claim to historical
importance: it was another of Fisher's great pioneer ventures in
econometrics. There was presented his early work in price-index
numbers. There appeared his index of the Volume of Trade and
other creations that were then novel, among them his ingenious
method of estimating the velocity of money.[15] Also, there was an
elaborate attempt at statistical verification of results.[16] All these
pieces of research are among the classics of early econometrics. The
really important thing, however, is that the whole argument of the
book is geared to the criterion of statistical operationality and that
it avoids any concept or proposition that is not amenable to statistical measurement. Once more, for better and for worse, Fisher nailed
his flag to the econometric mast.

It is less easy to show that the book is the most important link
between the older theories of money and those of today. As was his
habit, he made no claims to originality. The book is dedicated to
Newcomb, and other predecessors could be readily mentioned. Yet
the central chapters, iv, v, and vi, represent a contribution that was
more than synthesis. Fisher accepted without question what then
was still a new theory of bank credit. He assigned a pivotal role to

[15] Fisher's first paper on this subject—which harks back to Petty, but
had been taken up again by Kemmerer—appeared in December 1909 in the
Journal of the Royal Statistical Society. Kinley's work followed, largely inspired by Fisher's.
[16] Fisher subsequently published estimates of the items that enter the
equation of exchange for a number of years.

the lag of the interest rate in the credit cycle. He explicitly recognized the variability of velocity—remember that the postulate of constant velocity used to be considered, and is sometimes considered even now, as the main characteristic as well as blemish of the 'old' monetary theories. And he took due account of a host of factors (some of which combined under the label 'conditions of production and consumption') that help to determine purchasing power. All this does not amount to a full integration of the theory of money with the theory of prices and distributive shares, still less with the theory of employment. But it constitutes a stepping stone between money and employment.

If that be so, why was it that friends and foes of *The Purchasing Power of Money* saw nothing in it but another presentation, statistically glorified, of the oldest of old quantity theories—that is, a monument of an obsolescent theory that was to become quite obsolete before long? The answer is simple: because Fisher said so himself—already in the Preface and then repeatedly at various strategic points. Nor is this all. He bent his forces to the task of arriving actually at a quantity-theory result, viz. that at least 'one of the normal effects' of an increase in the quantity of money is an 'exactly proportional increase in the general level of prices.' For the sake of this theorem he discarded his recognition of the fact that variations in the quantity of money might ('temporarily') exert an influence upon velocity and reasoned after all on the hypothesis that the latter was an institutional constant. For the same reason he postulated that deposit currency tends to vary proportionately with legal-tender (reserve) money. All the rich variety of factors that do interact in the monetary process was made to disappear—as 'indirect' influences— behind the five factors (quantities of basic money and deposits, their two velocities, and volume of trade) to which he reserved the role of 'direct influences' upon the price level which thus became the dependent variable in the famous Equation of Exchange. And it was *this* theory which he elaborated with an unsurpassable wealth of illustrations, whereas he shoved all his really valuable insights mercilessly into Chapters IV, V, VI, and disposed of them semicontemptuously as mere disturbances that occur during 'transition periods' when indeed the quantity theory is 'not strictly true' (Chapter VIII, §3). In order to get at the core of his performance, one has first to scrap the façade which was what mattered to him and to both his admirers and opponents and on which he had lavished his labors.

But why should he have thus spoiled his work? His own verification though declared satisfactory does not bear out the more rigid of his formulations (see, e.g. the result arrived at for 1896-1909, p. 307 of the revised edition). Several of his own arguments in *The Theory of Interest* and in his writings on business cycles clash with them. It cannot be urged that much of his or any quantity theory can in fact be salvaged by interpreting it strictly as an equilibrium proposition [17]—valid, as it were, for a sort of Marshallian long-run normal. For, on Fisher's own showing, this equilibrium is not arrived at by a mechanism that could be fully understood in terms of his five factors alone. It can only be summed up but it cannot be 'causally explained' in terms of these. Moreover, he applied the equation of exchange year by year, hence also to conditions that were certainly far removed from any equilibrium. I cannot help thinking that the scholar was misled by the crusader. He had pinned high hopes to the Compensated Dollar. His reformer's blood was up. His plan of stabilizing purchasing power had to be simple—as were the ideas he was to take up later on, Stamped Money and Hundred Percent—in order to convince a recalcitrant humanity, and so had to be its scientific base. This is enough in order to suggest my own solution for what has always seemed to me an enigma.[18] I have no wish to pursue the subject of economists' crusading any further. Let me, however, ask the reader: in this case at least, if in no other, what did Fisher himself, or economics, or this country, or the world gain by this crusade?

[17] In justice to Fisher we must never forget that most of the current objections to it are derived from phenomena that belong to Fisher's transition periods. Also the problem of verification looks somewhat more hopeful if this point be taken into account.

[18] The fact that his was an essentially 'mechanistic' mind is also relevant, of course.

VI

The monetary reformer also stepped in to impair both the scientific and the practical value of Fisher's contributions to business-cycle research. But in themselves they are much more important than most of us seem to realize.[19] They are, once more, models of econometric research and have perhaps influenced the development of its standard procedure. Fisher's econometrics there took a definitely dynamic turn: the paper of 1925 suggested an explicitly dynamic model (see last footnote), several years before the boom in such models set in. Finally, with admirable intuition, he listed all the more important 'starters' of the cyclical movement, the modus operandi of which need only be worked out to yield a satisfactory explanatory schema.

But in order to realize this, we must again perform an operation of 'scrapping the façade.' The 'starters' are not where they belong, viz. in the place of honor at the beginning. They are shoved into Chapter IV. On the surface, we have overindebtedness and the process of its deflation, 'the root of almost all the evils.' Or, in other words, everything is being reduced to a mechanically controllable surface phenomenon with the result that Fisher actually deprecated the use of the term 'cycle' as applied to any actual historical event (p. 58). And expansion and contraction of debt, associated as they are with rising and falling price levels, land us again in monetary reform, the subject Fisher was really interested in when he wrote the book. This time the Compensated Dollar, while still recom-

---

[19] Fisher's first contributions in this field are to be found in *The Rate of Interest* and *The Purchasing Power of Money*. Then came several important papers, chiefly 'The Business Cycle Largely a Dance of the Dollar' (*Journal of the American Statistical Association,* December 1923) and 'Our Unstable Dollar and the So-called Business Cycle' (ibid., June 1925). I wonder whether I am right in believing that the latter paper was the first economic publication to present a dynamic schema—$T(t + w) = a + m^2 P'(t)$—in which fluctuations were shown to result from factors that do not fluctuate themselves ('oscillators'). It was therefore a curious slip when Fisher wrote in 1932 (*Booms and Depressions,* Preface) that the field of business cycles was 'one which I had scarcely ever entered before.' His name would stand in the history of this field even if he had ceased to write in 1925.

mended, received but modest emphasis. Instead of the vigorous advocacy of this particular plan that we found in *The Purchasing Power of Money,* we find in Part III of *Booms and Depressions* (entitled Factual) a simple and popularly worded survey of means of monetary control in which hardly any economist will find much matter for disagreement and which includes practically all the policies of 'reflation' that were either adopted or proposed in the subsequent years. I do not want to belittle the merit, or to question the wisdom, of almost everything Fisher wrote there. On the contrary, considering the date of publication, I believe him to be entitled to more credit than he received. But I do wish to emphasize that this was not the only merit of the book and that, though but imperfectly sketched, something much larger and deeper looms behind the façade.[20]

VII

The *Investigations, Appreciation and Interest, The Nature of Capital and Income, The Theory of Interest, The Purchasing Power of Money, Booms and Depressions,* are the pillars and arches of a temple that was never built. They belong to an imposing structure that the architect never presented as a tectonic unit. From Cantillon through A. Smith, J. S. Mill, and Marshall, leaders of economic thought made their impression, on their epoch and on posterity, by systematic treatises. Fisher never expounded his thought in this way. The busy crusader had no time for it. And nevertheless this would have been the only way to rally his American fellow economists to his teaching. As it was, whatever the reason, he formed no school. He had many pupils but no disciples. In his crusades, he joined forces with many groups and individuals. In his

[20] This could be established still more convincingly from his paper 'The Debt-Deflation Theory of Great Depressions' (*Econometrica,* vol. I, October 1933, pp. 337-57). In itself, debt deflation is nothing but a piece of mechanism, the familiar spiral that we all of us understand well enough. If this were all the paper would not be worth noticing, But it is not all. In fact, the theory of the 'starters' and its implications stand out much better than they do in the book.

scientific work, he stood almost alone. Thus, he had to do without all the benefits that schools, protecting, interpreting, developing their master's every word, confer upon their chosen protagonist. There are no Fisherians in the sense in which there have been Ricardians or Marshallians and in which there are Keynesians. Strange as it may seem in the case of a man of such monolithic purity of purpose, of such width of social sympathies, of such unqualified adherence to one of the ruling slogans of his day—stabilization—he always remained outside of the current and always failed to convince either his contemporaries or the rising generations. But those pillars and arches will stand by themselves. They will be visible long after the sands will have smothered much that commands the scene of today.

WESLEY CLAIR MITCHELL*
1874-1948

$\mathbf{M}$ ITCHELL died on October 29, 1948—active to the last, 'in harness,' as he once wrote me he would be.[1] We mourn a character of singular purity, a fellow worker of firm convictions and at the same time of infinite gentleness, a teacher who was wholeheartedly devoted to duty, an incorruptible servant of truth who was impervious to all temptations, even those subtle ones that proceed from warm and elevated social sympathies, a leader who led by example and performance, without ever asserting his authority or indeed any claims of his own. The aura of such a personality can be, and has been, felt by all who came near him, but it is as difficult to put into words as is the wide range of his interests or the effective ser-

* This article was completed by Professor Schumpeter only two weeks before his death, which occurred on January 8, 1950. [Ed.] Reprinted from *The Quarterly Journal of Economics,* vol. LXIV, no. 1, February 1950. Copyright 1950 by the President and Fellows of Harvard College.
[1] The unfinished manuscript, entitled *What Happens During Business Cycles,* on which he was working at the time of his death, has been mimeographed and communicated to the participants in the National Bureau of Economic Research Conference on Business Cycles that was held in New York, November 25-27, 1949.

vice he devoted to so many causes—to all of them with a profound seriousness which never succeeded in extinguishing the humorous twinkle in his eyes. We loved him and we know that we shall not meet his like again.

This is all I shall say about the man. For the rest, this memoir will be devoted exclusively to an attempt to survey his work and to formulate what it means to the scientific economics of our age, if it is indeed possible to separate the work from the man in the case of a scholar whose greatest contribution was the moral message which speaks to us from every page he wrote.[2]

I

Is there anything in the theory that a man's position in the sequence of 'generations' is determined by the influences that impinged upon him during his twenties? If there is, we should look for formative factors in the decade that preceded Mitchell's migration, in 1903, to the University of California. This decade of scientific adolescence centered in his work at Chicago, where he took his Ph.D. in 1899. But he was of the oak and not of the willow: his own mental and moral texture—traceable, if you wish, to his New England background and an eminently healthy youth on the paternal farm—was presumably too strong to be greatly influenced by his teachers in economics, though a good course on English economic history and J. Laurence Laughlin's guidance in matters of money

---

[2] For all that is thus lacking in this memoir the reader is referred to the large number of obituary tributes which have appeared. I wish to mention specifically several memoirs by Professor Arthur F. Burns—particularly the one contained in the 29*th Annual Report of the National Bureau of Economic Research*—and Professor Frederick C. Mills's memorial address at the 61st Annual Meeting of the American Economic Association (see *American Economic Review,* June 1949), to both of which I am indebted for various pieces of information (as I am also to several communications from Professor Burns); and the memoirs by Professor J. Dorfman (*Economic Journal,* September 1949) and Professor Kuznets (*Journal of the American Statistical Association,* March 1949). Also, the present memoir should be compared with Professor Alvin H. Hansen's in *Review of Economics and Statistics,* November 1949. A bibliography has been compiled by the National Bureau.

and currency policy did leave discernible traces. Veblen was much more to the taste of a mind that was nonconformist by nature, of a quick intelligence that resented dogma and stuffiness more than anything else, that preferred the paddock to the stable, and thoroughly enjoyed, though rarely produced, sarcasms and paradoxes. However, before long he also took Veblen's measure and, if for the rest of his life he continued to emphasize the difference between making goods and making money, he soon tired of the glitter of the more dubious Veblenite gems. But John Dewey and Jacques Loeb opened new vistas that were never to pall. They opened the avenues to a social science much broader than professional economics in which he loved to dwell. This being important in order to understand Mitchell's economics and the nature of his personal contribution, let us call a halt in order to cross a few t's and to dot a few i's.

The 1890's were the first of the three decades of what may be called the Marshallian epoch. However, since not every reader, and specially not every American reader, will agree with all that this phrase implies, let me spell out what I mean by it. Three tendencies then came of age and produced the New Economics of 1900. There was first a novel preoccupation with, and a novel attitude toward, problems of social reform, best exemplified by German *Sozialpolitik*. Second, economic history, amidst surf and breakers, established itself within the precincts of academic economics. Third, a new organon of economic theory—it is really difficult to decide which of the names affixed to it, marginalism, neoclassicism, et cetera, is the least misleading one—came into its own after a struggle which had lasted for a quarter of a century. But, with the possible exception of England where Marshall's leadership succeeded to some extent in uniting them all, those three tendencies were at war everywhere not only among themselves but also with the views and methods of a preceding period to which large parts of the national professions clung tenaciously. In the United States in particular, where the economic profession enjoyed tropical growth, the backward glance discerns little else but the outmoded textbook—improved no doubt by the work of such men as F. Walker but outmoded nevertheless—and, for the rest, chaos—fertile chaos perhaps, but still chaos. Without meaning disrespect to forgotten or half-forgotten worthies, we can easily understand that a youngster entering the Chicago department of economics around 1895 found nobody there to show him the wealth of ideas and research programs that lives under the smooth surface of Marshall's *Principles,* the only work from which Marshall's teaching could have been learned then without going to Cambridge and listening to him.[3] And it would have taken a teacher of supreme ability to present, in 1895 or even later, J. B. Clark's teaching in any really useful manner. So *Sozialpolitik* went by default, economic history remained on a side track, the new theoretical organon was easily disposed of as 'marginalism' or 'neoclassicism,' and the dry-as-dust textbook—more or less shaped on the Millian model—triumphed to drive more active minds into 'institutionalist' revolt.[4]

The curve on which Mitchell's own work was to move can, I believe, be readily interpreted as the intersection of two surfaces: one which represents these environmental conditions and another which represents the propensities of his own mind. A man of his ability was bound to be dissatisfied with the state of things he beheld, a man of *his type of ability* was bound to look for the remedy in the ocean of social facts of which economists seemed to him to absorb but a few miserable inlets. He wanted to swim and not to wade, to explore and not to turn round and round on a small piece of arid land. And two more points will finish off the picture. First, he was as suspicious of logical rigors as the colt is of bridle and saddle and soon spied behind the work of the tillers of that arid plot not only unrealistic 'postulates' framed for the sake of methodological convenience and

[3] For that matter—how many people know *now* what Marshall's critical presentation of the 'doctrine of maximum satisfaction' did to the scientific basis of laissez-faire? Or how much Marshall did to pave the way for modern econometrics?

[4] In Mitchell's case, there was a year of study in Halle and Vienna to interrupt his work in Chicago. But it left no visible mark. And—again without disrespect to anyone's memory, least of all to that of the great Menger—this is what we should expect.

to be discarded at will, but also 'preconceptions' (ideologies) which enslave the research worker instead of serving him.[5] Second, quite apart from this, his type of mind was not made to enjoy or to appreciate what he called 'playing' with the postulates: the work on this arid ground was vitiated by political prejudice or metaphysical beliefs; but even if it had not been, it would still have seemed to him otiose.

If this defines the institutionalist position, then Mitchell was and always remained an institutionalist. I do not wish to enter the discussion about the precise meaning of that elusive concept, a discussion that still flares up from time to time and has produced such gems as the statements that Veblen was no institutionalist at all or that he was the only one. This would be the more unprofitable because everyone who participated in the 'revolt' alluded to above filled in the blanks left by its essentially negative criticism with a positive program of his own. But Mitchell's own methodological position can and must be scrutinized more closely both because of the outstanding importance of his work and because it has repeatedly, and even recently, been discussed in a manner that seems to me not entirely satisfactory. We have to consider three different things: Mitchell's views on the proper attitude of the scientific economists toward 'policy'; his views on the proper method of protecting the scientific result from ideological vitiation; and his views on 'theory.' His opinions on all three subjects changed but little throughout his adult life. And we may conveniently survey them now.

II

As regards the first, his practice is a shining example to all of us. Like other institutionalists, he resented the political alliance that existed between the economics of his formative years and laissez-faire liberalism. But he was one of the few who did so for the right reason. Although social sympathies and a sense of the practical inadequacy of straight laissez-faire programs presumably contributed to making

[5] For a characteristic quotation see Mills, op. cit. p. 734, notes 4 and 5.

.

him averse to that particular alliance, it is much more important that he felt that economists had no business to enter any such alliance. Economics was to be an objective science that puts a storehouse of carefully ascertained facts and inferences from such facts at the disposal of anyone who cares to use them. This did not induce him to shut himself up in an ivory tower. On the contrary he was always ready to render public service whenever called upon to do so. His work with the Immigration Commission in 1908, with the Bureau of Labor Statistics and the War Industries Board during the First World War, and later on, his work as chairman of President Hoover's Committee on Social Trends (1929-33), as a member of the National Planning Board, the National Resources Board, the Federal Emergency Administration of Public Works (1933), and as chairman of the Commitee on the Cost of Living (1944) are sufficient proof of this. But the nature of this work only serves to bear out my point; it always fell in with his conception of his scientific mission—always consisted in observing and interpreting the facts of a situation, in presenting objectively what was actually happening. In cases where ends may be taken for granted he did not fight shy of practical recommendations. But he never went beyond the reserve that, like him, I think appropriate for the man who devotes himself to the analyst's task, and he never peddled any recipes, never advocated 'policies.'

As regards the second point, the ideological danger, his very awareness of it must be recorded as a signal merit. The only questions that can arise in this connection are, on the one hand, whether he was not too prone to suspect ideology ('preconceptions') in authors whose methods and results he did not approve; and on the other hand, whether the remedy he invoked was adequate. Thus, there are plenty of shortcomings in Ricardo's analysis; but if we neglect his policy recommendations and take account of the level of abstraction on which he moved, we do not find many ideologically vitiated statements—as Karl Marx readily recognized. And Mitchell's remedy—careful and 'objective' investigation of facts—will indeed destroy many preconceptions but not all; no amount of care will protect research from the evil spirits that dwell in the investigator's very soul and never announce themselves to him. Never mind—this does not alter the fact that Mitchell was one of the very few economists who have seen the problem in all its depth and who have realized that preconceptions in our field are no mere matter of political prejudice or of sponsorship of some special interest.

The third point, the subject of 'Mitchell and Economic Theory,' presents much greater difficulties than the two others. In part, these difficulties proceed from an ambiguity in the meaning of the word. When in his main publications on business cycles, Mitchell, while listing a large number of theories of the phenomenon and declaring his readiness to avail himself of any *suggestions* they might convey to him, made it quite clear that he did not propose to ally himself with any one of them or to fetter himself by constructing one of the same type for his own purposes, he clearly used the word 'theory' in the sense of 'explanatory hypothesis.' And what he meant may be expressed by the unchallengeable statement that such a hypothesis should result from, or be suggested by, detailed factual study rather than be posited at the start of the investigation. Fairly interpreted, this is a tenable position, and in particular not open to the objection that such a program is logically impossible because, in any case, we must first identify the phenomenon to be investigated and in doing so must inevitably introduce elements that will exert some guiding influence upon our factual research; in other words that there is no such thing as factual investigation, or, in particular, 'measurement' without any 'theory' at all. This is also true; but when we say it we become aware of the fact that we are now using the word 'theory' in a different sense, namely in the sense of 'conceptual tool.' And in this sense Mitchell certainly did not wish to exclude 'theory' from any stage of either his own or anyone else's work. This will be illustrated as we proceed. But it is not all.

Though Mitchell never committed the absurd mistake of objecting on principle to the use of conceptual tools or schemata, he did object to the ones that were actually in use in the 'classic' literature with which he included also the post-classical literature available in his formative period.[6] And this for two reasons, one of which is closely connected with his personal achievement as a leader of economic thought, and the other of which indicates a limitation that prevented his achievement from extending his leadership over a still wider domain.

He strove no doubt to widen the frontiers of economics so as to include the province that is best called Economic Sociology—the analysis of social institutions or of 'prevalent social habits.'[7] The institutions of the 'monetary' (capitalist) economy were not to be accepted as data—though changeable ones—from other disciplines, but were to be made part of the economist's research material. But the essential point was that he did not think of this material, or of generalizations therefrom, as a complement to traditional theory but as a substitute for it. The theory of the economic process itself was to remain a theory, but it was to become a theory built from the results of detailed observation of actual behavior and—since he did not exclude on principle either introspection or psychological inter- pretation inspired by introspection—motivation. We shall readily understand why this approach should have led Mitchell to look upon economic life as a process of change, and why from this stand- point the analysis of business cycles should have appeared to him as the first step toward realistic analysis of the economic process in general. We shall not wonder at, but on the contrary admire him for, his emphasis upon sequences that characterized his thought from first to last. And we shall hail him—that is, the Mitchell of be-

[6] By classic literature I mean the publications of the leading English authors from 1776 to 1848. As regards the literature available in his formative period, we must not forget that Walras (except perhaps the dubious philos- ophy that surrounds the core of Walras' work) hardly existed for him and that Marshall's teaching, as indicated above, never became a living reality to him.

[7] The practice of discussing social institutions together with the eco- nomic processes that, controlled and controlling, take place within them, may be traced to the scholastic doctors and to Aristotle. J. S. Mill devoted about one-third of his *Principles* to what I call Economic Sociology above. But the subject had become dry and unprogressive, at least in this country, when, under the influence of Veblen, Mitchell attempted to infuse new life into it.

fore 1913—as a forerunner of modern dynamics. But, having applauded his premises, we shall question one of the conclusions he drew from them, namely, that the economic logic of what he agreed with others to call the neoclassical theory should therefore go overboard.

When we study the mimeograph of his famous course on the history of economic thought—*Types of Economic Theory* which I hope to see published some day—we are struck by the fact that he objected to his authors' 'postulates' quite as much as he objected to their 'preconceptions.' Up to a point he was right once more: quite obviously, logical schemata or models are not the whole of economics or even of economic theory in his sense and in addition there is plenty to criticize in the manner in which these models have been set up and in the postulates or assumptions that are basic to them. But Mitchell did not object to individual postulates—or complete models—in order to replace them by others. He objected to them *qua* postulates or models and shrugged his shoulders at the people who were concerned about such questions as their determinacy and consistency. And he thought that 'my grandaunt's theology; Plato and Quesnay; Kant, Ricardo, and Karl Marx; Cairnes and Jevons and even Marshall, were much of a piece.'[8] It should be superfluous, at this hour of the day, to dwell on the error involved in this or to point out precisely where a fundamentally sound methodological instinct drove him into error. The simple fact is that it takes many types of mind to build a science; that these types hardly ever understand one another; and that preference for the work one is made for easily shades off into derogatory judgments about other work which is then hardly ever looked at seriously. But it is not superfluous to point out the damage this attitude did to Mitchell's work and to the range of its influence. His aversion to making his theoretical schemata explicit makes it difficult for any but the most fervently sympathetic interpreter to see that they are there—the basic idea of his book of 1913 could be put into a dynamic schema that even enjoys the property of 'completeness'—and such

[8] Quoted from Mills, op. cit. p. 733*n*.

passages as that in which he disposed of the static theory of equilibrium as a 'dreamland' makes it easy for any not-so-sympathetic critic to renounce his leadership on the ground that evidently he failed to grasp its meaning or the nature and meaning of models in general. He never would listen to the argument that rational schemata aim at describing the *logic* of certain forms of behavior that prevail in every economy geared to the quest of pecuniary gain—a concept he understood so well—and do not at all imply that the subjects of this rationalistic description feel or act rationally themselves. And I shall never forget his speechless surprise when I tried to show him that his great book of 1913, so far as the bare bones of its argument are concerned, was an exercise in the dynamic theory of equilibrium.[9] I am not writing these sentences in order to discount the fame of a man whom I not only loved but also admired. I am writing them simply in order to remove what I believe have been misunderstandings on all sides and to open up the way to him for a still larger crowd of potential followers.

III

We turn to the core of his work. The first thing to strike us is its imposing unity. It may have been a happy coincidence that Laughlin suggested to him the Greenback episode as the subject of his doctor's thesis. But, apart from the implications of the fact that the willful candidate accepted the suggestion, it seems safe to suppose that Mitchell would have found the way to his Rome whatever starting point he might have chosen. In his hands, that subject became an investigation into the economic processes of the Greenback episode—of the ways in which the processes reacted to the impact of war finance, and to which the effects of the Greenback issue themselves were but an approach. The fact that, following Laughlin's

[9] For what else are his 'recurring readjustments of prices' to which he returned again and again but imperfect movements of the economic system in the direction of a state of equilibrium? If he failed to avail himself of the apparatus of equilibrium theory, so the (successors of the) builders of the equilibrium theory failed to avail themselves of his facts.

teaching, he gave a bad grade to the quantity theory—which he was soon to modify [10]—is a minor matter. The really important thing to notice in the two works that grew out of this thesis [11] is the vision of the monetary—or 'capitalist'—economy which they reveal. On the one hand, he integrated the monetary phenomena with the rest, thus anticipating tendencies that have asserted themselves of late; and, on the other hand, he analyzed the relations that bind 'prices together in a system of responses through time' [12] which led him quite naturally to the study of business cycles as a first step toward a general *theory* of the money economy of today, his real topic throughout his adult life.[13]

The volume on *Business Cycles* that appeared in 1913 had been simmering since 1905 though the conscious resolve to write a treatise on this subject seems to have been made only in 1908.[14] It is a landmark in the history of American economics—though its influence upon scholars spread far beyond the United States—and cannot be praised too highly. The product of its author's prime, of the span of years when freshness and vigor are unimpaired as yet but already matched by analytic experience and wide acquirements, it was both his masterpiece in this word's original meaning—the piece of work

[10] An almost unqualifiedly negative verdict upon that 'theory' was rendered in what I believe was Mitchell's earliest publication, 'The Quantity Theory of the Value of Money,' which he contributed to the *Journal of Political Economy,* March 1896, while still a student. It is characteristic of the man that he amended that verdict and condemned his early notions on the subject before long ('The Real Issues in the Quantity Theory Controversy,' ibid. June 1904).

[11] *A History of the Greenbacks, with Special Reference to the Economic Consequences of their Issue:* 1862-65, 1903; and *Gold, Prices and Wages under the Greenback Standard,* 1908.

[12] See Burns, op. cit. p. 13.

[13] This important point had better be established. Reference to Burns (op. cit. pp. 20-22) suffices for this purpose. Mitchell conceived the plan of a Theory of the Money Economy, and began to work out its 'skeleton,' in December 1905. Professor Burns's quotation from a letter of that date makes it quite clear that he set about it in the true Mitchellian fashion which made the study of business cycles, as Burns aptly said, a necessary *Vorarbeit* for the larger plan.

[14] See Burns, op. cit. p. 22; Mitchell was then 34.

by which the medieval journeyman proved himself to be a master of his craft—and the code that embodied the law of all the work that was to follow.[15] The essentials of the plan of the book reappear in the volume of 1927. Even *Measuring Business Cycles* (1946) carries out, on a higher and wider plane, part of the ideas that first saw the light of publicity in 1913. Even most of the work of the National Bureau of Economic Research is in very truth their lengthened shadow.[16] Both the methods and the results of 1913 stood the test of the huge amount of research that was brought to bear upon them, although Mitchell, in his single-minded devotion to truth, always stood ready to modify them.[17]

Having defined, as best I could, the place of *Business Cycles* in Mitchell's individual evolution, I have now to define its place in the evolution of the science. This task I approach with considerable diffidence. First, as pointed out before, Mitchell's creative efforts were not simply directed toward the cyclical phenomena *per se,* but rather toward a new economics—or as he himself said, a new economic theory—to be inspired by the 'ideas developed in the study of business fluctuations.' [18] This makes his work incommensurable with the work of most students of business cycles. Second, like the majority of creative workers, Mitchell did not easily come to grips

[15] The reader will understand that this is meant to apply to his essential work only and not to all the parerga. But it applies more widely than one might think at first sight. The two most important exceptions, Mitchell's work on index numbers and in the field of the history of economic thought are readily seen, the first as a part of the general program outlined—and indeed already carried into effect, to some extent, in the book of 1913—the latter as the critical complement (see below, p. 257) of his positive work. And even most of the parerga are elements in the great mosaic.

[16] This turn of phrase is a slightly transformed version of Professor Mills's '. . . the National Bureau of Economic Research, an institution which in very truth is the lengthened shadow of Wesley Mitchell' (F. C. Mills, op. cit. p. 735).

[17] The most important change in method consisted in what is known as the National Bureau method of time-series analysis (see below, p. 258). The most important modification of results consisted in the diminishing emphasis that he came to place upon the role of increasing costs in bringing prosperities to an end and of decreasing costs in stimulating recovery.

[18] *Business Cycles: The Problem and Its Setting,* 1927, p. 452.

with the work of people who were, or seemed to him to be, widely removed from him in attitudes or methods. He was the most generous of men. He read widely. But, preoccupied with his own task at which for prolonged spells he worked with all but feverish zeal, he did not easily penetrate beyond a certain level into structures not his own. This makes it necessary, in justice to his mental stature, to fall back upon a distinction, the necessity of which has often impressed itself upon me in my researches into the history of economic analysis—the distinction between subjective and objective priority. And third (as in the case of the discovery—or invention—of the calculus, and many similar ones) there is the fact that men's minds, at any given time, are apt to converge in similar views but in such manner as to make these men—and their pupils—see secondary differences between one another more clearly than the essential similarites. In the case before us, workers were under the impression that the number of different 'explanations' was increasing, whereas the fact is that a certain family likeness in their conceptions of the problem—of cycles versus 'crises'; their methods—involving increasing appeal to statistical material; and their results—such as emphasis upon a generalized form of what we call now the acceleration principle, became more strongly marked all the time. No one author led in this movement and none seems to have been greatly influenced by the others. But the date of Mitchell's volume assures to it an outstanding position in the history of the movement.[19]

[19] To mention but a few others: Aftalion's work, written in a kindred spirit as regards method though differing from Mitchell's in a few interpretative *nostra,* appeared also in 1913; Spiethoff's, though foreshadowed in some articles published during the first decade of this century, was not available in any well-rounded form and did not reveal the massive basis of fact on which it rested until 1925; Pigou did not definitely reveal his affinity to Mitchell's approach until 1927; D. H. Robertson not until 1915; Cassel (whose explanation acquired different traits later on) not before the publication of his treatise on general economics. Professor Haberler calls Tugan-Baranowski a forerunner of Spiethoff (*Prosperity and Depression,* 1941, p. 72), but I prefer to exclude him from this group. Let me emphasize that I am not trying to discount the theoretical differences within it. Their affinity in spirit and approach is all that I wish to emphasize.

There was of course a forerunner to all these authors, Clément Juglar—the great outsider who may be said to have created modern business-cycle analysis. So far as Mitchell is concerned, Juglar was his forerunner in theory as well as in method. Not only did he write a 'great book of facts' which spurned contemporaneous theory and made clear the necessity of passing from 'crises' to 'cycles,' [20] but he also indicated with truly Mitchellian reserve important principles of interpretation which he believed to rise directly from observation and which culminated in the famous dictum: the only cause of depression is prosperity, or, if I read this sentence aright, depression is the reaction to what happens in prosperity. This seems to me to be the first, though partial, formulation of the theory that every phase of the economic process engenders the next phase and that, in particular, stresses which accumulate in the system during prosperity lead to recession (which in turn creates the conditions for a new spell of prosperity). Mitchell, who independently adopted a similar schema, did not hesitate to call it a 'theory' (see e.g. *Business Cycles,* p. 583, or Burns's résumé, op. cit. p. 26), and this is exactly what it is if we take the term in its proper—that is, instrumental—sense: a schema that must derive justification, if at all, 'in an independent effort to use it in interpreting the ceaseless ebb and flow of economic activity.' And it formulates one of the two— there are only two—fundamentally different groups of cycle theories. There is the 'theory' that the economic process is essentially non-oscillatory and that the explanation of cyclical as well as other fluctuations must therefore be sought in particular circumstances (monetary or other) which disturb that even flow. Marshall stands out in the large crowd that represents this 'hypothesis.' And there is the 'theory' that the economic process itself is essentially wavelike—that cycles are the form of capitalist evolution—the theory to which Mitchell was to lend the weight of his authority. I think it may be said that he went a step further than this: on the ground

[20] See Mitchell's own comment in the volume of 1927, pp. 11-12, where Mitchell also noticed Wade, Overstone, and others who paved the way toward this step, but not Marx.

that the capitalist economy is a profit economy in which economic activity depends upon the factors which affect present or prospective pecuniary profits—equivalent, I believe, to the Keynesian marginal efficiency of capital—he declared that profits are the 'clue' to business fluctuations, which seems to tally substantially not only with the 'theory' adumbrated in Chapter 22 of Keynes's *General Theory*[21] but also with the theories of a group of business-cycle students that is almost as large as the group that looks upon cycles as inherent in the capitalist process. Beyond this Mitchell did not commit himself. In particular he did not go on to say that profits are evidently—somehow, but in any case closely—connected with the processes of investment. But even so we have before us a definite, if only verbal, schema that stands at the back of his factual work. If this schema seems to be less in evidence in the last stage of his work this is because the end caught him in midstream, that is, in the 'factual' phase of his work and before he was able to co-ordinate the fruits of his labors completely.

Exactly like the volume of 1927, the one of 1913 starts with a brief survey of existing explanations. In both cases, they are presented, to say the least, succinctly and with a surprising detachment. Mitchell found them all 'plausible' but also 'perplexing.' He classified them, but without attempting to criticize them systematically. Though he raised an objection here and there, the reader gets the impression that he looked upon them as so many statements of partial truths each of which was pretty much as good as any other and all of which had, on a common plane, to await trial in the court of facts. This impartiality also reveals one of the characteristics of Mitchell's methodological bent that has been mentioned above: for him there was nothing, or at all events nothing important, *between* the explanatory hypothesis and the facts; there was, in particular, no logical criterion that might rule out a theory before it came up for factual trial. But, given Mitchell's distrust of

[21] There are differences no doubt that are emphasized by the reserve of one of the authors and the trenchancy of the other. But the 'clue' or proximate cause of cyclical fluctuations is in the element of profits for both of them.

'neoclassical' economics, such impartiality had its virtues. And it did not, as has been repeatedly stated, leave him without a compass for his voyage across the ocean of statistical facts.

Also like the volume of 1927, the one of 1913 next unfolded Mitchell's vision of the money economy. In both cases, these chapters are in fact introductory treatises on general economic theory as he conceived it. Closely knit and unadorned, lacking effective conceptualization, they have never received their due. To mention one example only: how many people know that the theory of money flows, which these chapters indicate rather than present, anticipates much of what is best in modern income accounting and aggregative analysis? And of course we have here the 'theoretical background' that so many critics miss and which is further developed in Part III of the 1913 volume.[22] No doubt, this background exposition needs amplification and, in addition, the editorial services of a professional theorist. But it is a great performance all the same.

Part II of the 1913 volume, however, needs no editing by anyone. It is a gem and a pioneer achievement. Mitchell not only knew how to use statistical material but also how to develop it—how to get what he wanted, even if it was not already there. Perception of a need that proceeded from a comprehensive vision; diagnosis of the available means to satisfy it; and attack upon the problem—these things must have followed one another, between 1908 and 1913, with the speed of lightning. Many men have had comprehensive visions. Many men have had a passion for detail. But he was one of the few to whom it is given to harness their visions into the service of their work on detail, and their passion for detail into the service of their visions.

[22] This Part III, reprinted in 1941 under the title *Business Cycles and their Causes,* contains several points which, or the importance of which, Mitchell ceased to believe in later on. Nevertheless, in writing it he came as near to a fully articulate rendering of his theory of the business cycle as he ever did. The unpublished manuscript mentioned (note 1, p. 239) is not only incomplete; it is the product of an uphill fight against unmanageable masses of material and against time.

IV

For the rest, no more need be said here about the volume of 1927 except that much more definitely than the volume of 1913 it was in the nature of a survey of work done and of a program for work to be done.[23] His labors during the years from 1908 to 1913 had taught him that the huge task he had attempted to accomplish was altogether beyond the possibilities of single-handed effort. His activities during the subsequent years that produced, among other things,[24] his investigations into the subject of price and production index numbers,[25] taught him that he was gifted, as few people ever have been, for the task of leading teams in which, though he knew how to keep direction, he always participated as a fellow worker— throwing his mind into the common pool and spreading the spirit of intellectual fellowship. And so, quite naturally, in 1920 this work issued into the work of the National Bureau of Economic Research of which he was one of the founders and, to his death, the moving spirit, the kindly leader who led but never drove, who inspired but never crushed the initiative of his associates. This 'bold experiment' was an act of self-realization. Its unqualified success is a monument to his intellectual and moral qualities.

The Bureau produced, and from the outset planned to produce, a series of investigations, starting from the famous study on the size and distribution of national income, which in appearance went far beyond business cycles and topics closely related to business cycles.[26] But Mitchell's conception of the phenomenon encom-

[23] The reader is referred to my review article, 'Mitchell's Business Cycles' in *The Quarterly Journal of Economics*, November 1930.

[24] The most important of the studies that should but cannot be noticed here were republished by Professor Joseph Dorfman in the volume entitled *The Backward Art of Spending Money*, 1937.

[25] See especially Bulletins No. 173 and 656 of the Bureau of Labor Statistics. *The History of Prices during the War*, a series of publications of the War Industries Board, was edited by Mitchell, who contributed himself the bulletin on *International Price Comparisons* and the *Summary*. The latter contains his production index.

[26] For details, see the annual reports or at least Professor Burns's brief story, op. cit. pp. 31 *et seq.*

passed the whole of the economic process and thus made all that happens in it relevant to the 'theory' of business cycles. Considerations of means and opportunities determined only the time sequence of the individual projects, all of which had their place in his comprehensive plan. This must be kept in mind in any appraisal of Burns's and Mitchell's *Measuring Business Cycles* (1946).

The authors of this volume do not profess to have written a treatise on business cycles but only to present a 'plan for measuring business cycles' or rather of the Economic Process in Motion. This 'declaration of intention' fits the first eight chapters better than the remaining four (which deal with results rather than mere measurements) but I prefer to formulate the contents of the book somewhat differently: the aim is to make the phenomenon stand up before us and *by so doing to show us what there is to explain.* This endeavor is presided over by a set of analytic decisions which constitute an improved version of the ones we find in the volume of 1913 but which can hardly be called a definition. Here they are: 'Business Cycles are a type of fluctuations found in the aggregate economic activity of nations that organize their work mainly in business enterprises: a cycle consists of expansions occurring at about the same time in many economic activities, followed by similarly general recessions, contractions, and revivals which merge into the expansion phase of the next cycle; this sequence of changes is recurrent but not periodic; in duration business cycles vary from more than one year to ten or twelve years; they are not divisible into shorter cycles of similar character with amplitudes approximating their own' (p. 3). There is a lot of 'theory' in this, besides anticipation of several subsequent factual findings. The last sentence, in particular, boldly adopts a single-cycle *hypothesis* which makes it difficult to distinguish different kinds of fluctuations, the existence of which is not a matter of hypothesis-making but of direct observation.[27] However this and other points are, to some extent,

---

[27] The second sentence seems to suggest that there is some point in recognizing four cyclical phases. As we shall see, this suggestion is not embodied in the pattern of the cyclical stages subsequently adopted. The reader

matters of individual judgment and expository convenience, and we shall not go into them any further.

From Mitchell's general point of view it was right and proper to analyze *all* the time series—over a thousand—that the united forces of the National Bureau were able to unearth and to treat. For business cycles, considered as the form of the capitalist process, are of necessity 'congeries of interrelated phenomena' coextensive with that process itself, and even if it were possible to imagine an element that has, in itself, nothing to do with cycles, it would still be necessary to investigate how it is affected by the cyclical movement.[28] If nevertheless, and in spite of all the qualms about the theoretical considerations involved, it proved necessary to make selections—as e.g. in the four last chapters of *Measuring Business Cycles*—this was a concession to the limitations of the means available and not a matter of principle. However, Mitchell was well aware that even the most complete array of statistics would not do what he wanted. So, in order to check as well as to light up his statistical material and the inferences to be drawn from it, he hit upon the idea of collecting what he called business annals, as far back and for as many countries as possible. The well-known book by W. L. Thorpe (1926) was the result. In a statistical age, the methodological merit in this recognition of the importance of non-

will realize that Mitchell's old aversion to the use of the equilibrium concept—or even to its counterpart in the world of business, the 'normal state of trade' which he declared to be a 'figment' in the volume of 1927, p. 376—may be the reason, or one of the reasons, for this. For the four-phase pattern has in fact little value unless we interpret expansions (prosperities) and contractions (depressions) as movements away from, and recessions and revivals as movements toward, comparatively equilibrated (and in this though in no other sense, 'normal') conditions.

[28] Mitchell's conception of a cyclical situation may, I think, be best rendered by an analogy. The members of a family circle produce a certain moral atmosphere which, in a sense, is the result of their individual behavior. But nevertheless this atmosphere, once created, is in itself an objective fact that in turn influences the behavior of the members of the family: the members of the National Bureau's family of time series jointly produce the cyclical situations, but they are all of them also being shaped by the existing cyclical situation.

statistical historical material cannot be emphasized too strongly. Though, as the years went by, Mitchell's confidence in this source of information seems to have decreased, and though it has been inadequately exploited from the first, it still redeems his work from the statisticism that threatens to swamp the field.

By now, everyone is familiar with what has come to be called the National Bureau method. Nevertheless, the ingenious idea that underlies this representation of cyclical behavior should be restated once more. On the one hand, every series, corrected for seasonal fluctuations, is treated by itself and its average behavior during its own expansions and contractions is brought out (specific cycles): each such cycle, identified by marking off the troughs and peaks in the series, is divided into intervals or stages for which the values of the series are expressed as percentages of its average value for each cycle—a judicious compromise between eliminating trend and leaving it in—and the averages of these percentages then serve to draw a picture of the typical specific cycle of the series. On the other hand, in order to display the behavior of each individual series in periods of expansion and contraction of the whole economic system, dates are derived for the peaks and troughs of general business activity, both from the approximate 'consensus' of all series included and from the nonnumerical information presented in the business annals. The behavior of each series is then studied in each of the (nine) intervals or stages into which this 'reference cycle' is divided, the 'standing' of the series in each stage of its reference cycle being also expressed as a percentage of its average value during the whole reference cycle. The typical reference cycle of the series is produced by averaging the standings of the series in each stage of all the cycles covered. The comparison of the specific and the reference cycles of each series is perhaps the most illuminating of the operations or measurements possible within this schema. This dual representation of (potentially) every bit of statistical information is extremely well devised in order to marshal business-cycle facts so far as this can be done without postulating *a priori* any particular relations between them. Even so, many a Gordian knot had to be cut. And the engine naturally works with greater friction in the last four chapters where a sample of seven relatively long time series is made to bear a heavy burden of concrete inferences. But the purpose of presenting facts so as to make it possible to confront them with theories stands out impressively throughout.

Of course, this volume was only a beginning. And if Mitchell had been able to complete his unfinished manuscript, this also would have been no more than a beginning. Work of this kind has no natural end and of necessity always points further ahead into an indefinite future. This is true of the whole of the work of Mitchell's life. And it is this which makes its greatness and defines its unique position in the history of modern economics. Here was a man who had the courage to say, unlike the rest of us, that he had not all the answers; who went about his task without either haste or rest; who did not care to march along with flags and brass bands; who was full of sympathy with mankind's fate, yet kept aloof from the market place; who taught us, by example and not by phrase, what a scholar should be.

JOHN MAYNARD KEYNES*
1883-1946

In HIS sparkling essay on the Great Villiers Connection,[1] Keynes revealed a sense of the importance of hereditary ability—of the great truth, to use Karl Pearson's phrase, that ability runs in stocks—that fits but ill into the picture many people seem to harbor of his intellectual world. The obvious inference about his sociology is strengthened by the fact that in his biographical sketches he was apt to stress ancestral backgrounds with unusual care. He would therefore understand my regret at my inability, owing to lack of time, to probe into the past of the Keynes Connection. Let us hope that someone else will do this, and content ourselves with an admiring glance at the parents. He was born on the fifth of June 1883, the eldest son of Florence Ada Keynes, daughter of the Reverend John Brown, D.D., and of John Neville Keynes, Registrar of

---

* Reprinted from *The American Economic Review,* vol. XXXVI, no. 4, September 1946. Copyright 1946 by American Economic Association.

[1] The essay, a review of W. I. J. Gun, *Studies in Hereditary Ability,* was published in *The Nation and Athenaeum,* March 27, 1926, and has been reprinted in the volume *Essays in Biography,* 1933. This volume sheds more light on Keynes the man and Keynes the scholar than does any other publication of his. I shall accordingly refer to it more than once.

the University of Cambridge—a mother of quite exceptional ability and charm, one-time mayor of Cambridge, and a father who is known to all of us as an eminent logician and author, among other things, of one of the best methodologies of economics ever written.[2]

Let us note the academic-clerical background of the subject of this memoir. The implications of this background—both the eminently English quality of it and the gentry element in it—become still clearer when we add two names: Eton and King's College, Cambridge. Most of us are teachers, and teachers are prone to exaggerate the formative influence of education. But nobody will equate it to zero. Moreover, there is nothing to show that John Maynard's reaction to either place was anything but positive. He seems to have enjoyed a thoroughly successful scholastic career.[3] In 1905 he was elected President of the Cambridge Union. In the same year he emerged as twelfth Wrangler.

Theorists will notice the latter distinction which cannot be attained without some aptitude for mathematics plus hard work—work hard enough to make it easy for a man who has gone through that discipline to acquire any more advanced technique he may wish to master. They will recognize the mathematical quality of mind that underlies the purely scientific part of Keynes's work, perhaps also the traces in it of a half-forgotten training. And some of them may wonder why he kept aloof from the current of mathematical economics which gathered decisive momentum at just about the time when he first entered the field. Nor is this all. Though never definitely hostile to mathematical economics—he even accepted the presidency of the Econometric Society—he never threw the weight

[2] *Scope and Method of Political Economy* (1891). The well-earned success of this admirable book is attested by the fact that a reprint of its fourth edition (1917) was called for as late as 1930; in fact, so well has it kept its own amidst the surf and breakers of half a century's controversies about its problems that even now students of methodology can hardly do better than choose it for guide.

[3] Eton always meant much to him. Few of the honors of which he was the recipient later on pleased him so much as did his election, by the masters, as their representative on Eton's governing board.

of his authority into its scale. The advice that emanated from him was almost invariably negative. Occasionally his conversation revealed something akin to dislike.

Explanation is not far to seek. The higher ranges of mathematical economics are in the nature of what is in all fields referred to as 'pure science.' Results have little bearing—as yet, in any case—upon practical questions. And questions of policy all but monopolized Keynes's brilliant abilities. He was much too cultivated and much too intelligent to despise logical niceties. To some extent he enjoyed them; to a still greater extent he bore with them; but beyond a boundary which it did not take him long to reach, he lost patience with them. *L'art pour l'art* was no part of his scientific creed. Wherever else he may have been progressive, he was not a progressive in analytic method. We shall see that this also holds in other respects that are unconnected with the use of higher mathematics. If the purpose seemed to justify it, he had no objection to using arguments that were as crude as those of Sir Thomas Mun.

II

An Englishman who entered adult life from Eton and Cambridge, who was passionately interested in the policy of his nation, who had conquered the presidential chair of the Cambridge Union in the symbolic year 1905 that marked the passing of an epoch and the dawn of another [4]—why did such an Englishman not embark upon a political career? Why did he go to the India Office instead? Many pro's and con's enter into a decision of this kind, money among others, but there is one point about it which it is essential to grasp. Nobody could ever have talked to Keynes for an hour without discovering that he was the most unpolitical of men. The political game as a game interested him no more than did racing—or, for that matter, pure theory *per se*. With quite unusual gifts for debate and with a keen perception of tactical values, he yet seems to have been impervious to the lure—nowhere anything

[4] The Campbell-Bannerman victory was won and a parliamentary Labour Party emerged in January 1906.

like as strong as it is in England—of the charmed circle of political office. Party meant little or nothing to him. He was ready to co-operate with anyone who offered support for a recommendation of his and to forget any past passage of arms. But he was not ready to co-operate with anyone on any other terms, let alone to accept any-one's leadership. His loyalties were loyalties to measures, not loyalties to individuals or groups. And still less than a respector of persons was he a respector of creeds or ideologies or flags.

Was he not, therefore, cut out for the role of an ideal civil servant, by nature made to become one of those great permanent Under-secretaries of State whose discreet influence counts for so much in the shaping of England's recent history? Anything but that. He had no taste for politics, but he had less than no taste for patient routine work and for breaking in, by gentle arts, that re-fractory wild beast, the politician. And these two negative pro-pensities, the aversion to the political arena and the aversion to red tape, propelled him toward the role for which he was indeed by nature made, for which he quickly found the form that suited him to perfection, and from which he never departed throughout his life. Whatever we may think of the psychological laws which he was to formulate, we cannot but feel that, from an early age, he thoroughly understood his own. This is, in fact, one of the major keys to the secret of his success—and also to the secret of his happi-ness: for unless I am much mistaken his life was an eminently happy one.

Thus, after two years at the India Office (1906-8) he went back to his university, accepting a fellowship at King's (1909), and quickly established himself in the circle of his Cambridge fellow economists and beyond. He taught straight Marshallian doctrine with the Fifth Book of the *Principles* as the center, the doctrine that he mastered as few people did and with which he remained identi-fied for twenty years to come. A picture survives in my memory of how he then looked to a casual visitor to Cambridge—the picture of the young teacher of spare frame, ascetic countenance, flashing eyes, intent and tremendously serious, vibrating with what seemed to that visitor suppressed impatience, a formidable controversialist whom nobody could overlook, everybody respected, and some liked.[5] His rising reputation is attested by the fact that as early as 1911 he was appointed editor of the *Economic Journal* in succession to its first editor, Edgeworth. This key position in the world of economics he filled without interruption and with unflagging zeal until the spring of 1945.[6] Considering the length of his tenure of this office and all the other interests and avocations in the midst of which he filled it, his editorial performance is truly remarkable, in fact, almost unbelievable. It was not only that he shaped the general policy of the *Journal* and of the Royal Economic Society, of which he was secretary. He did much more than this. Many articles grew out of his suggestions; all of them received, from the ideas and facts presented down to punctuation, the most minute critical attention.[7] We all know the results, and everyone of us has—no doubt—his own opinion about them. But I feel confident of speaking for all of us when I say that, taken as a whole, Keynes the editor has had no equal since Du Pont de Nemours managed the *Ephémérides*.

The work at the India Office was not more than an apprenticeship that would have left few traces in a less fertile mind. It is highly revealing not only of the vigor but also of the type of Keynes's talent that it bore fruit in his case: his first book—and first success—was on *Indian Currency and Finance*.[8] It appeared in 1913, when he was also appointed member of the Royal Commission on Indian Finance and Currency (1913-14). I think it fair to

[5] My own acquaintance with Keynes, productive of a totally different impression, dates only from 1927.

[6] Edgeworth served once more, as joint editor, 1918-25. He was succeeded by D. H. Macgregor, who served, 1925-34, to be in turn succeeded by Mr. E. A. G. Robinson (who had been appointed assistant editor in 1933).

[7] Once he patiently explained to a foreign contributor that, while it is permissible to abbreviate *exempli gratia* into e.g., it is not permissible to abbreviate 'for instance' into *f. i.*—and would the author sanction the alteration?

[8] In 1910-11 he gave lectures on Indian Finance at the London School of Economics. See F. A. Hayek, 'The London School of Economics, 1895-1945,' *Economica* (Feb. 1946), p. 17.

call this book the best English work on the gold exchange standard. Much more interest attaches, however, to another question that is but distantly related to the merits of this performance taken by itself; can we discern in it anything that points toward the *General Theory?* In the Preface to the latter, Keynes himself claimed not more than that his teaching of 1936 seemed to him 'a natural evolution of a line of thought which he had been pursuing for several years.' On this I shall offer some comments later on. But now I will make bold to assert that, though the book of 1913 contains none of those characteristic propositions of the book of 1936 that have been felt to be so 'revolutionary,' the general attitude taken toward monetary phenomena and monetary policy by the Keynes of 1913 clearly foreshadowed that of the Keynes of the *Treatise* (1930).

Monetary management was then no novelty, of course—which is precisely why it should not have been heralded as a novelty in the 20's and 30's—and preoccupation with Indian problems was particularly likely to induce awareness of its nature, necessity, and possibilities. But Keynes's vivid appreciation of its bearing not only upon prices and exports and imports, but also on production and employment was nevertheless something new, something that, if it did not uniquely determine, yet conditioned his own line of advance. Moreover, we must remember how closely his *theoretical* development in post-war times was related to the particular situations in which he offered practical advice and which neither he nor anyone else foresaw in 1913; add the theoretical implications of the English experience in the 20's to the theory of *Indian Currency and Finance,* and you will get the substance of the Keynesian ideas of 1930. This statement is conservative. I could go further—a little—were I not afraid of falling into an error that is very common among biographers.

III

In 1915, the potential public servant in the academic gown turned into an actual one: he entered the Treasury. English finance

during the First World War was eminently 'sound' and spelled a
moral performance of the first order. But it was not conspicuous
for originality, and it is possible that the brilliant young official
then acquired his dislike of the Treasury Mind and the Treasury
View that became so marked later on. His services were, however,
appreciated, for he was chosen to serve as Principal Representative
of the Treasury at the Peace Conference—which might have been
a key position if such a thing could have existed within the orbit
of Lloyd George—and also as Deputy for the Chancellor of the
Exchequer on the Supreme Economic Council. More important
than this, speaking from the biographer's standpoint, is his abrupt
resignation in June 1919, which was so characteristic of the man and
of the kind of public servant he was. Other men had much the same
misgivings about the peace, but *of course* they could not possibly
speak out. Keynes was made of different stuff. He resigned and told
the world why. And he leapt into international fame.

Economic Consequences of the Peace (1919) met with a
reception that makes the word Success sound commonplace and
insipid. Those who cannot understand how luck and merit inter-
twine will no doubt say that Keynes simply wrote what was on
every sensible man's lips; that he was very favorably placed for
making his protest resound all over the world; that it was this protest as such and not his particular argument that won him every
ear and many thousands of hearts; and that, at the moment the
book appeared, the tide was already running on which it was to
ride. There is truth in all this. Of course, there was an unique
opportunity. But if we choose, on the strength of this, to deny the
greatness of the feat, we had better delete this phrase altogether
from the pages of history. For there are no great feats without
pre-existing great opportunities.

Primarily the feat was one of moral courage. But the book is
a masterpiece—packed with practical wisdom that never lacks depth;
pitilessly logical yet never cold; genuinely humane but nowhere
sentimental; meeting all facts without vain regrets but also without hopelessness: it is sound advice added to sound analysis. And

it is a work of art. Form and matter fit each other to perfection. Everything is to the point, and there is nothing in it that is not to the point. No idle adornment disfigures its wise economy of means. The very polish of the exposition—never again was he to write so well—brings out its simplicity. In the passages in which Keynes tries to explain, in terms of the *dramatis personae,* the tragic failure of purpose that produced the Peace, he rises to heights that have been trodden by few.[9]

The economics of the book, as well as of *A Revision of the Treaty* (1922) that complements and in some respects amends its argument, is of the simplest and did not call for any refined technique. Nevertheless, there is something about it that calls for our

---

[9] See pp. 26-50, on the Council of Four, republished, with an important addendum, the Fragment on Lloyd George, in the *Essays in Biography.* It is painful to report that, at the time, some opponents of Keynes's views, in full retreat before his victorious logic, seem to have resorted to sneers about his presentation of certain facts and his interpretation of motive, neither of which, so they averred, he was in a position to judge. Since this indictment of Keynes's veracity has been repeated recently in a *causerie* published in an American magazine, it is first of all necessary to ask the reader to satisfy himself that not a single result of Keynes's analysis and not a single recommendation of his depends on the correctness or incorrectness of the picture he drew of the motives and attitudes of Clemenceau, Wilson, and Lloyd George. But, secondly, since it is part of the purpose of this memoir to delineate a character, it is further necessary to prove that there is absolutely no foundation for the aspersion that Keynes indulged in a flight of 'poetic fantasy' and that he pretended to an intimate knowledge of 'arcana' that cannot have been known to him—which, at best, would convict him of petty vanity and, at worst, of more than that. But the proof in question is not difficult to supply. If the reader will refer to that masterly sketch, as I hope he will, he is bound to find that Keynes claimed no intimacy with those three men and personal acquaintance only with Lloyd George. He said nothing about the private meetings of the four (the fourth was Orlando), but merely described scenes at the regular meetings of the Council of Four, which, along with all other leading experts, he must have normally attended in his official capacity. Moreover, his presentation of the personal aspects of the steps on the road that led to the disastrous result is amply supported by independent evidence: his brilliant story is nothing but a reasonable interpretation of a course of events that is common knowledge. Finally, critics had better bear in mind that this interpretation is distinctly generous and perfectly free from traces of any resentment, however justifiable, that Keynes may have felt.

attention. Before embarking on his great venture in persuasion, Keynes drew a sketch of the economic and social background of the political events he was about to survey. With but slight alterations of phrasing, this sketch may be summed up like this: Laissez-faire capitalism, that 'extraordinary episode,' had come to an end in August 1914. The conditions were rapidly passing in which entrepreneurial leadership was able to secure success after success, propelled as it had been by rapid growth of populations and by abundant opportunities to invest that were incessantly re-created by technological improvements and by a series of conquests of new sources of food and raw materials. Under these conditions, there had been no difficulty about absorbing the savings of a *bourgeoisie* that kept on baking cakes 'in order not to eat them.' But now (1920) those impulses were giving out, the spirit of private enterprise was flagging, investment opportunities were vanishing, and bourgeois saving habits had, therefore, lost their social function; their persistence actually made things worse than they need have been.

Here, then, we have the origin of the *modern* stagnation thesis—as distinguished from the one which we may, if we choose, find in Ricardo. And here we also have the embryo of the *General Theory*. Every comprehensive 'theory' of an economic state of society consists of two complementary but essentially distinct elements. There is, first, the theorist's view about the basic features of that state of society, about what is and what is not important in order to understand its life at a given time. Let us call this his vision. And there is, second, the theorist's technique, an apparatus by which he conceptualizes his vision and which turns the latter into concrete propositions or 'theories.' In those pages of the *Economic Consequences of the Peace* we find nothing of the theoretical apparatus of the *General Theory*. But we find the whole of the vision of things social and economic of which that apparatus is the technical complement. The *General Theory* is the final result of a long struggle *to make that vision of our age analytically operative.*

IV

For economists of the 'scientific' type Keynes is, of course, the Keynes of the *General Theory*. In order to do some justice to the straight-line development which leads up to it from the *Consequences of the Peace,* and of which the main stages are marked by the *Tract* and by the *Treatise,* I shall have to brush aside ruthlessly many things that ought not to go unrecorded. Three foothills of the *Consequences* are, however, mentioned in the note below,[10] and a few words must be said on *A Treatise on Probability* which he published in 1921. There cannot be, I fear, much question about what Keynes means for the theory of probability, though his interest in it went far back: his fellowship dissertation had been on the subject. The question that is of interest to us is what the theory of probability meant for Keynes. Subjectively, it seems to have been an outlet for the energies of a mind that found no complete satisfaction in the problems of the field to which, as much

[10] These are: his article on population and the ensuing controversy with Sir William Beveridge (*Econ. Jour.,* 1923); his pamphlet, *The End of Laissez-Faire* (1926); and his article on the 'German Transfer Problem' in the *Econ. Jour.* (March 1929), with subsequent replies to the criticism of Ohlin and Rueff. The first attempts to conjure Malthus' ghost—to defend (at the threshold of the period of unsalable masses of food and raw materials!) the thesis that, since somewhere about 1906, nature had begun to respond less generously to human effort and that overpopulation was the great problem or one of the great problems of our time—is perhaps the least felicitous of all his efforts and indicative of an element of recklessness in his makeup which those who loved him best cannot entirely deny. All that needs to be said about *The End of Laissez-Faire* is that we must not expect to find in this piece of work what the title suggests. It was not at all what the Webbs wrote in that book of theirs that invites comparison with Keynes's. The article on German reparations reveals another side of his character: it was evidently dictated by the most generous motives and by unerring political wisdom; but it was not good theory and Ohlin and Rueff found it easy to deal with it. It is difficult to understand how Keynes can have been blind to the weak spots in his argument. But, in the service of a cause he believed in, he would sometimes, in noble haste, overlook defects in the wood from which he made his arrows. Perusal of the collection entitled *Essays in Persuasion* (1931) is perhaps the best method of studying the quality of his reasoning in the not-quite-professional part of his work.

from a sense of public duty as from taste, he devoted most of his time and strength. He entertained no very high opinion about the purely intellectual possibilities of economics. Whenever he wished to breathe the air of high altitudes, he did not turn to our pure theory. He was something of a philosopher or epistemologist. He was interested in Wittgenstein. He was a great friend of that brilliant thinker who died in the prime of life—Frank Ramsey, to whose memory he erected a charming monument.[11] But no merely receptive attitude could have satisfied him. He had to have a flight of his own. It is highly revelatory of the texture of his mind that he chose probability for the purpose—a subject bristling with logical niceties yet not entirely without utilitarian connotation. His indomitable will produced what, seen as I am trying to see it, was no doubt a brilliant performance, whatever specialists, non-Cambridge specialists particularly, might have to say about it.

We are drifting from the work to the man. Let us then use this opportunity for looking at him a little more closely. He had returned to King's and to his prewar pattern of life. But the pattern was developed and enlarged. He continued to be an active teacher and research worker; he continued to edit the *Journal;* he continued to make the public cares his own. But though he strengthened his ties with King's by accepting the important (and laborious) function of Bursar, the London house, at 46 Gordon Square, became second headquarters before long. He acquired an interest in, and became chairman of, *The Nation*—which superseded the *Speaker* in 1921, absorbed the *Athenaeum,* and was, in 1931, merged with *The New Statesman* (*The New Statesman and Nation*)—to which he directed a current stream of articles that would have been fulltime work for some other men. Also, he became chairman of the National Mutual Life Assurance Society (1921-38) to which he gave

[11] In *The New Statesman and Nation,* October 3, 1931, republished in the *Essays in Biography*. To this essay, the most warm-hearted thing he ever wrote, is appended an anthology of gleanings from Ramsey's notes. These express Ramsey's views, of course, and not Keynes's, but, for an occasion like this, nobody would choose passages that do not strike a sympathetic note. Thus, Ramsey's sayings become indicative of Keynes's philosophy.

much time, and managed an investment company, earning a considerable income from such business pursuits. There was no nonsense about him, in particular no nonsense about business and money making: he frankly appreciated the comforts of a proper establishment; and not less frankly he used to say (in the 20's) that he would never accept a professorial appointment because he could not afford to do so. In addition to all this, he served actively on the Economic Advisory Council and on the Committee on Finance and Industry (Macmillan Committee). In 1925, he married a distinguished artist, Lydia Lopokova, who proved a congenial companion and devoted helpmate—'in sickness and in health'—to the end.

That combination of activities is not unusual. What made it unusual and, indeed, a marvel to behold is the fact that he put as much energy in each of them as if it had been his only one. His appetite and his capacity for efficient work surpass belief, and his power of concentration on the piece of work in hand was truly Gladstonian: whatever he did, he did with a mind freed from everything else. He knew what it is to be tired. But he hardly seems to have known dead hours of cheerlessness and faltering purpose.

Nature is wont to impose two distinct penalties upon those who try to beat out their stock of energy to the thinnest leaf. One of these penalties Keynes undoubtedly paid. The quality of his work suffered from its quantity and not only as to form: much of his secondary work shows the traces of haste, and some of his most important work, the traces of incessant interruptions that injured its growth. Who fails to realize this—to realize that he beholds work that has never been allowed to ripen, has never received the last finishing touch—will never do justice to Keynes's powers.[12] But the other penalty was remitted to him.

[12] The most obvious example for this is his most ambitious venture in research, the *Treatise on Money,* which is a shell of several pieces of powerful but unfinished work, very imperfectly put together (see below, p. 277). But the instance that will convey my meaning best is the biographical essay on Marshall (*Econ. Jour.,* Sept. 1924). He evidently lavished love and care upon it. As a matter of fact, it is the most brilliant life of a man of science I have

In general, there is something inhuman about human machines that fully use every ounce of their fuel. Such men are mostly
cold in their personal relations, inaccessible, preoccupied. Their
work is their life, no other interests exist for them, or only interests
of the most superficial kind. But Keynes was the exact opposite of
all this—the pleasantest fellow you can think of; pleasant, kind, and
cheerful in the sense in which precisely those people are pleasant,
kind, and cheerful who have nothing on their minds and whose one
principle it is never to allow any pursuit of theirs to degenerate
into work. He was affectionate. He was always ready to enter with
friendly zest into the views, interests, and troubles of others. He
was generous, and not only with money. He was sociable, enjoyed
conversation, and shone in it. And, contrary to a widely spread
opinion, he could be *polite,* polite with an old-world *punctilio* that
costs time. For instance, he would refuse to sit down to his lunch,
in spite of telegraphic and telephonic expostulation, until his guest,
delayed by fog in the Channel, put in appearance at 4 P.M.

His extracurricular interests were many, and each of them
he pursued with joyful alacrity. But this is not all of it. Once more,
people are not uncommon who, in spite of absorbing avocations,
enjoy some recreative activities in a passive way. The Keynesian
touch is that with him recreation was creative. For instance, he
loved old books, niceties of bibliographic controversy, details of the
characters, lives, and thoughts of men of the past. Many people
share this taste which may have been fostered in him by the classical
ingredients in his education. But whenever he indulged it, he took
hold like the workman he was, and we owe to his hobby several
not unimportant clarifications on points of literary history.[13] He
also was a lover and, up to a point, a good judge of pictures, to a

---

ever read. And yet, the reader who turns to it will not only derive much
pleasure and profit, but also see what I mean. It starts beautifully, it ends
beautifully; but in order to be perfect, it would have needed another fort-
night's work.

[13] The literature of philosophy and economics attracted him most. In
this pursuit Professor Piero Sraffa became to him a much-appreciated ally.
The best example I can offer of results is the edition of Hume's abstract of his

modest extent also a collector. He thoroughly enjoyed a good play, and founded and generously financed the Cambridge Arts Theatre, which no one who went to it will forget. And, once upon a time, an acquaintance of his received the following note from him, evidently dashed off in high good humor: 'Dear . . . , if you wish to know what at the moment *exclusively* occupies my time, look at the enclosed.'[14] The enclosure consisted of a program or prospectus of the 'Carmago Ballet.'

V

I return to the highway. As stated above, our first stop is at the *Tract on Monetary Reform* (1923). Since, with Keynes, practical advice was the goal and beaconlight of analysis, I will do what in the case of other economists I should consider an offense to do, viz. invite readers to look first at what it was he advocated. It was, in substance, stabilization of the domestic price level for the purpose of stabilizing the domestic business situation, secondary attention being paid also to the means of mitigating short-run fluctuations of foreign exchange. In order to achieve this he recommended that the monetary system created by the necessities of warfare should be carried over into the peace economy, the boldest of the various suggestions offered—with an evident trepidation quite unlike him—being the separation of the note issue from the gold reserve which he wished, however, to retain and of which he was anxious to emphasize the importance.

There are two things in this piece of advice that should be carefully noticed: first, its specifically English quality; second, ex

Treatise on Human Nature 'reprinted with an Introduction by J. M. Keynes and P. Sraffa,' 1938. The Introduction is a curious monument of philological ardor.

[14] The acquaintance, a most disorderly person, does not keep letters. The exact wording of Keynes's note can therefore not be verified. But I am positive that it contained a single brief sentence and that the import of this sentence was as stated. It must have been about ten or fifteen years ago, perhaps more.—In his last years, those artistic activities and tastes led to his being elected trustee of the National Gallery and Chairman of the Council for the Encouragement of Music and the Arts. More work!

visu *of England's short-run interests and of the kind of Englishman
the adviser was,* its sober wisdom and conservativism.[15] It cannot
be emphasized too strongly that Keynes's advice was in the first
instance always English advice, born of English problems even
where addressed to other nations. Barring some of his artistic tastes,
he was surprisingly insular, even in philosophy, but nowhere so
much as in economics. And, he was fervently patriotic—of a patri-
otism which was indeed quite untinged by vulgarity but was so
genuine as to be subconscious and therefore all the more powerful
to impart a bias to his thought and to exclude full understanding
of foreign (also American) viewpoints, conditions, interests, and
especially creeds. Like the old free-traders, he always exalted what
was at any moment truth and wisdom for England into truth and
wisdom for all times and places.[16] But we cannot stop at this. In
order to locate the standpoint from which his advice was given it is
further necessary to remember that he was of the high intelligentsia
of England, unattached to class or party, a typical prewar intellectual, who rightly claimed, for good and ill, spiritual kinship with
the Locke-Mill connection.

What was it, then, that this patriotic English intellectual
beheld? The generalization we have already noticed in the pages
of the *Consequences.* But England's case was more specific than
that. She had not emerged from the war as she had emerged from
the war of the Napoleonic era. She had emerged impoverished; she
had lost many of her opportunities for the moment and some of
them for good. Not only this, but her social fabric had been weak-
ened and had become rigid. Her taxes and wage rates were incompatible with vigorous development, yet there was nothing that could
be done about it. Keynes was not given to vain regrets. He was not
in the habit of bemoaning what could not be changed. Also he was
not the sort of man who would bend the full force of his mind to
the individual problems of coal, textiles, steel, shipbuilding (though

[15] It should surprise no one that he was eventually (1942) elected di-
rector of the Bank of England.
[16] This also explains what his opponents called his inconsistency.

he did offer some advice of this kind in his current articles). Least of all was he the man to preach regenerative creeds. He was the English intellectual, a little *deraciné* and beholding a most uncomfortable situation. He was childless and his philosophy of life was essentially a short-run philosophy. So he turned resolutely to the only 'parameter of action' that seemed left to him, both as an Englishman and as the kind of Englishman he was—monetary management. Perhaps he thought that it might heal. He knew for certain that it would sooth—and that return to a gold system at pre-war parity was more than *his* England could stand.

If only people could be made to understand this, they would also understand that practical Keynesianism is a seedling which cannot be transplanted into foreign soil: it dies there and becomes poisonous before it dies. But in addition they would understand that, left in English soil, this seedling is a healthy thing and promises both fruit and shade. Let me say once and for all: all this applies to every bit of advice that Keynes ever offered. For the rest, the advocacy of monetary management in the *Tract* was anything but revolutionary. There was, however, a novel emphasis on it as a means of general economic therapeutics. And concern with the saving-investment mechanism is indicated in the first lines of the Preface and throughout the first chapter.[17] Thus, though the immediate task before the author prevented him from going very far into these matters, the book does indicate further advance toward the *General Theory*.

Analytically, Keynes accepted the quantity theory which 'is fundamental. Its correspondence with facts is not open to question' (p. 81). All the more important is it for us to realize that this acceptance, resting as it does on the very common confusion between the quantity theory and the equation of exchange, meant

---

[17] See, e.g. the highly characteristic passages on p. 10, and also the description of the 'investment system' on p. 8, which anticipates some of the very inadequacies of the analysis of the *General Theory*. Even then, and indeed from first to last, Keynes displayed a curious reluctance to recognize a very simple and obvious fact and to express it by the no less simple and obvious phrase, that typically industry is financed by banks.

much less than it seems to mean exactly as Keynes's later repudiation of the quantity theory means much less than it seems to mean. What he intended to accept was the equation of exchange—in its Cambridge form—which, whether defined as an identity or as an equilibrium condition, does not imply any of the propositions characteristic of the quantity theory in the strict sense. Accordingly, he felt free to make velocity—or k, its equivalent in the Cambridge equation—a variable of the monetary problem, very properly giving Marshall credit for this 'development of the traditional way of considering the matter' (p. 86). This is the Liquidity Preference in embryonic form. Keynes overlooked that this theory can be traced back to Cantillon—at least—and that it had been developed, though sketchily, by Kemmerer,[18] who said that 'large sums of money are continually being hoarded' and that 'the proportion of the circulating medium which is hoarded . . . is not constant.' We cannot go into the many excellent things in the *Tract*, e.g. the masterly section on the Forward Market in Exchanges (chap. III, sec. IV) and on Great Britain (chap. V, sec. I) which it is impossible to admire too highly. We must hurry on to our 'second stop' on the road to the *General Theory*, the *Treatise on Money* (1930).

With the exception of the *Treatise on Probability*, Keynes never wrote another work in which the hortatory purpose is less visible than it is in the *Treatise on Money*. It is there all the same, and not confined to the last book (VII), in which, among other things, we find all the essentials of Bretton Woods—what an extraordinary achievement! Primarily, however, those two volumes

---

[18] E. W. Kemmerer, *Money and Credit Instruments* (1907), p. 20. But on p. 193 of the *Tract*, Keynes commits himself to the untenable statement that 'the internal price level is mainly determined by the amount of credit created by the banks' and from this he never departed. To the end, this credit remained for him an independent variable, given to the economic process, though determined, not by gold production as it was of old but either by the banks or by the 'monetary authority' (Central Bank or Government). This, however—considering quantity of money as 'given'—is one of the characteristic features of the quantity theory in the strict sense. Hence my statement in the text that he never abandoned the quantity theory as completely as he thought he did.

are no doubt Keynes's most ambitious piece of genuine research, of research so brilliant and yet so solid that it is a thousand pities that the harvest was garnered before it was ripe. If only he had learned something from Marshall's craving for 'impossible perfection' instead of lecturing him about it! (*Essays in Biography,* pp. 211-12).[19] Moreover, Professor Myrdal's gentle sneer at 'that Anglo-Saxon kind of unnecessary originality' is amply justified.[20] Nevertheless, the book was the outstanding performance in its field and day. All I can do, however, is to collect the most important signposts that point toward the *General Theory*.[21]

There is, first, the conception of the theory of money as the theory of the economic process as a whole that was to be fully developed in the *General Theory*. This conception is, second, embedded in the vision or diagnosis of the contemporaneous state of the economic process that never changed from the *Consequences*. Third, saving and investment decisions are resolutely separated, quite as resolutely as in the *General Theory,* and private thrift is

[19] A semi-apologetic passage in the Preface of the *Treatise* shows that he was not unaware of the fact that he was offering half-baked bread.

[20] Gunnar Myrdal, *Monetary Equilibrium* (English translation, by Bryce and Stolper [1939], of a German version of the Swedish original that appeared in the *Ekonomisk Tidskrift* in 1931), p. 8. Myrdal's protest was not, of course, made on his own behalf but on behalf of Wicksell and the Wicksellian group. But a similar protest would have been in order on behalf of Böhm-Bawerk and his followers, especially of Mises and Hayek. The latter's *Geldtheorie und Konjunkturtheorie* had been published, it is true, only in 1929. But Böhm-Bawerk's work was available in English, and Taussig's *Wages and Capital* dates from 1896. Nevertheless, Keynes wrote the capital theory of Book vi exactly as if they had never lived. But there was no obliquity in this. He simply did not know. Proof of his good faith is the ample credit he gave to all authors he did know, Pigou and Robertson among them.

[21] This, of course, involves injustice to the work as a whole, and in particular to the first two books: the conventional but nonetheless brilliant introduction (Nature of Money, Book i) and the almost independent treatise on price levels (Value of Money, Book ii) which is full of suggestive ideas. It must be remembered—and this is really the most fundamental difference between the *Treatise* and the *General Theory*—that the work professes to be an analysis of the dynamics of price levels, 'of the way in which the fluctuations of the price level actually come to pass' (vol. i, p. 152), though in reality it is much more than this.

well established in its role of villain of the piece. The recognition extended to the work of 'Mr. J. A. Hobson and others' (vol. I, p. 179) is highly significant in this respect. And we learn that a thrift campaign is not the way to bring down the rate of interest (e.g. vol. II, p. 207). Differences in conceptualization—sometimes only in terminology—obscure but do not eliminate the fundamental identity of the ideas the author strives to convey. Thus, fourth, much of the argument runs in terms of the Wicksellian divergence between the 'natural' and the 'money' rate of interest. To be sure, the latter is not yet *the* rate of interest, and neither the former nor profits are as yet turned into the 'marginal efficiency of capital.' But the argument clearly suggests both steps. Fifth, the emphasis upon expectations, upon the 'bearishness' that is not yet liquidity preference from the speculative motive, and the theory that the fall in money wage rates in depression ('reduction in the rate of efficiency-earnings') will tend to re-establish equilibrium *if and because it will act on interest (bank rate) by reducing the requirements of Industrial Circulation*—all these and many other things (bananas, widows' cruses, Danaïdes' jars) read like imperfect and embarrassed first statements of *General Theory* propositions.

VI

The *Treatise* was not a failure in any ordinary sense of the word. Everybody saw its points and, with whatever qualifications, paid his respects to Keynes's great effort. Even damaging criticism, such as Professor Hansen's criticism of the Fundamental Equations,[22] or Professor von Hayek's criticism of Keynes's basic theoretical structure,[23] were as a rule tempered with well-deserved eulogy. But from Keynes's own standpoint it was a failure, and not

[22] Alvin H. Hansen, 'A Fundamental Error in Keynes' Treatise on Money,' *The American Economic Review*, 1930; and Hansen and Tout, 'Investment and Saving in Business Cycle Theory,' *Econometrica*, 1933.

[23] F. A. von Hayek, 'Reflections on the Pure Theory of Money of Mr. Keynes,' I and II, *Economica*, 1931 and 1932. Hayek went so far as to speak of an 'enormous advance.' Nevertheless Keynes replied not without irritation. As he himself remarked on another occasion, authors are difficult to please.

only because its reception did not measure up to his standard of success. It had somehow missed fire—it had not really made a mark. And the reason was not far to seek: he had failed to convey the essence of his own personal message. He had written a treatise and, for the sake of systematic completeness, overburdened his text with material about price indices, the *modus operandi* of bank rates, deposit creation, gold and what not, all of which, whatever its merits, was akin to current doctrine and hence, for his purpose, not sufficiently distinctive. He had entangled himself in the meshes of an apparatus that broke down each time he attempted to make it grind out his own meanings. There would have been no point in trying to improve the work in detail. There would have been no point in trying to fight criticisms, the justice of many of which he had to admit. There was nothing for it but to abandon the whole thing, hull and cargo, to renounce allegiances and to start afresh. He was quick to learn the lesson.

Resolutely cutting himself off from the derelict, he braced himself for another effort, the greatest of his life. With brilliant energy he took hold of the essentials of his message and bent his mind to the task of forging a conceptual apparatus that would express these and—as nearly as possible—nothing else. He succeeded to his satisfaction. And so soon as he had done so—in December 1935—he buckled on his new armor, unsheathed his sword and took the field again, boldly claiming that he was going to lead economists out of errors of 150 years' standing and into the promised land of truth.

Those around him were fascinated. While Keynes was remodeling his work, he currently talked about it in his lectures, in conversation, in the 'Keynes Club' that used to meet in his rooms at King's. And there was a lively give and take. '. . . I have depended on the constant advice and constructive criticism of Mr. R. F. Kahn. There is a great deal in this book which would not have taken the shape it has except at his suggestion' (*General Theory,* Preface, p. viii). Considering all the implications of Richard Kahn's article on 'The Relation of Home Investment to Unemployment,' published in the *Economic Journal* as early as June 1931, we shall certainly not suspect those two sentences of overstatement. Some credit was also given, in the same place, to Mrs. Robinson, Mr. Hawtrey, and Mr. Harrod.[24] There were others—some of the most promising young Cambridge men among them. And they all talked. Glimpses of the new light began to be caught by individuals all over the Empire and in the United States. Students were thrilled. A wave of anticipatory enthusiasm swept the world of economists. When the book came out at last, Harvard students felt unable to wait until it would be available at the booksellers: they clubbed together in order to speed up the process and arranged for direct shipment of a first parcel of copies.

VII

The social vision first revealed in the *Economic Consequences of the Peace,* the vision of an economic process in which investment opportunity flags and saving habits nevertheless persist, is theoretically implemented in the *General Theory of Employment, Interest, and Money* (Preface dated December 13, 1935) by means of three schedule concepts: the consumption function, the efficiency-of-capi-

---

[24] Mr. Hawtrey's relation to the book can never have been any other than that of an understanding and, up to a point, sympathetic critic. He never was, of course, a Keynesian. From the *Tract* to the *Treatise,* Keynes was a Hawtreyan. Mr. Harrod may have been moving independently toward a goal not far from that of Keynes, though he unselfishly joined the latter's standard after it had been raised. Justice imposes this remark. For that eminent economist is in some danger of losing the place in the history of economics that is his by right, both in respect to Keynesianism and in respect to Imperfect Competition. Not less do I feel bound to advert to Mrs. Robinson's claims. It is highly revelatory of the attitude of the academic mind to women that she was excluded from the seminar mentioned above (at least she was not invited on the one occasion when I addressed it). But she was in the midst of things. Proofs of this are her 'Parable on Saving and Investment' (*Economica,* February 1933), an article which was a most skillfully fought rear-guard action covering retreat from the *Treatise;* and, still more significant of her role in the evolution of the *General Theory,* her 'Theory of Money and the Analysis of Output,' published as early as October 1933, in the *Review of Economic Studies.*

tal function, and the liquidity-preference function.[25] These together with the given wage-unit and the equally given quantity of money 'determine' income and *ipso facto* employment (if and so far as the latter is uniquely determined by the former), the great dependent variables to be 'explained.' What a *cordon bleu* to make such a sauce out of such scanty material! [26] Let us see how he did it.

(1) The first condition for simplicity of a model is, of course, simplicity of the vision which it is to implement. And simplicity of vision is in part a matter of genius and in part a matter of willingness to pay the price in terms of the factors that have to be left out

[25] Distinctive terminology helps to drive home the points an author wishes to make and to focus his readers' attention. This (though nothing else) justifies the re-naming of Irving Fisher's marginal rate of return over cost—the priority of which Keynes fully recognized—and also the use of the phrase, liquidity preference, instead of the usual one, hoarding. Consumption function is certainly a better shell for Keynes's meaning than the Malthusian phrase, Effective Demand, which he also used, for nothing but confusion can come from using the concepts of Demand and Supply outside of the domain (partial analysis) in which they carry rigorously definable meaning. It is not without interest to note that Keynes called his assumptions about the forms of the consumption and liquidity preference functions Psychological Laws. This was of course, another emphasizing device. But no tenable meaning can be attached to it, not even so much meaning as attaches to the 'law of satiable wants.' In this, as in some other respects, Keynes was distinctly old-fashioned.

[26] It is really an injustice to Keynes's achievement to reduce it to the bare bones of its logical structure and then to reason on these bones as if they were all. Nevertheless, great interest attaches to the attempts that have been made to cast his system into exact form. I want in particular to mention: W. B. Reddaway's review in the *Economic Record*, 1936: R. F. Harrod, 'Mr. Keynes and Traditional Theory,' *Econometrica*, January 1937; J. E. Meade, 'A Simplified Model of Mr. Keynes' System,' *Review of Economic Studies*, February 1937; J. R. Hicks, 'Mr. Keynes and the "Classics," ' *Econometrica*, April 1937; O. Lange, 'The Rate of Interest and the Optimum Propensity to Consume,' *Economica*, February 1938; P. A. Samuelson, 'The Stability of Equilibrium,' *Econometrica*, April 1941 (with dynamical reformulation); and A. Smithies, 'Process Analysis and Equilibrium Analysis,' *Econometrica*, January 1942 (also a study in the dynamics of the Keynesian schema). In the hands of writers less in sympathy with the spirit of Keynesian economics, some of the results presented in these papers might have been turned into serious criticisms. This is still more true of F. Modigliani, 'Liquidity Preference and the Theory of Interest and of Money,' *Econometrica*, January 1944.

of the picture. But if we place ourselves on the standpoint of Keynesian orthodoxy and choose to accept his vision of the economic process of our age as the gift of genius whose glance pierced through the welter of surface phenomena to the simple essentials that lie below, then there can be little objection to his aggregative analysis that produced his results.

Since the aggregates chosen for variables are, with the exception of employment, monetary quantities or expressions, we may also speak of monetary analysis and, since national income is the central variable, of income analysis. Richard Cantillon was the first, I think, to indicate a *full-fledged* schema of aggregative, monetary, and income analysis, the one worked out by François Quesnay in his *tableau économique*. Quesnay, then, is the true predecessor of Keynes, and it is interesting to note that his views on saving were identical with those of Keynes: the reader can easily satisfy himself of this by looking up the *Maximes*. It should, however, be added that the aggregative analysis of the *General Theory* does not stand alone in modern literature: it is a member of a family that had been rapidly growing.[27]

(2) Keynes further simplified his structure by avoiding, as much as possible, all complications that arise in process analysis. The exact skeleton of Keynes's system belongs, to use the terms proposed by Ragnar Frisch, to macrostatics, not to macrodynamics. In part this limitation must be attributed to those who formulated his teaching rather than to his teaching itself which contains several dynamic elements, expectations in particular. But it is true that he had an aversion to 'periods' and that he concentrated attention upon considerations of static equilibrium. This removed an important barrier to success—a difference equation as yet affects economists as the face of Medusa.

(3) Furthermore, he confined his *model*—though not always his argument—to the range of short-run phenomena. While points

[27] The quickest way to learn how far aggregative analysis had progressed before the publication of the *General Theory* is to read Tinbergen's survey article in *Econometrica,* July 1935.

(1) and (2) are commonly emphasized, it does not seem to be realized sufficiently how very strictly short run his model is and how important this fact is for the whole structure and all the results of the *General Theory*. The pivotal restriction is that not only production functions and not only methods of production but also the quantity and quality of plant and equipment are not allowed to change, a restriction which Keynes never tires of impressing upon the reader at crucial turns of his way (see, e.g., p. 114 and p. 295).[28]

This permits many otherwise inadmissible simplifications: for instance, it permits treating employment as approximately proportional to income (output) so that the one is determined as soon as the other is. But it limits applicability of this analysis to a few years at most—perhaps the duration of the '40 months' cycle'—and, in terms of phenomena, to the factors that *would* govern the greater or smaller utilization of an industrial apparatus *if* the latter remains unchanged. *All the phenomena incident to the creation and change* in this apparatus, that is to say, the phenomena that dominate the capitalist processes, are thus excluded from consideration.

As a picture of reality this model becomes most nearly justifiable in periods of depression when also liquidity preference comes nearest to being an operative factor in its own right. Professor Hicks was therefore correct in calling Keynes's economics the economics of depression. But from Keynes's own standpoint, his model derives additional justification from the secular stagnation thesis. Though it remains true that he tried to implement an essentially long-run vision by a short-run model, he secured, to some extent, the freedom for doing so by reasoning (almost) exclusively about a stationary process or, at all events, a process that stays at, or oscillates about, levels of which a stationary full-employment equilibrium is the ceiling. With Marx, capitalist evolution issues into breakdown. With J. S. Mill, it issues into a stationary state that works without hitches. With Keynes, it issues into a stationary state that constantly

[28] Strictly, some change in the quantity of equipment must be admitted, but it is conceived of as so small, at any given point of time, that its effect upon the existing industrial structure and its output can be neglected.

threatens to break down. Though Keynes's 'breakdown theory' is quite different from Marx's, it has an important feature in common with the latter: in both theories, the breakdown is motivated by causes inherent to the working of the economic engine, not by the action of factors external to it. This feature naturally qualifies Keynes's theory for the role of 'rationalizer' of anti-capitalist volition.

(4) Quite consciously, Keynes refused to go beyond the factors that are the *immediate* determinants of income (and employment). He himself recognized freely that these immediate determinants which may 'sometimes' be regarded as 'ultimate independent variables . . . would be capable of being subjected to further analysis, and are not, so to speak, our ultimate atomic independent elements' (p. 247). This turn of phrase seems to suggest no more than that economic aggregates derive their meaning from the component 'atoms.' But there is more to it than this. We can, of course, greatly simplify our picture of the world and arrive at very simple propositions if we are content with arguments of the form: *given* A, B, C . . . then D will depend upon E. If A, B, C . . . are things external to the field under investigation, there is no more to be said. If, however, they are part of the phenomena to be explained, then the resulting propositions about what determines what may easily be made undeniable and acquire the semblance of novelty without meaning very much. This is what Professor Leontief has called implicit theorizing.[29] But for Keynes, as for Ricardo,[30] arguments of this type were but emphasizing devices: they served to single out and by so doing to emphasize a particular relation. Ricardo did not say: 'Under present English conditions, as I see them, free trade in foodstuffs and raw materials will, everything considered, tend to

---

[29] Cf. his article under that title in the *Quarterly Journal of Economics,* vol. 51, pp. 337-51.
[30] The intellectual affinity of Keynes with Ricardo merits notice. Their methods of reasoning were closely similar, a fact that has been obscured by Keynes's admiration of Malthus' anti-saving attitude and by his consequent dislike of Ricardo's *teaching.*

raise the rate of profit.' Instead he said: 'The rate of profit depends upon the price of wheat.'

(5) Forceful emphasis on a small number of points that seemed to Keynes to be both important and inadequately appreciated being the keynote of the *General Theory,* we find other emphasizing devices besides the one just mentioned. Two we have noticed already.[31] Another is what critics are apt to call overstatements—overstatements, moreover, which cannot be reduced to the defensible level, because results depend precisely upon the excess. But it must be remembered not only that, from Keynes's standpoint, these overstatements were little more than means to abstract from non-essentials but also that part of the blame for them lies at our own door: we, as a body, simply will not listen unless a point be hammered in with one-sided energy. Granting, for the sake of argument, that the points in question were actually important enough to merit being hammered in, and remembering that the gems of unqualified overstatement do not occur in the *General Theory* itself but in the writings of some of Keynes's followers, we shall appreciate this method of flavoring what I have described as the sauce.

Three examples must suffice. First, every economist knows— if he did not he could not help learning it from conversation with businessmen—that any sufficiently general change in money wage rates will influence prices in the same direction. Nevertheless, it was not the practice of economists to take account of this in the theory of wages. Second, every economist *should* have known that the Turgot-Smith-J. S. Mill theory of the saving and investment mechanism was inadequate and that, in particular, saving and investment decisions were linked together too closely. Yet, had Keynes presented a properly qualified statement of their true relation, would he have elicited more from us than a mumble to the effect: 'Yes . . . that's so . . . of some importance in certain cyclical situations. . . What of it?' Third, let any reader look up pages 165 and 166 of the *General Theory*—the first two pages of Chapter 13, on the 'General Theory of Interest.' What will he find? He will find that the theory, accord-

[31] See above, n. 25.

ing to which the investment demand for savings and the supply of
savings that is governed by time-preference ('which I have called
the propensity to consume') is equated by the rate of interest 'breaks
down' because 'it is impossible to deduce the rate of interest merely
from a knowledge of these two factors.' Why is this impossible?
Because the decision to save does not *necessarily* imply a decision
to invest: we must also take account of the possibility that the
latter does not follow or not follow promptly. I will lay any odds
that this perfectly reasonable improvement in the tenor of current
teaching would not have greatly impressed us had he left the matter at this. It had to be liquidity preference to the fore—and interest
nothing but the reward for parting with money (which cannot be
so on the showing of his own text)—and so on in a well-known
sequence in order to make us sit up. And we were made to sit up
to some purpose. For many more of us will now listen to the proposition that interest is a purely monetary phenomenon than were
ready to listen thirty-five years ago.

But there is one word in the book that cannot be defended on
these lines—the word 'general.' Those emphasizing devices—even
if quite unexceptionable in other respects—cannot do more than
individuate very special cases. Keynesians may hold that these
special cases are the actual ones of our age. They cannot hold more
than that.[32]

(6) It seems evident that Keynes *wished* to secure his major
results without appeal to the element of rigidity, just as he spurned
the aid he might have derived from imperfections of competition.[33]
There were points, however, at which he was unable to do so,
especially the point at which the rate of interest has to become rigid
in the downward direction because the elasticity of the liquidity-
preference demand for money becomes infinite there. And at other
points, rigidities stand in reserve, to be appealed to in case the

[32] This has first been pointed out by O. Lange, op. cit., who also paid
due respect to the only truly general theory ever written—the theory of Léon
Walras. He neatly showed that the latter covers Keynes's as a special case.
[33] The latter factor was, however, inserted by Mr. Harrod.

front-line argument fails to convince. It is, of course, always possible
to show that the economic system will cease to work if a sufficient
number of its adaptive organs are paralyzed. Keynesians like this
fire escape no more than do other theorists. Nevertheless, it is not
without importance. The classical example is equilibrium underemployment.[34]

(7) I must, finally, advert to Keynes's brilliance in the forging
of individual tools of analysis. Look, for instance, at the skillful use
made of Kahn's multiplier or at the felicitous creation of the concept of user cost which is so helpful in defining his concept of income and may well be recorded as a novelty of some importance.
What I admire most in these and other conceptual arrangements
of his is their *adequacy:* they fit his purpose as a well-tailored coat
fits the customer's body. Of course, precisely because of this, they
possess but limited usefulness irrespective of Keynes's particular
aims. A fruit knife is an excellent instrument for peeling a pear.
He who uses it in order to attack a steak has only himself to blame
for unsatisfactory results.

VIII

The success of the *General Theory* was instantaneous and, as
we know, sustained. Unfavorable reviews, of which there were
many, only helped. A Keynesian school formed itself, not a school

---

[34] I have sometimes wondered why Keynes attached so much importance to proving that there may—and under his assumptions generally will—
be less than full employment in *perfect equilibrium of perfect competition*.
For there is such an ample supply of verifiable explanatory factors to account
for the actual unemployment we observe at any time that only the theorist's
ambition can induce us to wish for more. The question of the presence of
involuntary unemployment in perfect equilibrium of perfect competition, a
state that even the straw man whom Keynes called 'classical economist' never
believed in as a reality, is no doubt of great theoretical interest. But practically,
Keynes should have fared equally well with the unemployment that may
exist in a permanent state of disequilibrium. As it is, he clearly failed to
prove his case. But inflexibility of wages in the downward direction stands
ready to lend its aid. The theoretical question itself is the subject of a discussion that suffers from the failure of participants to distinguish between
the various theoretical issues involved. But we cannot enter into this.

in that loose sense in which some historians of economics speak of a French, German, Italian school, but a genuine one which is a sociological entity, namely, a group that professes allegiance to One Master and One Doctrine, and has its inner circle, its propagandists, its watchwords, its esoteric and its popular doctrine. Nor is this all. Beyond the pale of orthodox Keynesianism there is a broad fringe of sympathizers and beyond this again are the many who have absorbed, in one form or another, readily or grudgingly, some of the spirit or some individual items of Keynesian analysis. There are but two analogous cases in the whole history of economics—the Physiocrats and the Marxists.

This is in itself a great achievement that claims admiring recognition from friends and foes alike and, in particular, from every teacher who experiences the enlivening influence in his classes. There cannot be any doubt, unfortunately, that in economics such enthusiasm—and correspondingly strong aversions—never flare up unless the cold steel of analysis derives a temperature not naturally its own from the real or putative political implications of the analyst's message. Let us therefore cast a glance at the ideological bearings of the book. Most orthodox Keynesians are 'radicals' in one sense or another. The man who wrote the essay on the Villiers Connection was not a radical in *any* ordinary sense of the word. What is there in his book to please them? In an excellent article in *The American Economic Review,* Professor Wright [35] has gone so far as to say that 'a conservative candidate could conduct a political campaign largely on quotations from the *General Theory*.' True, but true only if this candidate knows how to use asides and qualifications. Keynes was no doubt too able an advocate ever to deny the obvious. To some extent, though probably to a small extent only, his success is precisely due to the fact that even in his boldest rushes he never left his flanks quite unguarded—as unwary critics

[35] D. McC. Wright, 'The Future of Keynesian Economics,' *Am. Econ. Rev.,* vol. xxxv, no. 3 (June 1945), p. 287. This article, in spite of some differences of opinion, usefully complements my own in many points into which considerations of space forbid me to enter.

of either his policies or his theories are apt to discover to their cost.[36] Disciples do not look at qualifications. They see one thing only—an indictment of private thrift and the implications this indictment carries with respect to the managed economy and inequality of incomes.

In order to appreciate what this means, it is necessary to recall that, as a result of a long doctrinal development, saving had come to be regarded as the last pillar of the bourgeois argument. In fact, old Adam Smith had already disposed pretty much of every other: if we analyze his argument closely—I am speaking, of course, only of the ideological aspects of his system—it amounts to all-around vituperation directed against 'slothful' landlords and grasping merchants or 'masters' plus the famous eulogy of parsimony. And this remains the keynote of most non-Marxist economic ideology until Keynes. Marshall and Pigou were in this boat. They, especially the latter, took it for granted that inequality, or the existing degree of inequality, was 'undesirable.' But they stopped short of attack upon the pillar.

Many of the men who entered the field of teaching or research in the twenties and thirties had renounced allegiance to the bourgeois scheme of life, the bourgeois scheme of values. Many of

[36] This is why there is such ample room for that turn of phrase that occurs so often in the Keynesian literature: 'Keynes did not *really* say this' or 'Keynes did not *really* deny that.' In the *General Theory* most of the explicit qualifications occur in chapters 18 and 19. But the only possible reference to all the implicit ones is *passim*. The logic of the classical system is not *really* impugned (p. 278). Even Say's law (in the sense defined on p. 26) is not completely thrown out; even the existence of a mechanism that tends to equilibrate saving and investment decisions—and the role of interest rates in this mechanism—and even the possibility that a reduction of money wages may stimulate output is not absolutely denied; though, to be sure, only in application to very special cases, the validity of the first and the existence of the other two are occasionally recognized. Critics are therefore in constant danger of being convicted of 'gross misrepresentation' exactly as unwary critics of Malthus' first *Essay* invariably run into a volley of quotations from the second edition—in which, in fact, Malthus went far toward explaining away Malthusianism. But it is impossible to go into all this here. In the article quoted, Professor Wright offers instructive examples.

them sneered at the profit motive and at the element of personal performance in the capitalist process. But so far as they did not embrace straight socialism, they still had to pay respect to saving— under penalty of losing caste in their own eyes and ranging them- selves with what Keynes so tellingly called the economist's 'under- world.' But Keynes broke their fetters: here, at last, was theoretical doctrine that not only obliterated the personal element and was, if not mechanistic itself, at least mechanizable, but also smashed the pillar into dust; a doctrine that may not actually say but can easily be made to say both that 'who tries to save destroys real capital' and that, *via* saving, 'the unequal distribution of income is the ultimate cause of unemployment.' [37] *This* is what the Keynesian Revolution amounts to. Thus defined, the phrase is not inappropriate. And *this,* and only this, explains and, to some extent, justifies Keynes's change of attitude toward Marshall which is neither understandable nor justifiable upon any scientific ground.

But though this attractive wrapper made Keynes's gift to scientific economics more acceptable to many, it must not divert attention from the gift itself. Before the appearance of the *General Theory,* economics had been growing increasingly complex and in- creasingly incapable of giving straightforward answers to straight- forward questions. The *General Theory* seemed to reduce it once more to simplicity, and to enable the economist once more to give simple advice that everybody could understand. But, exactly as in the case of Ricardian economics, there was enough to attract, to inspire even, the sophisticated. The same system that linked up so well with the notions of the untutored mind proved satisfactory to the best brains of the rising generation of theorists. Some of them felt— still feel for all I know—that all other work in 'theory' should be scrapped. All of them paid homage to the man who had given them a well-defined model to handle, to criticize, and to improve—

---

[37] And, after all, a glance at pp. 372-3 and 376 of the *General Theory* will convince anyone that Keynes actually came pretty near to authorizing both statements. One must be as punctiliously conscientious as is Professor Wright in order to say that he did not actually do so.

to the man whose work symbolizes at least, even though it may not embody, what they wanted to see done.

And even those who had found their bearings before, and on whom the *General Theory* did not impinge in their formative years, experienced the salutary effects of a fresh breeze. As a prominent American economist put it in a letter to me: 'It (the *General Theory*) did, and does, have something which supplements what our thinking and methods of analysis would otherwise have been. It does not make us Keynesians, it makes us better economists.' Whether we agree or not, this expresses the essential point about Keynes's achievement extremely well. In particular, it explains why hostile criticism, even if successful in its attack upon individual assumptions or propositions, is yet powerless to inflict fatal injury upon the structure as a whole. As with Marx, it is possible to admire Keynes even though one may consider his social vision to be wrong and every one of his propositions to be misleading.

I am not going to grade the *General Theory* as if it were a student's examination book. Moreover, I do not believe in grading economists—the men whose names one might think of for comparison are too different, too incommensurable. Whatever happens to the doctrine, the memory of the man will live—outlive both Keynesianism and the reaction to it.

At this I will leave it. Everyone knows the stupendous fight the valiant warrior put up for the work that was to be his last.[38] Everyone knows that during the war he entered the Treasury again (1940) and that his influence grew, along with that of Churchill, until nobody thought of challenging it. Everyone knows of the honor that has been conferred upon the House of Lords. And, of course, of the Keynes Plan, Bretton Woods, and the English loan. But these things will have to engage some scholarly biographer who has all the materials at his disposal.

[38] His last great work, that is. He wrote many minor pieces almost to his dying day.

APPENDIX

G. F. KNAPP *
1842-1926

T HE death of Professor Knapp on February 20 has removed from the German scientific world one of the most striking figures of what may be termed the third epoch of political economy in Germany—the first being the 'cameralistic,' the best-known names of which were Seckendorff and Justi; the second corresponding to the classic period in England and culminating in such works as those of Thünen and Hermann—the outstanding features of which were 'Sozialpolitik' and 'Historical Method.' Along with Schmoller, Wagner, Bücher, Brentano, although different from everyone of them in many ways, George Frederic Knapp will always be associated with all its merits and some of its shortcomings.

Few words suffice for his uneventful life. He was born on March 7, 1842, in Giessen, the son of a professor and author of a very successful textbook on Technology. Studying in Munich, Berlin, and Göttingen, he made himself a statistician, quite unusually equipped, for that time, in mathematics. In 1867 he became head of the Statistical Bureau of the Municipality of Leipzig and

* Reprinted from *The Economic Journal*, vol. XXXVI, no. 143, September 1926.

earned, during the following years, much deserved praise by the efficiency of his management of that office, amply proved by the excellence of what the Bureau published under him. In 1869 he was made 'extraordinary' professor—a title but imperfectly equivalent to 'assistant' professor—at the University of Leipzig, whence he was called to Strassburg in 1874 and promoted to a full professorship. There he remained until he retired from his chair—really longer still, until 1919, when he had to leave what had become a foreign town.

Whatever he did was done wholeheartedly with all the concentration of a character of singular strength. To trace the outline of the work of his life is therefore much easier than this task usually is in the case of a man of so much mental vitality. Until 1874 he was—if we may pass by two papers of less importance, his doctoral thesis on Thünen and one on questions of taxation—a statistician only. Apart from his practical work in this field he made contributions to the theory of the subject, some of which, named below,[1] may repay perusal even now. It is only the standard he has set for himself elsewhere that prevents us from dwelling on the honorable position due to him—if not in the first rank, at least near to it—on that account alone.

But as an historian of economic life and as an economist of 'institutional' complexion he was truly great. His two volumes, published in 1887, on the emancipation of peasants and the origin of the rural worker in the older parts of Prussia (*Bauernbefreiung und der Ursprung der Landarbeiter in den ältern Teilen Preussens*) are his masterpiece and the standard work in the matter. They have helped to mould the minds of many followers and created what almost amounts to a special branch of our science. The reason for this does not lie in any new historical technique nor in the mastering of any material of special difficulty. In these respects Knapp was

[1] *Uber die Ermittlung der Sterblichkeit aus den Aufzeichnungen der Bevölkerungsstatistik*, 1868. *Die neueren Ansichten über Moralstatistik*, 1871. *Theorie des Bevölkerungswechsels: Abhandlungen zur angewandten Mathematik*, 1874.

not equal to such men as Meitzen or Hanssen. But he had other
qualities, beyond comparison, higher and rarer. He had a clear, I
should like to say a passionate, vision of the essence of things, which
pierced far below the surface. He *saw* the processes and problems
of history and grasped them more firmly than most men do the facts
surrounding them. And he based his historical analysis on a comprehensive knowledge of present-day facts. The sources of such sketches
as his *Landarbeiter in Knechtschaft und Freiheit,* 1891, and his
Grundherrschaft und Rittergut, 1897, are only in part historical;
partly they flow from a study of what German landowners and their
laborers, their mentality and methods and their lives really are
today. The quality I am striving to define goes far toward making
the historian; but it is everything for him who does not look for
the romance, but for the problems of history.

Like the farmer who by changing his crops conserves the
fertility of his soil, Knapp about 1895 dropped this work and took
up, once more, an entirely different set of problems. And, in some
respects, it was then that he made his most successful hit. His *Staat-
liche Theorie des Geldes,* recently translated into English under the
auspices of the Royal Economic Society, was published for the first
time in 1905. It undoubtedly raised him to international fame. A
host of disciples gathered round it, and admirers and opponents
contributed equally—the latter by the wrath of their attacks not
less than the former by their eulogies—toward a striking success.
Still, much as there is to admire in the book, the largeness of conception, the independence of execution, the freshness of its style, it
is impossible to deny that in handling what are fundamentally
questions of economic theory it went wrong, and that its influence
on monetary science in Germany has been, in the main, an unfortunate one. But if it shows that economic theory, whatever its
shortcomings may be, cannot safely be despised, it also serves to
show, once more, the strength of this remarkable man, who convinced so many of what he could not prove and often fascinated
even where he did not convince.

FRIEDRICH VON WIESER*
1851-1926

T HE last of the three founders of what has been called the Austrian School passed away on July 23, 1926, a few days after having
completed his seventy-fifth year, still full of vigor of mind and
body.

Baron Friedrich von Wieser, born on July 10, 1851, the son
of the Privy Councillor Baron Leopold von Wieser, was educated
in Vienna, where he took his degree in 1872. Up to this time his
favorite studies had been historical, but in 1872 he came across
Menger's *Grundsätze,* the perusal of which made him a convert to
economic theory. He continued along the path thus opened up before him during his years of study at the universities of Heidelberg,
Jena, and Leipzig which followed, and during his short employ in
the Civil Service preceding his becoming 'Privatdozent' at the University of Vienna in 1883 and his being called to the University of
Prague in 1884, whence he returned to Vienna in 1903, succeeding
Karl Menger. Passing by minor events of his career, I would only
mention that he entered the *Herrenhaus* (House of Lords) as a life

* Reprinted from *The Economic Journal,* vol. xxxvii, no. 146, June 1927.

member in 1917, and that he took Cabinet office as Minister of
Commerce in the same year. After his resignation he returned
again to his chair and to his scientific work.

It is not easy to convey to anyone who did not know him
an adequate impression of this eminent man, who fascinated
wherever he went. His fine presence, his singular and quite unconventional charm and dignity of manner, something which gave
weight to his every word, something else indefinably artistic about
his personality, a sublime repose in whatever he said or did expressive of wide horizons—all this defies description. Perhaps the only
thing I can do is to relate that, when we were celebrating his seventieth birthday, three speakers, myself included, compared him, independently of each other, to Goethe. He was always active, never in a
hurry, interested in everything—among other things he was a prominent connoisseur and sedulous patron of art—upset by nothing.
There was some charmed recess within him into which no public
or private misfortune seemed able to cut. Every honor or success
came to him naturally and without effort and clothed him as if he
had never been without it—yet did not seem to mean anything to
him. He never fought for or against anything—but every difficulty
seemed to give way before him. And old age itself, the destroyer of
other men, to him only added, as it were, finishing touches, improving a picture which it always was an aesthetic pleasure to
look at.

It is still more difficult to define within a short page or two
the character of his scientific work, especially to English readers;
for his way of expressing himself was strikingly un-English, and it
is to be feared that even the well-known translation and interpretation of part of his work by Professor Smart has done but little
to impress his real importance on the English and American public.
He was deficient in technique and is one of the few examples of
clear thinking not implying concise writing. An appendix to the
best of the obituary notices which have so far appeared, the one by
F. A. von Hayek in the *Jahrbücher für Nationalökonomie und
Statistik,* 1926, contains a full list of his writings, running to sixty-

two items. We must confine ourselves to indicating briefly the
general trend of his thought.

He was a theorist first of all. What Menger did for him was
not so much giving him an *idea* as the *impulse* to develop his own
ideas. Few men have thought so deeply on the fundamentals of the
theory of value or have had so clear a vision of the groundwork
of economics. And the best part of the energy of his prime was
given to working out patiently the views and methods summed up
in his book entitled *Der Natürliche Wert* (1889), to which he led
up by his *Ursprung und Hauptgesetze des wirtschaftlichen Güterwertes* (1884), containing a first exposition of his theories of the
'Grenznutzen,' of cost of production explained by 'indirect utility'
(the theorem which has been called Wieser's law by Pantaleoni),
and of 'imputation' (*Zurechnung*). These things are well known.
But what I should like to insist upon is not the importance of any
single instrument or theorem of his, but the fertility and grandeur
of his conception of economic life as a whole, well brought out
by the device of reasoning about a communistic society. Much
progress has since been made in the theory of the equilibrium of
prices, but of late, if I am not very much mistaken, questions are
cropping up which may force us to go back again to those fundamental ideas which many of us now believe to be obsolete.

After the publication of his *Natural Value* he dropped this
line of thought for twenty years. But once more he returned to it
in 1909, and in 1914 he published, in that encyclopedic *Grundriss
der Sozialökonomik,* his 'Theorie der gesellschaftlichen Wirtschaft,'
his last and ripest message on pure theory which, owing to the war,
is only now beginning to to make its influence felt.

Much like Walras and others, he had turned meanwhile to
the theory of money, building up slowly and from within—not
looking at what other people wrote—what will always rank with
the best performances of our age in this field. His first utterance on
the subject was his inaugural address given in 1903 after his election to the chair of Menger, his last the article on Money in the
Handwörterbuch der Staatswissenschaften, which he finished but

a short time before he died. He approached the subject by way of investigating into historical changes in the purchasing power of money, and aimed at giving to the quantity theorem the same sort of foundation which his theory of value had given to the law of cost. Those who really understand monetary theory are none too numerous. Among them there is happily very much in common, and what differences remain are partly little more than differences in taste and technique. Therefore Wieser's treatment necessarily runs parallel with that of others for a considerable part of the way. But in some points—developed later by such men as F. X. Weiss and L. v. Mises—it seems to me to pierce further below the surface than any other.

The chief work of his later years, however, centered in sociology, in the sense in which it may be defined as an analysis of history, or, as he himself defined it with that power he had of coining striking words, as 'history without names.' Historical Sociology, or Sociological History, had been his first interest, and it was to be his last. After toiling at it with youthful energy for years, he published, when seventy-four years of age, his great sociological book, entitled *Das Gesetz der Macht*—thus achieving what he had in his mind to do when still at school, and gathering in the harvest of his thought in that field.

So there was nothing casual or incomplete or devious or distorted about this life. Every element of it formed part of an harmonious whole, which unfolded itself slowly and grew organically to an imposing height and breadth.

LADISLAUS VON BORTKIEWICZ*
1868-1931

V ON BORTKIEWICZ, by far the most eminent German statistician since Lexis, whose pupil he was in important respects, was not a German by descent. He came from one of those Polish families which had made their peace with Poland's Russian lords, and was brought up in St. Petersburg, his birthplace, where he also went to the University and where he later on taught for a time. Connections formed during a prolonged stay in Germany, where in 1895 he had become a Privatdozent in the University of Strassburg, led to his being appointed, in 1901, to an 'extraordinary' (assistant) professorship at Berlin. Characteristically enough, this eminent man was never thought of as a candidate for one of the great chairs, either in Berlin or at any other university, and it was not until 1920, when by a measure intended to 'democratize' faculties *all* extraordinary professors became full professors *ad personam,* that he obtained that rank, without, however, ceasing to be entirely isolated.

There were several reasons for this. He was a foreigner. Although not a clumsy speaker or writer, he was not a good lecturer, and his lectures, which he elaborated with a minute and conscien-

* Reprinted from *The Economic Journal,* vol. XLII, no. 166, June 1932.

tious attention to details all his own, were said to be delivered to rather empty classrooms. His critical acumen made people fear him, but it hardly contributed to making them love him. Those colleagues whose duty it would have been to propose his name to the Ministries of Education were hardly in a position to understand his contributions. He did not seem to mind, but kept aloof in dignified reserve, enjoying the respect, with which everyone looked upon him, and a quiet scientific life to be cut short in the fullness of his powers by an unexpected death. A bibliography of (as far as I can see) his whole published work has been drawn up by Professor Oscar Anderson,[1] to which I refer the reader.

Nature—it is not often that the goddess makes up her mind so decidedly—had made him a critic, so much so that even his original contributions assumed the form of criticisms, and that critique became his very breath. This critical faculty, or rather passion, which did not stop short at small blunders in numerical examples, stands out particularly in his work as an economist. Here he was not an originator, and I believe he just missed greatness by refusing to put to full use the mathematical tools at his command, which at the time of his prime might have made him rival the fame of Edgeworth or of Barone. But he upheld the flag of economic theory—professing the Marshallian creed—at an epoch and in a country in which hardly anyone would hear of it, and he cleared the ground of many battlefields by his powerful sword. By far his most important achievement is his analysis of the theoretical framework of the Marxian system (*Archiv für Sozialwissenschaft,* vols. xxiii and xxv, and *Conrads Jahrbücher,* 1907), much the best thing ever written on it and, incidentally, on its other critics. A similar masterpiece is his paper on the theories of rent of Rodbertus and Marx (*Archiv für die Geschichte des Sozialismus,* vol. i).

[1] *Zeitschrift für Nationalökonomie,* vol. iii, no. 2. In writing about a man who was a paragon of conscientiousness I may perhaps allow myself for once to follow the example set by him, and to point out a misprint occurring on p. 279, sub. no. 2, of the list of his economic papers: He did not, in his critique of Pareto's *Cours,* reproach the marginal utility school with fostering an 'ultra-*radical*' economic policy, but an ultra-*liberal* one.

Where blunders are secondary and fundamentals sound, as in the cases of Walras, Pareto, and Böhm-Bawerk, the stern critic shows to less advantage. As a writer on monetary theory and policy, he ranks high among German authors. The subjects of the gold standard, of banking credit, of velocity of circulation owe much to him. The best he did in this field, however, is his work on index numbers (*Nordisk Statistik Tidskrift,* 1924), a masterly review of Irving Fisher's work amounting to an original contribution in the matter of tests.

In the field of statistical method, his ἀριστεία among Germans is, of course, undoubted. As the discoverer of the 'law of small numbers' (1898) and the leader of the Lexian school, he has won an international name which will go down to posterity. His book on probability (*Die Iterationen,* 1917), his only 'book'—he had so great an inhibition on giving to the public that he lost some of the claims to high originality which he would otherwise have had—is an admirable piece of work even when looked at without any predilection for the fundamental conception of probability that underlies it. It is impossible, nor would it be proper in an economic journal, to unfold the long list of Bortkiewicz's contributions to the theory of statistics. A few instances of special importance to the economist must suffice. No one has done more to clear up the important subject of the measures of inequality of incomes (nineteenth session of the Institut International de Statistique). Most of us will read with profit and pleasure those excellent papers on the quadrature of empirical curves (*Skandinavisk Aktuarie Tidskrift,* 1926) and on homogeneity and stability in statistics (ibid. 1918), or the one on variability under the Gaussian law (*Nordisk Statistisk Tidskrift,* 1922) or on the property common to all laws of error (*Sitzungsberichte der Berliner math. Gesellschaft,* 1923), or on the succession in time of chance events (*Bulletin de l'institut international de statistique,* 1911)—not to mention any of his papers on mortality and insurance, some of which are treasures of their kind.

But in order to give an idea of the compass of his mind it is necessary to point to one more opusculum of his, far removed though it is from economics: his pamphlet on 'Radio-aktive Strahlung als Gegenstand wahrscheinlichkeitstheoretischer Untersuchungen,' Berlin, 1913. In turning over the pages of this parergon, one seems to discern the true contour lines of the mind of the *economist* who wrote it, and one begins to wonder whether one can rely on what he published as a measure of the range of his possibilities.